Legal Issues in Public School Employment

Joseph Beckham
and
Perry A. Zirkel,
Editors

Phi Delta Kappa, Bloomington, Indiana

cover design by Nancy Rinehart

Table of Contents

Introduction

The relationship between public schools and their employees is one of the most frequently litigated aspects of American education. The annual review of U.S. judicial decisions in the *Yearbook of School Law* typically chronicles more than 300 cases involving employment and labor-related legal issues in public schools. Since most of these cases are appellate court decisions, the actual number of cases decided at the trial court level is far higher. Add to this list those employment issues that are the subject of grievance arbitration proceedings, local board hearings, or state administrative review, and the actual number of employment disputes in public school settings takes on extraordinary proportions.

We live in a litigation-prone society, and school districts are not exempt from such litigation because conflict is inherent in resolving ambiguities in contracts of employment. Furthermore, adverse economic conditions, declining enrollments, demands for educational accountability, and recent interpretations of constitutional and statutory entitlements have all contributed to the trend of school employees seeking redress in state and federal courts. Therefore, it is not surprising that the employment relationship has become a frequent issue for judicial intervention.

A better understanding of how the courts resolve public school employment issues will familiarize educators as to what steps can be taken to avoid or to reduce litigation and to mitigate liability. Judicial opinions do much more than simply provide a ruling in a case. When carefully analyzed, these opinions provide a basis for proper professional practice. Judges often suggest procedures that will ensure appropriate standards of due process and reduce the likelihood of arbitrary or capricious conduct.

The chapters in this text present a comprehensive and current report of legal issues in public school employment. The authors have undertaken extensive reviews and analyses of judicial decisions in state and federal courts and related legislative and regulatory mandates involving the public school employment relationship. Where appropriate, they have extrapolated legal principles that inform as well as guide the practice of teachers, staff specialists, administrators, and board members.

Chapter topics range from federal constitutional issues to documentation of employment practices, offering both legal and operational guidelines for the educator. The authors, who include principals, professors of school law, and practicing attorneys, have recognized expertise in their respective chapter topic. Each provides a national perspective but also incorporates statutory problems associated with selected state jurisdictions.

The editors have sought to strike a balance between readability and legal accuracy. The language is largely non-technical to assist those readers without legal training, and a glossary is provided for a few specialized terms. Ample citations to illustrative cases have been provided for practitioners who may wish to review the complete text of a given case in order to amplify the legal principles identified.

The general applicability of the legal guidelines will be apparent to the practicing educator, but two caveats are in order. First, the outcome of litigation in public school employment settings is highly dependent on the facts involved. Subtle distinctions of fact can influence the interpretation of law. Consequently, educators are admonished to preserve a documentary record of employment decisions and to recognize that each case may carry nuances of fact that contribute to a different judicial decision. Second, while the emphasis in this book has been upon legal issues of national prominence, state and local standards may vary. Careful review and reference to state legislative and judicial mandates, board regulation and policy, and the collective or individual contract of employment are essential in the interpretation and application of legal guidelines outlined in the chapters that follow. While this book is a useful starting point, consultation with knowledgeable counsel should be undertaken when dealing with a specific case.

1
Critical Elements of the Employment Relationship

Joseph Beckham

The employment relationship in public schools is governed by constitutional mandates, federal and state statutes, administrative regulations, and contractual obligations. Federal constitutional and statutory provisions that apply across state jurisdictions are treated in other chapters of this book. This chapter will deal with fundamental aspects of the employment relationship, which are influenced by legal principles derived from state law, local district policy and practice, and the unique terms of a particular employment contract.

Although there is great variation in the application of legal standards from one state jurisdiction to another, four elements of the public school employment relationship bear special scrutiny: employment qualifications, contractual obligations, tenure, and discipline.

Qualifications of Faculty and Staff

Each state has adopted its own statutory and regulatory requirements to ensure that only qualified personnel teach or administer in public schools. Generally, the administration of a certification program and the enforcement of other employment qualifications is the responsibility of the state board of education under authorization of the legislature. In most states, professional preparation requirements such as training and

---

Joseph Beckham is an associate professor at Florida State University.

experience are established by the state education agency. State statutes or regulatory provisions may also mandate additional requirements such as good moral character, minimum age, and citizenship.

A local school board usually has discretionary authority to establish other reasonable qualifications for positions in addition to those mandated under state law.[1] In establishing the "reasonableness" of any qualification, the school board should demonstrate that a valid relationship exists between the qualification, the job to be performed, and the legitimate purposes of the public education system.[2]

Loyalty Oaths

The U.S. Supreme Court has considered a number of cases involving the requirement that a loyalty oath be executed by the teacher as a condition of employment. While the high court has observed that a state may require teachers to be of "patriotic disposition,"[3] the Court has struck down loyalty oaths that make membership in an allegedly subversive organization grounds for employment disqualification because such a provision was deemed unconstitutionally vague.[4]

However, the Supreme Court has recognized the constitutionality of a limited loyalty oath as a condition of employment, provided that the oath requires no more than that the prospective employee swear or affirm support for the state and federal constitutions and faithfully discharge the duties of the position to which the employee is assigned. The high court's view is that such oaths are strictly limited to an affirmation of support for constitutional government and a pledge not to act forcibly to overthrow the government.[5]

Competitive Examinations

The use of competitive examinations as a qualification for employment has been upheld where the examination procedures were uniformly applied to all candidates and validly related to job requirements.[6] However, employment qualification requirements involving a standardized examination have been subject to close judicial scrutiny where allegations of discrimination or denial of due process of law are involved.[7] For example, South Carolina requires graduates of teacher-training institutions to make a minimum score on a standardized objective test before receiving a teaching certificate. To ensure that the test was a reasonable measure of subject matter taught in the state's teacher-training institutions, state authorities conducted content validation studies, pilot tested the instrument, and submitted the test items to a review panel. Another review panel determined the minimum score requirement, which was later lowered by the state department of education. Nevertheless, a group of black teacher candidates filed suit, since a disproportionate number of blacks, particularly those educated in predominantly black colleges, did not meet the minimum score requirement.

A three-judge federal district court reviewed the procedures used to develop and implement the test and found no violation of the equal protection clause of the 14th Amendment or of the applicable standards of Title VII of the Civil Rights Act of 1964. Since the validation procedure demonstrated that the test was related to the content of academic subject matter found in the state's teacher-training institutions, the court regarded the test as rationally related to a valid state purpose, i.e., ensuring that certified teachers would have a minimum level of knowledge necessary for effective teaching.[8]

Professional Growth Requirements

A school board may require that a teacher meet reasonable requirements for professional growth, although the reasonableness of the requirements may be challenged where they exceed scholastic training requirements fixed under state statute. For example, in *Harrah Independent School District* v. *Martin* the U.S. Supreme Court upheld the dismissal of a tenured teacher who refused to comply with a professional growth policy.[9] The policy compelled teachers with a bachelor's degree to earn at least five semester hours of college credit every three years. In previous years the board had denied salary increments to teachers who did not meet the requirement, but when this option was foreclosed by state statute, the board's only recourse was termination.

Residency Requirements

The New Hampshire Supreme Court struck down a requirement that teachers reside within the boundaries of the school district in which they teach. The court held that the restriction violated the individual's fundamental right to equal protection of the laws under the state and federal constitutions. In balancing the denial of a fundamental constitutional right against the state's interest in maintaining the restriction, the court found no reasonable justification for the requirement that a teacher reside near his or her place of duty.[10]

More recently, however, the Sixth Circuit Court of Appeals sustained a residency requirement for public school teachers on the basis of the rational relationship test. The court found the residency requirement reasonable for Cincinnati, because resident teachers would more likely be committed to an urban educational system, would become more involved in activities with district parents and community leaders, and would be less likely to engage in strikes or to refuse to support tax levies.[11]

Certification Requirements for Hiring

Certification requirements may include evidence of specific job experience, satisfactory completion of educational requirements, minimum score requirements on job-related examinations, and such other requirements as are reasonably related to a valid state purpose. In determining whether candidates for certification meet state standards, courts grant considerable discretion to the administrative board charged with making such determinations, and are reluctant to overturn administrative decisions unless "clearly erroneous" or unsupported by substantial evidence.[12]

Certification or licensure ensures that the holder has met state requirements and is therefore qualified for employment in the specialization for which certification is granted. Generally, courts will interpret and enforce the standards established for certification with rigid conformity to literal construction and will decline to intervene where certification is denied.

A Michigan Department of Education rule requiring "at least one year of experience teaching handicapped people" was held to require that certification could be granted only where the teacher could document at least one year of teaching children in a self-contained, special education classroom.[13] Where state regulation required that only certified nurse-teachers could be employed by the school board, the Rhode Island Supreme Court declined to permit the hiring of noncertified nurses for certain limited nursing duties.[14] The Wyoming Supreme Court held that the state board of education is empowered by statute to administer certification of superintendents and acted within its scope of authority in denying certification to a proposed candidate who did not possess sufficient training or experience as a teacher in a recognized K-12 setting.[15]

The U.S. Supreme Court upheld a New York statute forbidding permanent certification as a public school teacher of any person who is not a United States citizen unless that person has manifested an intention to apply for citizenship.[16] The high court recognized a rational relationship between the statute and a legitimate state purpose. In the words of the opinion, the exclusion from certification was justified because:

> Within the public school system, teachers play a critical part in developing students' attitude toward government and understanding of the role of citizens in our society. . . . Further, a teacher serves as a role model for his students, exerting a subtle but important influence over their perceptions and values. Thus, through both presentation of course materials and the example he sets, a teacher has an opportunity to influence the attitudes of students toward government, the political process, and a citizen's social responsibilities. This influence is critical to continued good health of a democracy.[17]

Dismissal for Lack of Certification

Courts generally uphold dismissals for failure to acquire valid certification. The Washington Supreme Court held that it is the responsibility of the teacher to maintain valid certification, even where local school board officials had insisted that statutory certification could be waived.[18] Although school authorities had knowingly employed the teacher in an area for which she was not certified and assured her that lack of certification was not a problem, the Washington court ruled that the teacher was not entitled to equitable relief when she was dismissed for lack of legal qualifications. Similarly, the New York Court of Appeals sustained the dismissal of a teacher for "incompetency" because he failed to qualify for permanent certification during the statutorily required six-year period.[19]

Where lack of certification is attributable to the teacher, the lack of legal qualification is fatal to the validity of an employment contract.[20] However, where failure to maintain a valid teaching certificate is attributable to bureaucratic delay and other extenuating factors beyond the teacher's control, it has been held that dismissal for lack of proper legal qualification could not be maintained.[21]

Renewal of Certification

Requirements for renewal of certification, particularly when continuing education is required for renewal, have generally been upheld by courts as reasonable. A North Carolina State Board of Education regulation, which provided that certificates would expire after five years and that renewal would be permitted only upon completion of six units of credit during the five-year period preceding renewal, was upheld by that state's highest court.[22] Although contested as unreasonable, the regulation was found to have a reasonable basis in that the teacher's classroom performance would be improved if the teacher broadened his or her knowledge base through continued college coursework.

Certificate Revocation and Suspension

Revocation or suspension of the teaching certificate terminates the holder's right to teach and is distinguishable from dismissal by a local school board, since loss of the certificate forecloses all teaching opportunities within the state. Evidentiary standards and conformity to due process are usually more rigorous where the loss of a teaching certificate is involved.

Immoral conduct related to the commission of, or conviction for, a crime constitutes the most common basis for good cause revocation or suspension of certification. Typically, conviction of a crime is prima facie evidence of immoral conduct, as is an admission of guilt in a criminal prosecution. Certification revocation was affirmed in a Florida case involving an allegation of moral turpitude. A police officer in pursuit of vandals entered a teacher's residence and observed several marijuana plants. State revocation of the teaching certificate was justified on the basis of substantial evidence of illegal possession.[23] However, where a Florida teacher's certificate was initially suspended based on a police report that the teacher, clad only in trousers and socks, was found with a female student in the backseat of his car, the Florida court ruled that the evidence of impropriety was not sufficient to justify suspension.[24]

Where courts otherwise have been presented with the question of whether or not specific conduct of a teacher constitutes moral unfitness that would justify revocation or suspension of certification, they have generally required that the conduct must adversely affect the teacher's classroom performance or relations with students or colleagues. For example, the California Supreme Court ruled that a teacher who had engaged in homosexual conduct could not have his certificate revoked unless it was shown that the conduct indicated unfitness to teach or otherwise adversely affected performance as a teacher.[25] Incidents of extramarital heterosexual conduct, when balanced against years of highly rated teaching and the support of local board and school personnel, were held insufficient to justify revocation of certificate in Iowa.[26]

The Contract of Employment

The contract of employment is a critically important document that establishes the rights and responsibilities of contracting parties and provides essential guidelines for the administration of public schools. Contracts negotiated between a school district board of education and an employee are subject to provisions of state statutes and administrative regulations as well as express or implied terms of the contract agreement.

As a general rule, the express provisions of an employment contract are strictly enforced by courts. For example, the contract of employment between a teacher and a local Georgia school board stipulated that the employee could not resign without the local board's consent and added that resignation without board consent would authorize the local board to recommend a year's suspension of certificate. The local board refused to accept the teacher's resignation, sought to hold a hearing, then dismissed the teacher for immorality and recommended revocation of certification. On appeal, the teacher invoked the contract provisions that limited the board to recommend suspension for a year due to wrongful termination of the contract. The state school board's decision sustaining the teacher's position was affirmed on appeal; and the appellate court directed the local board to confine its action to proration of salary for the period served prior to the resignation, recommendation of the one-year suspension of certificate, and placement of a letter of reprimand in the teacher's personnel file.[27] A teacher who signed an agreement that he would not claim tenure by default if granted an additional year of probation was held to his agreement by a New York court. The board had been asked to reconsider denial of tenure and offered the teacher a contract with the option of an additional year as an alternative to nonrenewal. The offer of the board was found to have been made in good faith, and the agreement by the teacher was not considered coerced.[28]

A contract may be considered breached when one party acts unilaterally to change a material element of the original agreement. Under a negotiated agreement, a school district agreed to a salary schedule for a school year beginning August 23 and continuing for 180 days. Following the negotiations, the school board unilaterally altered the starting date of the school year. The change resulted in the loss of five working days, which reduced teachers' salaries under a salary computation formula devised by the board. The appellate court concurred with the trial court's judgment that the board's unilateral act of changing the starting date had effectively denied compensation under the terms of the negotiated agreement, and the board was liable for the salary losses plus interest.[29]

An employee's unforced resignation is normally considered a breach of the contract and prohibits that employee from claiming rights under the contract. A Utah teacher/coach, displeased with his reassignment to another school in the district, resigned. He contended that this resignation was from the school and not the district. Relying on the legal proposition that employment contracts can be altered only by mutual consent, the court held that the employee had resigned from employment in the district and thereby waived all rights to termination procedures.[30]

Several breach-of-contract cases brought against school districts have involved interpretation of oral agreements or implied contractual commitments. As a general rule, oral agreements cannot be considered as a contractual right to continued employment in a school district. When disputes arise, express contractual provisions are favored over implied contracts.

In Alabama, an oral contract between a clerk typist and the school board was held to create no property right for continued employment when her position was eliminated due to budget reductions.[31] Similarly, a Mississippi cafeteria manager could not rely on an oral contract to establish a property right to continued employment; the board could terminate her employment at will.[32]

A school board policy providing additional compensation to vocational education teachers who completed certification requirements was relied on as creating a de facto policy for additional compensation to already certified vocational education teachers in Arizona. The reviewing court rejected this reasoning, holding that where the certified teachers signed contracts, which called for specific salaries, the fact that other teachers were paid more was immaterial.[33]

Relationship of Local Contracts to State Statutes

The subordinate status of a local contractual agreement, when in conflict with the provisions of state statute, has regularly been recognized by courts. In a Pennsylvania case a teacher who had been tenured in one school district sought to require a second district to continue her as a substitute for an employee on leave of absence. The state's intermediate appellate court refused to order reinstatement. Although a professional employee contract had been negotiated, the court interpreted school code provisions defining "substitute" to mean that a professional employee could be hired devoid of rights to hearing and dismissal for cause and that a professional contract would not be controlling.[34] When agents of a New York school district requested that licenses be granted to teachers holding certificates of continuing eligibility for teaching classes for emotionally handicapped children, the court refused to grant the licenses on the grounds that state education statutes provided that no license could be validly issued absent a competitive examination.[35]

An employee who alleges that a school district is failing to comply with state statutory provisions governing employment contracts will normally have to carry the burden of proving noncompliance. California teacher aides who were not renewed due to financially depressed conditions in the district were unsuccessful in establishing a right to continued employment based on state statutes governing notice and layoff of classified employees, since the aides were not considered to come within the protection of the statutes.[36] When prospective principals sought to require a school board to appoint them to positions by rank order as determined by scores on administrative examinations, the Illinois Supreme Court ruled against them by interpreting statutory mandates requiring appointment "for merit only" as permitting the local board to exercise its discretion in the appointment of principals.[37]

Board Policies and Regulatory Provisions

A board of education's power to make and enforce policies applicable to employment agreements is discretionary, but must be exercised within the statutory authority granted to it for purposes related to the operation of schools. The board's power should be exercised in a reasonable manner and its policies should be uniformly applied throughout the district to avoid any allegation of arbitrary or capricious action.

Numerous cases illustrate the application of administrative regulations in situations involving the contractual rights of employees. In West Virginia an employee handbook promulgated by the state board of education provided that employees who met objective eligibility requirements for a vacant professional position had a right to an interview for the position. The court strictly construed the personnel regulations in favor of an employee who had applied for a position as an assistant state superintendent and ordered that the employee be given an interview before any denial of his application.[38] Similarly, a probationary special education teacher in New York City relied on regulations promulgated by the chancellor and the local board creating a right to be evaluated before discontinuation of her services. The court held that administrative rules that affect substantial rights of employees may not be waived by the local board and ordered evaluation and a new determination regarding continuation of employment.[39]

Numerous school board policies have been held to be reasonable directives for controlling contracts of employment. Failure to comply with a board's request that the teacher submit medical verification of her ability to resume teaching duties was held to be a reasonable basis for denying salary.[40] A school board policy that required teachers who received full pay while on military reserve leave to turn over to the board payments received for such reserve service was upheld in Colorado.[41] However, an Iowa school board policy requiring school employees to take vacation leave while participating in National Guard training was struck down as violating a state statute prohibiting discrimination against employees because of membership in the National Guard.[42]

Rules and regulations applicable to employment conditions in a school district should be spelled out in an employment contract. For example, if an employment contract between a local board and a teacher refers to regulatory provisions governing due process procedures for termination, then those provisions will govern the responsibilities of the parties involved in the event of a termination of employment.[43]

Noncontractual Duties

Certain duties not specified in an employment contract may be required of teachers in addition to regular classroom instruction. Depending on the jurisdiction, duties such as supervision of extracurricular activities, coaching, club sponsorship, monitoring, and related assignments may be assigned without reference to a specific contract obligation. However, noncontractual duties cannot be required where the activity is unrelated to a school program or educational objective.[44] Under New York law a school board may ask teachers to perform supervisory duties not required under the contract, provided that additional compensation is paid, duties are equitably assigned, and duties are related to respective subject matter fields in which the teachers have expertise.[45] Other courts have held general student supervisory duties to be within the implied requirements of a teaching contract.[46]

Teachers may not refuse to supervise extracurricular activities required as a condition of employment regardless of whether those duties are specified under contract. Courts have construed the refusal to assume extracurricular supervisory duties as an illegal strike or insubordination justifying nonrenewal.[47] The Illinois Court of Appeals has held that teachers could be required by the school board to supervise evening and weekend student activities, even when the rate of compensation for such supervisory services are below that for in-school supervision.[48] The Kansas Supreme Court upheld the validity of an employment contract provision that made acceptance by the teacher of a supplemental contract for supervision of extracurricular activities a prior condition to offering a teaching contract.[49]

An Alabama appeals court upheld a school board's decision dismissing a tenured guidance counselor for insubordination. After a review of evidence, it was established that the counselor refused to meet his assigned duty as a supervisor of children prior to the beginning of the school day. The supervision assignment was rotated among staff, but the counselor felt that guidance counselors should be exempt from this responsibility. A formal reprimand was issued; the counselor responded by filing a grievance. Although the grievance was sustained on a procedural error, the court considered the teacher's conduct in reaching its decision and concluded there was sufficient evidence of a willful refusal to obey a reasonable order of a superior official to justify dismissal.[50]

Tenure

Tenure or continuing contract provisions in state statute laws guarantee a property entitlement to professional staff. The nature and extent of the property right will depend on the interpretation of statute law in a specific jurisdiction, but it is generally accepted that the intent of tenure statutes is to compel procedural due process in dismissal or other adverse employment actions and thus to protect competent professional staff from unjust or arbitrary employment decisions.

Tenure has traditionally been considered the most substantial property right in employment that state statute or board policy could convey to the school employee. However, the security provided by tenured status is not absolute, as decisions relative to dismissal for cause and reduction in force make exceedingly clear.[51] Perhaps the single most significant benefit conveyed by tenure is the requirement that the school board carry the initial burden to provide sufficient evidence to warrant an adverse employment decision.

Probationary Period

Most tenure statutes specify a period during which the employee holds probationary status. The provisions typically establish dates by which time probationary teachers are to be notified of any decision not to renew their contracts and mandate evaluation of the probationary employee.

The requirement of a probationary period is strictly enforced by state courts, which generally insist that the employee meet the requirement of consecutive years of full-time service. For example, although a Kansas teacher had begun employment the previous year, she was not rehired for a second year, because of uncertain federal funding, until late September in a school year that began on August 22. According to the Kansas Supreme Court, this one-month gap in employment meant that the tenure "time clock" had to be reset, as consecutive service could not include the year of probationary employment prior to the gap.[52]

Tenure rights in most instances apply only to employment in the district where those rights were acquired. After having attained tenure status in one district, a Kentucky teacher resigned his position. He later accepted employment in another district where he taught three years before being notified that his contract would not be renewed. The teacher sued, charging that the board violated his tenure rights. The state supreme court disagreed, ruling that to gain tenure status, a teacher must be reemployed after serving four years in the district[53]

Tenure Eligibility for Other School Employees

The applicability of teacher tenure laws to other professional employees has been the subject of review in a number of appellate decisions. The Missouri Court of Appeals ruled that a school principal was ineligible for permanent status and not protected from nonrenewal under the state's teacher tenure provisions.[54] Under Alabama's law, a school counselor could not invoke the due process protections of the teacher tenure law in contesting his transfer from that position.[55] In Illinois an appellate court ruled that some physical education instructors were improperly suspended because they were protected by tenure and could be reassigned to teaching positions but not to coaching duties, since coaching responsibilities were not protected by the tenure statute.[56]

The Fourth Circuit Court of Appeals has held that a principal reassigned to the position of a teacher had no legitimate claim of entitlement to his position as principal, since his continuing contract was silent on the question of reassignment and state statute authorized school boards to reassign administrators without a showing of good cause.[57]

Minnesota statute law on teacher tenure includes all regularly employed principals, supervisors, and teachers. When declining enrollment required a school district to demote some principals, it followed a policy of demotion in inverse order of length of employment as a principal. The Minnesota Supreme Court found this action contrary to the statute and required that demotion and transfer be governed by seniority as an employee in the district.[58]

In Kentucky a court held that a school superintendent is not protected by the teacher tenure law. In this case, a teacher was appointed superintendent to serve the three remaining years of a former superintendent's contract. At the conclusion of the contract term, he was not reappointed as superintendent but instead was assigned a teaching position. The contention that he had served for some three years and had thereby achieved tenured status as superintendent was rejected.[59]

The employment status of a substitute teacher does not necessarily create an entitlement to continued employment,[60] nor can a teacher normally receive credit for substitute service in establishing a claim for tenured status.[61] However, the employee's status as a substitute must be clear and there must be no evidence of an intent to mislead the employee with respect to that status.[62]

Considerations relative to length of service and actual educational functions appear to be primary factors in determining eligibility for tenure. Thus certified remedial and supplemental teachers who were regularly employed on an hourly basis by a board of education in a state-funded and legislatively mandated special education program were held to be teaching staff members within the meaning of New Jersey's tenure law and entitled to acquire tenure.[63]

Acquisition of Tenure by Default or Acquiescence

An issue frequently addressed in court decisions involving tenure is the provision in some states for a so-called tenure by default or acquiescence. New York courts have been particularly lenient with probationary teachers seeking to establish this claim to continuing contract. In two New York cases, school employees successfully claimed they had acquired tenure by default. After serving as a fourth-grade reading teacher on probationary status for three years, an employee received notice that the board was not granting her tenure. However, she continued to teach as a part-time remedial reading teacher for two years and then three additional years at full-time. At that time she was again notified that tenure would not be granted and her contract would not be renewed. In her appeal, the teacher contended that she had acquired tenure by acquiescence at some point during this eight years of employment. Holding for the teacher, the appellate court remanded the case for determination of her tenure area.[64]

The facts of the other case were somewhat similar. In this instance a tenured assistant principal had accepted reassignment to the position of acting principal only after assurances from an assistant superintendent that this assignment was "to be considered an assignment continuous with your present one." Four years later he became a licensed principal and with the enactment of a new tenure law began serving a new probationary period. At the end of this period the board denied tenure. Overturning this action, the court said that after nine years in the position and because of the earlier assurances, he was entitled to tenure by acquiescence.[65]

Massachusetts had interpreted its tenure statute to grant a probationary teacher tenure by default where notice provisions informing of termination or nonrenewal were not met. A notice of termination, sent by the superintendent rather than the school committee, was held invalid and reinstatement with tenure was accorded to a teacher. The invalidity of the notice was predicated on the statutory requirement that only the school committee was empowered to deny tenure to the teacher.[66]

While decisions granting tenure by default are numerous, two court decisions seem to restrict the application of this extraordinary remedy. Both cases relate to the school employee's status as less than a full-time employee. In Illinois the court held that a teacher who had completed the required probationary period of two consecutive years was not eligible for tenure because the board, for reasons of declining enrollment, hired the teacher on a part-time basis for the third year.[67] In Arizona an appellate court affirmed the decision of a school district that refused to grant tenure to a certified employee who was neither a full-time teacher, a school principal devoting 50% of her time to classroom teaching, nor a supervisor of children's activities.[68]

Waiver of Tenure Rights

Whether an employee may be deemed to have waived tenure rights is dependent on the court's construction of state statutes and employment agreements. The Oregon Supreme Court concluded that a permanent teacher does not retain tenure when changing jobs as the result of a transfer to another district. The plaintiff in this case was a special education teacher who transferred to an intermediate district and after two years was dismissed.[69] However, under Tennessee law, a tenured teacher who resigns and then is reemployed by the district retains tenure status.[70] While Tennessee school employees do not waive tenure, the district is under no obligation to rehire them.

Under the terms of a Michigan collective bargaining agreement, if a teacher takes a leave of absence but fails to notify the school district of an intent to return, it would be considered a voluntary resignation. Provisions of the state law specified that a tenured teacher could not be denied continuing contract solely by taking a leave of absence, nor could a tenured teacher be terminated without mutual consent. The school district sought to terminate a tenured teacher on leave of absence when the teacher failed to notify the board of her intention to return within a contractually established deadline. The appellate court took note of the fact that the district failed to advise her of the contractual requirement to notify the board of an intent to return and concluded that the teacher's effort to immediately notify the board of that intention once she received notice that the deadline had passed was evidence that the teacher did not consent to termination and had not in fact resigned her tenure position.[71]

A teacher who had achieved tenured status was suspended due to a reduction in staff because of declining enrollment. In accepting part-time employment, the teacher was required to sign a provision that effectively denied any future employment rights beyond the one-year term of the employment contract. After nonrenewal at the end of the stipulated contract period, the teacher contested the provision as invalid when applied to a tenured teacher. The Iowa Supreme Court agreed, interpreting those provisions of the school code dealing with granting tenure and due process rights as being incorporated in the teacher's contract and thus nullifying the "one-year-only" clause. The clause was held not to constitute a waiver of tenure, nor would it be considered as a basis for good cause in nonrenewal of a tenured teacher's contract.[72]

A tenured teacher who suffered severe headaches was advised to take a medical leave and apply for disability retirement. Both were granted, but the teacher presented herself for work after successful neurological surgery and insisted on reclaiming her tenured status. The North Carolina appellate court held the teacher's employment as a career teacher terminated by operation of law when she elected and received the disability retirement benefits.[73]

Other Adverse Employment Decisions

It is well established that courts may review adverse employment decisions of school boards or administrative agencies to ensure compliance with statute law, contractual obligation, or evidentiary standards. While a court is reluctant to substitute its judgment for that of the school board, evidence that a school board acted arbitrarily and capriciously or failed to make findings of fact in support of its decision would justify court intervention.[74] In addition to dismissal decisions, other adverse employment decisions reviewable by courts include suspension, demotion, transfer, reclassification, reprimand, and failure to promote.

Suspension

The statutes of most states are silent on the authority of school boards to use disciplinary suspension. Nevertheless, there have been some cases challenging whether suspension may be imposed as a penalty for misconduct. In one case a teacher's refusal to submit to a required psychological examination to determine mental competency was a proper basis for a decision to suspend without pay under New York law.[75] However, a California court has ruled that continued suspension for refusal to submit to repeated or additional testing, absent a finding of mental incompetency, is unjustified.[76]

In a case from Illinois, an assistant football coach sought to invalidate a three-day suspension without pay imposed by the school board as a penalty for cursing a student during a football game. The Illinois Supreme Court interpreted the school code, which outlines the procedure to be applied when a board dismisses or removes a teacher, as implying authority to temporarily suspend a teacher, provided a hearing on any proposed suspension is granted.[77]

In a New York case, the state supreme court upheld a school board's imposition of a five-year disciplinary suspension. In overturning a judgment of the appellate court that had reduced the terms of the teacher's suspension to three years, the court noted:

> The courts should show particular deference in matters of internal discipline to determinations made by boards of education which possess a peculiar sensitivity to and comprehension of the complexities and nuances of personnel administration and have responsibility for appropriate accommodation for administration, teachers, pupils, parents and the community.[78]

Suspension may be imposed as a preliminary step in the dismissal process. South Carolina statutes authorize suspension prior to dismissal proceedings. The state supreme court found that a board of education had not violated a teacher's procedural rights by suspending him without providing time to correct deficiencies.[79] The superintendent had informed the teacher by letter of the reasons for the suspension, and the board had accorded him a fair and impartial hearing prior to dismissal.

An issue in many pre-dismissal suspension cases is the employee's right to pay during the period of suspension. An Arizona appellate court ruled that a board of education had no authority to suspend without pay even though the subsequent dismissal was proper.[80] Similarly, in two decisions, New York appellate courts held that a tenured teacher may not be suspended without pay pending final disposition of charges against him.[81]

Transfer and Demotion

Authority to transfer or demote is normally an implied statutory power of a school board, but challenges to this authority have increased. Frequently, courts are asked to determine whether these forms of school board employment decisions are violative of contractual obligations, arbitrary and capricious, or otherwise related to the denial of a specific constitutional or statutory employment right.

The question of whether a transfer constitutes a demotion that triggers statutory due process procedural protections is often a matter of fact to be determined at trial. Factors to be considered may involve more than a simple determination that the employee's salary remains unchanged. For example, an administrator who had been employed as director of vocational education received notice that, under a reorganization plan, his position as a school administrator was eliminated. He was given a new job description. It was held that this change in the job description, which reduced fringe benefits and made the former administrator subordinate to the principal, when previously the principal had been subordinate to him, constituted a demotion in position. The school board failed to show justification for the demotion, thus supporting the court's conclusion that demotion was arbitrary.[82]

Often, the predominant issue in a transfer case involves the extent of procedural due process required. In Georgia, three statutory considerations govern whether a transfer may be considered a denial of due process employment rights: responsibility, prestige, and salary. In a case involving a school principal's reassignment to director of an alternative school program, the lower court concluded that the principal's transfer reduced his prestige and responsibility, even though he received an increase in pay. The court held that such a transfer required a due process hearing. The Georgia Supreme Court reversed this decision, interpreting the statute to require all three features — less responsibility, less prestige, and less salary — not just one or two of them.[83]

The primary issue in a number of cases is whether or not the transfer was a demotion. The Pennsylvania Commonwealth Court ruled that an elementary principal had been demoted when he was reassigned to "auxiliary duties" in another elementary school, even though his salary remained the same. The court reasoned that he was no longer in complete charge and was no longer in a singular position.[84] Similarly, a tenured Massachusetts principal was held to have been demoted when the school committee assigned him full-time classroom teaching duties at a lower salary.[85]

Principals in Florida and Tennessee were unable to establish that their transfers were demotions. A Florida principal whose status was changed to "program coordinator" was unsuccessful in his claim that his new position was not similar and his salary was not the same, conditions necessary to grant a hearing according to statute.[86] In another case the principal's title and base salary remained unchanged, but since he now headed a smaller school with fewer teachers, his total compensation relative to fringe benefits was less. The court rejected his argument that the transfer required additional due process protections.[87]

If a transfer or demotion is a substantial penalty imposed for improper conduct, full due process rights should be accorded the employee. The Fourth Circuit Court of Appeals affirmed a North Carolina federal district court's decision upholding demotion of a "career" teacher to the position of "tutor." The demotion was a disciplinary penalty imposed because of an incident in the teacher's classroom in which she read to the class a confiscated student note containing three "vulgar colloquialisms." The court found no merit to the employee's claim that her First and 14th Amendment rights were violated. State statutes provided adequate notice of proscribed conduct, the hearings accorded met due process requirements, and the evidence refuted allegations of racial discrimination.[88]

All adverse employment cases require a prima facie proof that the employment decision is sufficiently adverse to justify a legal remedy. A claim that a change in teaching schedule was substantially motivated by a desire to retaliate against the teacher's exercise of free speech was not enough to establish a claim for violation of First Amendment rights. While a teacher's activity as a representative of her teaching association was considered to be protected under the First Amendment, a change in her teaching schedule was not considered a sufficient legal injury justifying relief. The federal district court reasoned that if a sanction is to be pleaded, it must be shown that the consequence of the sanction would have a chilling effect on the exercise of constitutionally protected rights. In the absence of a sufficiently adverse personnel action, such as reduction in rank or loss of pay, a teacher's claim would not be subject to court action, even though the administrative decision could be substantially motivated by a desire to curb the exercise of substantive constitutional rights.[89]

An employment decision may be sufficiently adverse to require that a school board provide a defensible basis for its decision, even when the decision involves a failure to promote. An Iowa statutory preference for school district employees did not justify the promotion of a school employee to a position as audiologist, where the evidence demonstrated that he possessed the requisite technical skills but lacked the ability to cooperate and coordinate his activities with others, was often abusive and insulting in professional relations, and contributed to discord and dissidence among staff.[90]

In an unusual administrative law case from New York, a teacher who was officially reprimanded by the school board for misconduct sought to overturn the board's decision as an excessive penalty. The appellate court took note that the reprimand was related to conviction for the felonious offense of drug possession and concluded that the reprimand was not excessive. Rather it was so lenient as to be arbitrary and capricious and an abuse of the board's discretion. The court ordered the board to reconsider its decision, presumably to enforce a more stringent penalty.[91]

Summary

Educators must be alert to the statutory mandates, regulatory provisions, and contractual obligations that are unique to their particular state or local school district. Local school boards must take care to exercise power within the scope of delegated constitutional or statutory authority for valid state purposes. Whether that purpose relates to the efficient management of the public schools, the education of pupils, the maintenance of appropriate discipline, or any other recognized state purpose, the principle of reasonableness should guide the deliberations of the school board or its agents.

Every aspect of the employment relationship, whether related to the evaluation of professional qualifications, the administration of contractual agreements, the awarding of tenure, or the determination of appropriate discipline, should emphasize the rational relationship between the legally defined mission of the public school and the rule or policy to be implemented. Judges will insist that public school officials be guided by principles of fairness, reasonableness, and good faith in dealings with public school employees.

Courts remain reluctant to intervene in the employment policies of school boards unless the employee can make an initial showing that the employment practice goes beyond the authority delegated to the board, was arbitrary or capricious, or otherwise violated the constitutional or statutory rights of the public school employee. If the employee is successful in carrying this initial burden of proof, then the school board must show that the policy or practice in question is within the scope of its authority and is fairly and reasonably applied. Consequently, it is important for the school board to have a clearly articulated basis for employment policies and to establish fundamental guidelines, through consultation and deliberation, to ensure fair and reasonable implementation of that policy.

Footnotes

1. *See, e.g.*, Steiner v. Independent School Dist., 262 N.W.2d 173 (Minn. 1978).
2. *See, e.g.*, Lenard v. Board of Educ. of Fairfield, 384 N.E.2d 1321 (Ill. 1979); Chester v. Harper Woods School Dist., 273 N.W.2d 916 (Mich. App. 1979).
3. Pierce v. Society of Sisters, 268 U.S. 510, 519 (1925).
4. *See, e.g.*, Weiman v. Updegraff, 344 U.S. 183 (1952). For a discussion of substantive constitutional rights, *see* chapter 3 *infra*.
5. *See, e.g.*, Cole v. Richardson, 405 U.S. 676 (1972); Connell v. Higginbotham, 403 U.S. 207 (1971).
6. *See, e.g.*, Council of Supervisors Ass'n v. Board of Educ., 297 N.Y.S.2d 547 (Sup. Ct. App. Div. 1969); Nelson v. Board of Examiners, 288 N.Y.S.2d 454 (Sup. Ct. App. Div. 1968).
7. *See, e.g.*, Armstead v. Starkville Municipal Separate School Dist., 461 F.2d 276 (5th Cir. 1972); Johnson v. Matzen, 210 N.W.2d 151 (Neb. 1926).
8. United States v. South Carolina, 445 F. Supp. 1094 (D.S.C. 1977), *aff'd*, 434 U.S. 1026 (1978).
9. 440 U.S. 194 (1979).
10. Donnelly v. Manchester, 274 A.2d 789 (N.H. 1971).
11. Werdwell v. Board of Educ. of Cincinnati, 529 F.2d 625 (6th Cir. 1976); *see also* Park v. Lansing School Dist., 233 N.W.2d 592 (Mich. 1975); Mogle v. Sever Cty. School Dist., 540 F.2d 478 (10th Cir. 1976).
12. *See, e.g.* Bay v. State Bd. of Educ., 379 P.2d 558 (Ore. 1963); In re Masiello, 138 A.2d 393 (N.J. 1958); Antell v. Board of Educ., 195 N.Y.S.2d 959 (Sup. Ct. 1959).
13. Golonka v. Michigan Dep't of Educ., 308 N.W.2d 425 (Mich. App. 1981).
14. Cranston Teachers' Ass'n v. Cranston School Comm., 424 A.2d 648 (R.I. 1981).
15. Wyoming State Dep't of Educ. v. Barber, 649 P.2d 681 (Wyo. 1982).
16. Ambach v. Norwick, 441 U.S. 68 (1979).
17. *Id.* at 78-79.
18. Granus v. Melrose-Mindoro Joint School Dist., 254 N.W.2d 730 (Wash. 1977).
19. Linton v. Board of Educ. of Yonkers, 417 N.Y.S.2d 246 (1979).
20. *See* Brubaker v. Community Unit School Dist. No. 16, 4 Ill. Dec. 853 (Ill. App. 1977).
21. Pintek v. Elk Lake School Dist., 360 A.2d 804 (Pa. Commw. 1976).
22. Guthrie v. Taylor, 185 S.E.2d 193 (N.C. 1971).
23. Adams v. State Professional Practices Council, 406 So. 2d 1170 (Fla. Dist. Ct. App. 1981).
24. Jenkins v. State Bd. of Educ., 399 So. 2d 103 (Fla. Dist. Ct. App. 1981).
25. Morrison v. State Bd. of Educ., 82 Cal. Rptr. 175 (1969).
26. Erb v. Iowa State Bd. of Pub. Instruction, 216 N.W.2d 339 (Iowa 1974).
27. Cobb Cty. Bd. of Educ. v. Vizcarrondo, 293 S.E.2d 13 (Ga. App. 1982).
28. Juul v. Board of Educ. of Hempstead, 428 N.Y.S.2d 319 (Sup. Ct. App. Div. 1980).

29. Monroe Cty. Commun. School v. Frohliger, 434 N.E.2d 93 (Ind. App. 1982).
30. Stringham v. Jordan School Dist., 588 P.2d 698 (Utah 1978).
31. Tripp v. Hall, 395 So. 2d 33 (Ala. 1981).
32. Brantley v. Surles, 404 So. 2d 1013 (Miss. 1981).
33. Rothery v. Cantrell, 635 P.2d 184 (Ariz. App. 1981).
34. Bitler v. Warrior Run School Dist., 437 A.2d 481 (Pa. Commw. 1981).
35. Bloomberg-Dubin v. Board of Educ., 439 N.Y.S.2d 956 (Sup. Ct. App. Div. 1981).
36. California School Employees v. King City Union Elementary School Dist., 172 Cal. Rptr. 368 (Cal. App. 1981).
37. Maiter v. Chicago Bd. of Educ., 415 N.E.2d 1034 (Ill. 1980).
38. State *ex rel.* Wilson v. Truby, 281 S.E.2d 231 (W.Va. 1981).
39. Lehman v. Board of Educ., 439 N.Y.S.2d 670 (Sup. Ct. App. Div. 1981).
40. Kurzius v. Board of Educ., 438 N.Y.S.2d 824 (Sup. Ct. App. Div. 1981).
41. Colorado Springs Teacher's Ass'n v. School Dist. No. 11, 622 P.2d 602 (Colo. App. 1980).
42. Belwey v. Villisca Commun. School Dist., 299 N.W.2d 904 (Iowa 1980).
43. *See* Rhodes v. Board of Educ. of Person Cty., 293 S.E.2d 295 (N.C. App. 1982).
44. *See, e.g.* Pease v. Millcreek Twp. School Dist., 195 A.2d 104 (Pa. 1963).
45. Parrish v. Moss, 106 N.Y.S.2d 577 (Sup. Ct. 1951).
46. *See, e.g.*, Johnson v. United School Dist., 191 A.2d 897 (Pa. 1963); McGrath v. Burkhard, 280 P.2d 864 (Cal. App. 1955).
47. *See* Board of Educ. of Asbury Park v. Asbury Park Educ. Ass'n, 368 A.2d 396 (N.J. Super. Ct. 1976) (illegal strike); Blair v. Robstown Indep. School Dist., 556 F.2d 1331 (5th Cir. 1977) (insubordination).
48. District 300 Educ. Ass'n v. Board of Educ., 334 N.E.2d 165 (Ill. App. 1975).
49. Riley Cty. Educ. Ass'n v. Unified School Dist., 592 P.2d 87 (Kan. 1979).
50. Jones v. Alabama State Tenure Comm'n, 408 So. 2d 145 (Ala. Civ. App. 1981).
51. See Chapters 8 and 9 *infra*.
52. Schmidt v. Unified School Dist. No. 497, 644 P.2d 396 (Kan. 1982).
53. Carpenter v. Board of Educ. of Owsley Cty., 582 S.W.2d 645 (Ky. 1979).
54. Duncan v. Reorganized School Dist. No. R-1, 617 S.W.2d 571 (Mo. App. 1981).
55. Smith v. Birmingham Bd. of Educ., 403 So. 2d 226 (Ala. 1981).
56. School Directors of Dist. U-46 v. Kossoff, 419 N.E.2d 658 (Ill. App. 1981).
57. Wooten v. Clifton Forge School Bd., 655 F.2d 552 (4th Cir. 1981).
58. McManus v. Independent School Dist., 321 N.W.2d 891 (Minn. 1982).
59. Floyd v. Board of Educ. of Greenup, 598 S.W.2d 460 (Ky. App. 1979).
60. *See* School Comm. of Providence v. Board of Regents for Educ., 429 A.2d 1297 (R.I. 1981); Pottsville Area School Dist. v. Marteslo, 423 A.2d 1336 (Pa. Commw. 1980). *But see* Robins v. Blaney, 451 N.Y.S.2d 853 (Sup. Ct. App. Div. 1982).
61. *See* Corrigan v. Donilon, 433 A.2d 198 (R.I. 1981); Johnson v. Board of Educ., 423 N.E.2d 903 (Ill. 1981).

62. Pottsville Area School Dist. v. Marteslo, 423 A.2d 1336 (Pa. Commw. 1980).
63. Spiewak v. Rutherford Bd. of Educ., 447 A.2d 120 (N.J. 1982).
64. Matthews v. Nyquist, 412 N.Y.S.2d 501 (Sup. Ct. App. Div. 1979).
65. Elsberg v. Board of Educ., 418 N.Y.S.2d 273 (Sup. Ct. 1979).
66. Farrington v. School Comm. of Cambridge, 402 N.E.2d 98 (Mass. App. 1980).
67. Johnson v. Board of Educ. of Decatur, 409 N.E.2d 139 (Ill. App. 1980).
68. Mish v. Tempe School Dist. No. 3, 609 P.2d 73 (Ariz. App. 1980).
69. Davis v. Wasco Intermediate Educ. Dist., 593 P.2d 1152 (Ore. 1979).
70. Cox v. Perkins, 585 S.W.2d 590 (Tenn. 1979).
71. Board of Educ. v. Cunningham, 317 N.W.2d 638 (Mich. App. 1982).
72. Bruton v. Ames Commun. School Dist., 291 N.W.2d 351 (Iowa 1980).
73. Meachan v. Montgomery Cty. Bd. of Educ., 267 S.E.2d 349 (N.C. App. 1980).
74. *See, e.g.*, Dobervich v. Central Cass Pub. School Dist., 302 N.W.2d 745 (N.D. 1981); Eskew v. Kanawha Cty. Bd. of Educ., 280 S.E.2d 297 (W.Va. 1981).
75. McNamara v. Commissioner of Educ., 436 N.Y.S.2d 406 (Sup. Ct. App. Div. 1981).
76. Buchan v. Las Vigenes Unified School Dist., 177 Cal. Rptr. 788 (Cal. App. 1981).
77. Craddock v. Board of Educ. of Annawan Commun. Unit School Dist., 405 N.E.2d 794 (Ill. 1980).
78. Sarro v. New York City Bd. of Educ., 419 N.Y.S.2d 483, 487 (1979).
79. McWhirter v. Cherokee Cty. School Dist., 261 S.E.2d 157 (S.C. 1979).
80. Fike v. Catalina-Foothills School Dist., 589 P.2d 1317 (Ariz. App. 1978).
81. Belluardo v. Board of Educ., 414 N.Y.S.2d 29 (Sup. Ct. App. Div. 1979); Bali v. Board of Educ., 416 N.Y.S.2d 933 (Sup. Ct. App. Div. 1979).
82. Jefferson Cty. DuBois Area Voc.-Tech. Dist. Schools v. Horton, 413 A.2d 36 (Pa. Commw. 1980).
83. Rockdale Cty. School Dist. v. Weil, 266 S.E.2d 919 (Ga. 1980).
84. School Dist. of York v. Allison, 406 A.2d 1197 (Pa. Commw. 1979).
85. Doherty v. School Comm. of Boston, 384 N.E.2d 228 (Mass. App. 1979).
86. Berkner v. School Bd. of Orange Cty., 373 So. 2d 54 (Fla. Dist. Ct. App. 1979).
87. McKenna v. Sumner Cty. Bd. of Educ., 574 S.W.2d 527 (Tenn. 1978).
88. Frison v. Franklin Cty. Bd. of Educ., 596 F.2d 1192 (4th Cir. 1979).
89. Reichert v. Draud, 511 F. Supp. 679 (E.D. Ky. 1981).
90. Bishop v. Keystone Area Educ. Agency, 311 N.W.2d 279 (Iowa 1981).
91. Riforgiato v. Board of Educ., 448 N.Y.S.2d 74 (Sup. Ct. App. Div. 1982).

2
Discrimination in Employment
Martha M. McCarthy

Public employment has not been immune to the problem of discrimination against various segments of our citizenry. Indeed, a substantial portion of educational employment litigation pertains to allegations of unlawful discrimination. Decisions regarding hiring, promotion, and a host of other concerns have generated charges that individuals have been discriminated against because of inherent traits rather than because of their qualifications and abilities.

This chapter provides an overview of litigation in which courts have interpreted educational employees' rights to nondiscriminatory treatment and employers' obligations to ensure equal employment opportunities. Specifically, protections against discrimination based on race, sex, national origin, religion, handicaps, and age are covered. Because of the range, volume, and complexity of the litigation in this area, the intent of this chapter is to identify applicable legal principles rather than to present a comprehensive analysis of all recent cases.[1]

Racial Discrimination

Claims of racial discrimination in educational employment have resulted in numerous lawsuits brought under the equal protection clause of the 14th Amendment and federal civil rights laws. The majority of the cases have involved hiring, promotion, job assignment, and staff reduc-

Martha M. McCarthy is a professor of education and associate dean of faculties at Indiana University.

tion practices that allegedly discriminate against minorities.[2] Also, the operation of affirmative action programs has resulted in claims of discrimination against the racial majority or so-called "reverse discrimination."

Hiring, Promotion, and Job Assignment

Many controversies involving hiring practices in the public sector have focused on prerequisites to employment that eliminate a disproportionate percentage of minorities from the applicant pool. The law is clear that a facially discriminatory racial classification, such as a governmental policy barring minorities from a certain position, violates the equal protection clause of the 14th Amendment unless justified by a compelling governmental interest. However, most allegations of racial discrimination in connection with prerequisites to public employment do not involve overt classifications; rather, they entail claims that facially neutral employment policies adversely affect minority employees. In such suits, aggrieved individuals must prove that they have been victims of purposeful discriminaton to gain relief under the equal protection clause.

Public employers can defend a constitutional charge of discriminatory intent by showing that the prerequisite to employment bears a rational relationship to a legitimate governmental goal. For example, in 1978 the U.S. Supreme Court affirmed a lower court's conclusion that a state's use of the National Teachers Examination for teacher certification and salary purposes satisfied 14th Amendment equal protection guarantees because the test was used for the legitimate purpose of improving the effectiveness of the state's teaching force and was not administered with any intent to discriminate against minority applicants for certification.[3] The trial court was convinced that the test was valid in that it measured knowledge of course content in teacher preparation programs. The court further reasoned that there was sufficient evidence to establish a relationship between the use of the test scores as a factor in determining teachers' placement on the pay scale and valid employment objectives such as encouraging teachers to upgrade their skills.

Because of the difficulty in proving unconstitutional intent, plaintiffs alleging racial discrimination in employment recently have relied primarily on Title VII of the Civil Rights Act of 1964. Title VII prohibits employers with 15 or more employees, employment agencies, and labor organizations from discriminating against employees on the basis of race, color, religion, sex, or national origin and covers hiring, promotion, and compensation practices as well as fringe benefits and other terms and conditions of employment.[4] The law allows employers to impose hiring restrictions based on sex, national origin, or religion (but not on race) if such characteristics are bona fide occupational qualifications.

In challenges to facially neutral policies with a disparate impact on groups protected by Title VII, proof of discriminatory intent is not necessary. After an initial inference of discrimination (prima facie case) is established, the burden shifts to the employer to prove that the policy is justified by a valid job necessity. In a Title VII disparate impact case, a rational or legitimate nondiscriminatory reason for the employment policy is insufficient to rebut an inference of discrimination; the policy must have a manifest relationship to the job. The Supreme Court has ruled that tests used as a prerequisite to employment that disproportionately eliminate minority applicants must be validated as assessing ability to perform the specific jobs for which they are used.[5]

In a significant 1982 decision, the Supreme Court ruled five-to-four that prerequisites to employment or promotion with a disparate adverse impact on minorities violate Title VII even though the "bottom line" of the hiring or promotion process results in an appropriate racial balance. While acknowledging that evidence of a nondiscriminatory work force might in some instances assist an employer in rebutting a constitutional charge of intentional discrimination, the Supreme Court majority reasoned that where "an identifiable pass-fail barrier denies an employment opportunity to a disproportionately large number of minorities and prevents them from proceeding to the next step in the selection process," that barrier must be shown to be job-related to satisfy Title VII.[6] The majority declared that Congress did not intend to give employers "license" to discriminate against some employees merely because other members of the employees' group are treated favorably.

However, the employer's burden of establishing a job necessity for policies with a disparate adverse impact is not impossible to satisfy. In 1981 the Fourth Circuit Court of Appeals found no Title VII violation in connection with a school district's use of certification grades based on scores on the National Teachers Examination to determine teachers' salaries.[7] Although the certification grades resulted in the denial of pay raises to a much larger proportion of black than white teachers, the appellate court reasoned that the practice was justified by the job necessity of attracting well-qualified teachers and encouraging self-improvement among low-rated instructional personnel. As discussed previously, this practice had already withstood constitutional challenge because intentional discrimination was not established.

In addition to challenges to facially neutral policies with a disparate *impact* on minorities, some employees have alleged that they have received discriminatory *treatment* because of their race or other protected characteristic in violation of Title VII. Plaintiffs carry a heavier burden of proof in substantiating disparate treatment in contrast to disparate impact under Title VII. In disparate treatment cases, plaintiffs must produce proof of the employer's intent to treat individuals differently relative to similarly situated members of another race, which is similar to the constitutional standard under the equal protection clause.

To establish a prima facie case of disparate treatment in connection with hiring and promotion practices, the plaintiff must first demonstrate membership in a group protected by Title VII. Then the individual must show that he or she applied for and was qualified to assume the job sought and was rejected despite such qualifications. The individual must also produce evidence that the position remained open after the rejection and that the employer continued to seek applicants with the plaintiff's qualifications.[8] Once a prima facie case is established, the employer can rebut the inference of discrimination by articulating a non-discriminatory reason for the action. The burden of persuasion remains with the plaintiff to prove by a preponderance of evidence that the legitimate reasons offered are mere pretexts for discrimination.

Courts have accepted employers' asserted nondiscriminatory reasons for denying employment or promotion to minorities and for other differential treatment if the individuals have not been certified or qualified for the positions sought or if the employment decisions have been based on quality of performance or other considerations unrelated to race.[9] However, minority plaintiffs have prevailed with evidence that the avowed nondiscriminatory reason was merely a pretext to mask discriminatory motive. For example, a black employee established a prima facie case of discrimination by establishing that a school district paid him less than his white counterpart for substantially equivalent work. The school district argued that the pay differential was based on nondiscriminatory reasons related to differences in performance and job responsibilities. But the appeals court concluded from the testimony that the differential was based primarily on racial considerations.[10]

Claims of discrimination in hiring and promotion have been particularly troublesome for the judiciary because of the subjective judgments involved. Courts have been reluctant to strip employers of their prerogative to base such decisions on personality and other subjective factors. Employers are not required to accord preference to minorities if nonminority applicants are considered better or merely equally qualified for available positions. The employer has discretion to choose among candidates with similar credentials, provided that the decision is not grounded in discriminatory motives. However, the judiciary also has recognized that "greater possibilities for abuse . . . are inherent in subjective definitions of employment selection and promotion criteria" because of the potential for masking racial discrimination.[11]

Statistical evidence often plays an important role in establishing a prima facie case of racial bias in connection with hiring practices. An inference of disparate treatment can be established by evidence of gross statistical disparities between an employer's work force and the availability pool or by evidence that minority employees have been confined primarily to a few schools with predominantly minority pupils. In 1982 the Fourth Circuit Court of Appeals ruled that if such a pattern or practice of employment discrimination is established, the burden of proof shifts to school authorities to rebut the discrimination charge.[12] Acknowledging that the plaintiff usually retains the burden of proof in a disparate treatment case, the appeals court reasoned that a finding of either intentional discrimination or a recent pattern of discrimination in a school district warrants placing the burden of persuasion on the employer to justify challenged practices.

Once unlawful discrimination is established in employment practices, federal courts have broad discretion in ordering equitable relief. In addition to requiring that victims of discrimination be hired, promoted, or reinstated in the next available positions, courts have awarded back pay to the date of the discriminatory act and have granted retroactive seniority under certain conditions to restore such employees to their rightful place.[13] However, bona fide seniority systems that are not negotiated or maintained with discriminatory intent are not vulnerable to attack under Title VII, even though they may perpetuate the effects of past intentional discrimination.[14]

Because legal proceedings in discrimination suits often are quite lengthy, some employers charged with discrimination in hiring have attempted to reduce their potential liability by remedying the alleged discriminatory practice before judicially ordered to do so. In 1982 the Supreme Court ruled that an employer can limit the accrual of back pay liability under Title VII by unconditionally offering the claimant the job previously denied without the promise of retroactive seniority.[15] The Supreme Court majority concluded that without such an opportunity to reduce back pay liability, employers would have no incentive to end discrimination through voluntary efforts when they have been accused of a discriminatory practice. Of course, if the employee ultimately wins a favorable judicial ruling, the court may award full compensation, including retroactive seniority.

Affirmative Action and Reverse Discrimination

The term "affirmative action" first was used in an Executive Order, issued by President Kennedy in 1961, to refer to a duty placed on employers to take steps to remedy past discrimination. There is some sentiment that without affirmative action plans, including goals to increase the representation of women and minorities in the work force, the effects of prior discriminatory practices cannot be eliminated. However, affirmative action goals are often stated in terms of hiring percentages, which have been criticized as causing "reverse discrimination" or discrimination against the majority. Although affirmative action programs are directed toward women, the handicapped, and certain categories of veterans as well as toward racial and ethnic minorities, most of the suits challenging such programs have focused on the preferential treatment of racial minorities.

Some courts have upheld the constitutionality of affirmative action plans in connection with a finding of de jure segregation. For example, in 1982 the First Circuit Court of Appeals upheld an affirmative action plan as part of a desegregation order in the Boston school district, and the Supreme Court declined to review the case.[16] Under the plan, minorities must maintain 20% of the teaching positions regardless of their seniority. The court reasoned that without such a plan, the efforts made in remedying intentional discrimination in the school district would be eradicated through layoffs necessitated by declining enrollments.

In contrast, in May 1983 the Sixth Circuit Court of Appeals reversed a federal district court's order that placed race over seniority in recalling teachers who had been released for financial reasons.[17] The appeals court held that the district court erred by imposing a quota of minority teachers (20%) that must be maintained by the Kalamazoo School District. Noting that racial hiring quotas per se are not improper to remedy a violation of students' constitutional rights, the court found that the school district had made a sustained good faith effort to recruit minority teachers to remedy the effects of prior segregation. The court concluded that "the record does not demonstrate that nullification of the seniority and tenure rights of white teachers is necessary to vindicate the students' constitutional rights."[18]

Even more controversial have been efforts to give employment preference to minorities in school systems that are not under court-ordered desegregation mandates. The judiciary has identified factors that should be evaluated in judging the constitutionality of voluntary affirmative action plans. These include the efficacy of alternative remedies, the envisioned duration of the plan, the relationship between the imposed percentage of minorities to be hired and the racial composition of the student population[19] or the relevant work force, and the availability of waiver provisions in the event that the quota is not met. Affirmative action plans that are temporary, do not exclude white employees from consideration for certain positions, and are not designed to maintain a rigid racial balance probably will survive judicial scrutiny, with evidence that such temporary preferential treatment is necessary to remedy the effects of past discriminatory practices.[20]

Sex Discrimination

Differential treatment of the sexes has a lengthy history, and only within the past few decades has such discrimination been legally challenged. Traditionally, distinctions based on sex were rationalized by an attitude of "romantic paternalism," which the Supreme Court characterized in 1973 as placing women "not on a pedestal but in a cage."[21] Until the 1970s, unequal treatment of male and female employees was not only prevalent, but also judicially sanctioned.

During the past decade courts have recognized that the 14th Amendment prohibits invidious governmental discrimination based on sex as well as on other inherent traits. Although gender classifications are not considered "suspect" as are those based on race, the judiciary recently has required facially discriminatory sex classifications to be substantially related to important governmental objectives to satisfy equal protection mandates.[22] However, the mere disparate impact of a facially neutral law on men or women is not sufficient to abridge the equal protection clause without proof of unlawful motive, even if the adverse impact of the statute was foreseeable at the time it was enacted.[23]

As with claims of racial discrimination, the difficult burden of establishing unconstitutional motive has caused most plaintiffs in sex bias suits to rely on federal statutory guarantees. Specifically, Title VII of the Civil Rights Act of 1964, the Equal Pay Act, and Title IX of the Education Amendments of 1972 have been the bases for most claims. A range of employment concerns has generated statutory sex bias suits, including conditions of employment, pregnancy-related policies, compensation practices, retirement benefits programs, and sexual harassment.

Conditions of Employment

Most allegations of sex bias in educational employment have been initiated by female plaintiffs contending that they have been treated unfairly solely because of their sex in violation of Title VII. In these cases plaintiffs often have attempted to establish a prima facie case of sex discrimination by presenting both specific and general statistical data. Specific data relates to the individual's qualifications for the job (or promotion) that was denied allegedly for discriminatory reasons. General data is presented to establish that a prevalent pattern or practice of sex bias exists in the institution. The judiciary has recognized that general statistical data are particularly helpful in the academic context where many hiring and promotion decisions are highly subjective. However, female plaintiffs have not been able to establish a prima facie case of sex discrimination if the labor market data presented do not reflect the number of women actually qualified for the specific job in question. Also, statistical disparity data have been rejected where factors other than sex, which might account for the employment decision, have not been considered.[24]

Educational employers have successfully rebutted a prima facie case of sex discrimination by showing that positions were filled by males who were better qualified than females who were rejected. In 1981 the Supreme Court further declared that employers are not legally obligated under Title VII to give preference to a female applicant when choosing between a male and female with similar qualifications.[25] Also, employers have prevailed by showing that promotion decisions were based on factors unrelated to sex, such as inadequate experience, scholarship, or performance.[26]

Plaintiffs have obtained relief for unlawful sex bias, however, if school authorities have been unable to articulate a nondiscriminatory reason for their actions. Title VII violations have been found with evidence that female applicants were better qualified for specific jobs but were rejected in favor of males because of stereotypic attitudes toward the capabilities of women. Courts similarly have awarded equitable relief where job advertisements have included the notation, "prefer men," or job descriptions have been specifically drafted to exclude qualified women.[27]

Even if the employer does produce a nondiscriminatory reason for the employment decision, the employee still might prove that the nondiscriminatory reason is merely a pretext. For example, in 1979 the First Circuit Court of Appeals ruled that a female university professor established that the legitimate reasons offered for her denial of promotion were a pretext for sex bias.[28] Evidence indicated that the plaintiff had been compared to a "school marm" and in other ways judged on her sex rather than merit. Moreover, the court found that evidence of a general atmosphere of sex bias in the institution, although not proof per se of disparate treatment, could be considered "along with any other evidence bearing on motive" in assessing whether the defendant's reasons were pretexts.

In addition to Title VII's prohibition against sex discrimination in employment, sex bias in federally funded education programs can be challenged under Title IX of the Education Amendments of 1972. While individuals have a private right to bring suit for injunctive relief under Title IX, the Act does not provide for personal remedies such as reinstatement and back pay. Instead, the sanction for a Title IX violation is termination of federal funds to the program where noncompliance is substantiated.

In June 1982 the Supreme Court settled a 10-year-old controversy when it ruled six-to-three that Title IX covers employees as well as students.[29] Acknowledging that the language of the Act does not expressly include employees, the Court majority noted that there is no specific exclusion to that effect in the law's list of exceptions. Also, the majority pointed out that Congress did not pass a resolution opposing the Title

IX employment regulations promulgated by the former Department of Health, Education and Welfare. Furthermore, Congress has rejected several bills that would have amended Title IX specifically to exclude employees. Although the Supreme Court endorsed the employment regulations, it held that Title IX is program specific in that it prohibits sex discrimination in educational programs directly receiving federal aid.

The Department of Education waited to respond to over 200 complaints, pending resolution of the Title IX employment jurisdiction issue. Yet, there is still ambiguity as to the actual reach of the law because the Supreme Court did not define a federally funded educational program. Lower courts recently have rendered conflicting opinions regarding whether "program" should be narrowly or broadly defined.[30] Even if the Supreme Court ultimately should endorse an expansive interpretation of a federally funded program, the prospects for aggrieved employees to gain relief under Title IX are not particularly promising. The Supreme Court recently declined to review two decisions in which the Seventh Circuit Court of Appeals held that proof of discriminatory intent is required to establish a Title IX violation and that individuals cannot seek damages under the law.[31] Although Title IX has served as a catalyst for many schools and colleges to change biased policies, the law has not yet posed a serious threat of sanctions for educational employers whose practices discriminate on the basis of sex.

Pregnancy-Related Policies

Law suits alleging discrimination against pregnant employees have been initiated under federal and state constitutional and statutory provisions. Since pregnancy affects only women, disadvantages in employment that accrue because of this condition have generated numerous charges of sex bias. Courts have been called on to address the treatment of pregnancy in disability benefits programs, in connection with leave and seniority policies, and as a basis for dismissing unwed female employees.

The exclusion of pregnancy-related disabilites from employee disability benefits programs elicited two Supreme Court rulings and stimulated congressional action in the mid-1970s. The Supreme Court ruled that the differential treatment of pregnancy in disability benefits packages does not constitute sex discrimination and thus satisfies both the U.S. Constitution and Title VII.[32] The Court held that the classification involved is based on pregnancy, not on sex, noting that nonpregnant employees contain both men and women. However, in 1978 Congress reacted to the Supreme Court's interpretation of Title VII by amending the law specifically to prohibit employers from excluding pregnancy benefits in comprehensive medical and disability insurance plans.[33] As of 29 April 1979, all employers with disability programs were required to be in compliance with this provision.

Maternity leave provisions also have been the source of considerable controversy. In 1974 the Supreme Court ruled that a school board policy, requiring teachers to take maternity leave at the beginning of the fifth month of pregnancy and prohibiting them from returning to work until one year after the birth of the child, created an irrebuttable presumption that teaching incompetency accompanies pregnancy and childbirth.[34] The denial of an opportunity for individual teachers to refute such a presumption was found to abridge the due process clause of the 14th Amendment. More recently, the Fifth Circuit Court of Appeals ruled that a school board's maternity leave provisions violated Title VII by vesting discretion in the superintendent to determine when a teacher could return to work from maternity leave, while employees themselves determined when to return to work from sick leave.[35] The board defended its policy as a business necessity, but the court ruled that there were less discriminatory alternatives to attain the district's fiscal objectives.

However, the Ninth Circuit Court of Appeals upheld a mandatory pregnancy leave policy, requiring pregnant employees to go on leave no later than the beginning of the ninth month, as a legitimate business necessity under Title VII.[36] Recognizing the impaired physical condition and abilities of teachers during the ninth month of pregnancy and the need to plan for teachers' absences, the court concluded that mandatory leave was necessary to attain administrative and educational objectives of the district. The court also rejected a 14th Amendment attack on the policy, reasoning that the provision did not impair the equal protection clause and was not irrational or arbitrary in contrast to the fifth-month rule invalidated previously by the Supreme Court. But the appellate court found that the school district's policy denying the use of accumulated sick leave to pregnant teachers created a prima facie case of discrimination. This portion of the ruling was remanded for additional proceedings to ascertain if the school district could demonstrate a business necessity for denying such use of sick leave. Other courts similarly have ruled that differential treatment of pregnancy within sick leave provisions violates Title VII unless justified as a business necessity.[37]

In addition to the use of sick leave for pregnancy-related absences, employees often take unpaid leave if additional time off is needed to recuperate from childbirth or to care for the new infant. The Supreme Court has recognized that the denial of accumulated seniority upon return from such maternity leave violates Title VII.[38] The judiciary also has held that school boards cannot exclude pregnancy leave while including other leaves in computing a teacher's probationary period toward the award of tenure and cannot otherwise discriminate against employees because of their prior pregnancies in the calculation of seniority.[39]

In some situations a teacher's pregnant status has been the basis for dismissal or nonrenewal. In 1979 the Fourth Circuit Court of Appeals found a Title VII violation where a school district had an unwritten policy that it would not renew the contract of any teacher who could not commit to a full-year's service, and this policy had been applied only to pregnant teachers.[40] Reversing the court below, the appellate court concluded that the pregnant plaintiff, whose contract had not been renewed, established a prima facie case of sex discrimination because of the disparate impact of the board's action on women. The court remanded the case for additional proceedings to ascertain whether the board could justify its practice as a business necessity.

Female employees have also relied on Title VII as well as their constitutional rights to privacy and equal protection of the laws in challenging dismissals which have been based on their unwed parenthood. In 1976 the Supreme Court declined to review a case in which the Fifth Circuit Court of Appeals held that a school board's rule prohibiting the hiring of parents of illegitimate children discriminated against women in violation of the equal protection clause.[41] The appeals court rejected the school district's contention that the policy was rationally related to a legitimate governmental interest. The court did not find that unwed parenthood per se constitutes immorality or that the employment of unwed parents in a school setting contributes to the problem of pregnancies among high school girls.

In 1982 the Fifth Circuit Court of Appeals ruled that if pregnancy out of wedlock is a substantial or motivating reason for a public school teacher's dismissal, the 14th Amendment equal protection clause is violated.[42] The federal district court had upheld a teacher's dismissal, reasoning that immorality based on the teacher's pregnant unwed status was only one of the grounds for the discharge. Because the dismissal was based in part on insubordination for the teacher's failure to adhere to board policy in notifying the superintendent of her pregnancy, the district court concluded that there was a legitimate nondiscriminatory reason that justified the discharge. Rejecting this conclusion, the appellate court recognized that a teacher's right to become pregnant out of wedlock is constitutionally protected and that the teacher carried her initial burden of substantiating that her unwed status was a motivating factor in the dismissal. The appeals court remanded the case for the district court to determine whether the school board could substantiate by a preponderance of evidence that the teacher would have been discharged in the absence of her unwed pregnancy.

Compensation

A source of considerable legal activity has been the discrepancy between mean wages for male and female workers. The Equal Pay Act of 1963 (EPA) requires equal pay for males and females for substantially equivalent work. Under EPA, employers are allowed to differentiate in compensation based on 1) seniority, 2) merit, 3) productivity, or 4) any other factor not related to sex. Successful plaintiffs can be awarded back pay and an additional equal amount in liquidated damages for willful discrimination. Most EPA cases have not involved school employees because the compensation of teachers and other school personnel is usually governed by salary schedules. However, some pay differentials among male and female public school employees have been challenged under this Act. For example, courts have relied on EPA in striking down a "head of household" supplement for only male teachers and lower compensation for female coaches who perform substantially equivalent duties as male coaches.[43]

To rebut a prima facie case of discrimination under EPA, an employer must do more than articulate a legitimate, nondiscriminatory reason for the action; evidence must be produced to substantiate that one of the four prescribed exceptions applies to the wage differential. In order to establish willful discrimination under the Act, a plaintiff need not prove that the employer had an evil purpose in mind. A discriminatory act is considered willful if the employer acted in bad faith or did not have reasonable grounds to believe that the salary differentials were in compliance with EPA.[44]

Despite the Equal Pay Act and comparable state statutory protections, the gap has widened in recent years between men and women as to their mean salaries. In 1955 working women took home 64 cents for every dollar earned by their male counterparts, but by 1980 female workers earned only 59 cents for every male dollar.[45] This increasing discrepancy is alleged to be caused by the fact that employment is predominantly sex-segregated and "women's jobs" continue to be lower in status and pay than comparable jobs populated primarily by males. Thus women recently have relied on Title VII in alleging sex discrimination because jobs of comparable worth in terms of skills, training, responsibility, and effort are not compensated equally.

The application of Title VII to sex-based discrimination in compensation has been controversial. When Congress added "sex" to the list of characteristics covered by Title VII, this action was accompanied by an amendment (the Bennett Amendment) stipulating that employers could differentiate in compensation under Title VII if the differential was authorized by the Equal Pay Act. Prior to 1981, some courts had reasoned that Title VII prohibits sex discrimination in compensation only involving unequal pay for substantially equivalent work, while other courts had interpreted the Bennett Amendment as incorporating EPA's affirmative defenses into Title VII, but not the equal work standard.[46] According to the latter position, Title VII's protection against sex-based discrimination in employment compensation is broader than the Equal Pay Act.

In 1981 the U.S. Supreme Court addressed the issue in *Gunther* v. *County of Washington*. In this five-to-four decision, the Court established the precedent that Title VII's prohibition against sex bias in compensation is not confined by the Equal Pay Act. The Court majority cautioned, however, that it was not substituting a "comparable" work standard for an "equal" work standard. It was simply extending Title VII coverage to claims beyond unequal pay for substantially equivalent work. The Court rejected the restrictive view of Title VII coverage because "a woman who is discriminatorily underpaid could obtain no relief — no matter how egregious the discrimination might be — unless her employer also employed a man in an equal job in the same establishment, at a higher rate of pay."[47] The Court noted that an employer's failure to adjust compensation based on the findings of its own job evaluation study can be used to substantiate a Title VII violation.

The concept of comparable worth, which has been called the women's issue of the Eighties, does not seem likely to receive judicial endorsement in the near future, given the massive economic implications. The Equal Employment Opportunity Commission (EEOC) announced in October 1982 that it does not plan to take action on the 226 claims involving comparable worth currently before it because the agency's authority in this area is unclear. However, the Supreme Court's expansive interpretation of Title VII's protection against sex bias in compensation is likely to cause employers to give greater attention to their justification for compensation differentials among jobs requiring comparable training, responsibility, skills, and effort.

Retirement Benefits

Differential treatment of men and women in retirement benefits programs has created extensive debate. Unlike stereotypic assumptions on which many discriminatory employment policies have been based in the past, the generalization is true that women as a class have a longer life expectancy than men. Because of this fact, employers often have required women to pay more into a retirement program in order to receive the same benefits or have required equal contributions and provided lower benefits to retired women.

In a significant 1978 decision, *City of Los Angeles Department of Water* v. *Manhart*, the Supreme Court struck down an employer's plan in which women made a larger contribution than men to receive comparable benefits upon retirement.[48] The Court rejected the contention that individuals were classified by longevity rather than sex, noting that gender was the only factor considered in predicting life expectancy. The Court found that to treat each individual female, who may or may not fit the generalization, as a class member for retirement benefits constituted sex discrimination in violation of Title VII. The Court, however, specifically limited its ruling to employer-operated pension plans requiring unequal contributions.

However, *Manhart* left unresolved the legality of pension plans that require equal contributions but award unequal benefits for retired men and women. On 6 July 1983 the U.S. Supreme Court settled the issue by invalidating an Arizona retirement program that used sex-segregated actuarial tables in a deferred compensation plan.[49] In *Arizona Governing Committee* v. *Norris* the Court majority agreed with the Ninth Circuit Court of Appeals that the plan violated Title VII because on retirement female employees receive lower monthly annuity payments than male employees contributing the same amount. Rejecting the argument that relief was barred because Title VII cannot be used to regulate the insurance business, the appeals court emphasized that it was not enjoining an insurance company from using sex-segregated annuity tables. Rather, it was barring an employer from contracting with an insurer to offer a fringe benefit which treats individuals differently because of their sex. The Supreme Court affirmed the lower court's order enjoining the state from applying sex-segregated tables to future contributions in calculating benefits. However, the Court held that the ban is not retroactive; contributions made prior to the ruling may be subjected to the sex-segregated tables.

Given the *Norris* ruling, the Teachers Insurance and Annuity Association and the College Retirement Equities Fund (TIAA-CREF) announced plans to convert to unisex tables in calculating retirement benefits on future contributions to the fund.[50] While women's advocacy groups are encouraged by recent developments, there is some disappointment that women nearing retirement will reap little benefit from the *Norris* ruling. Since only prospective relief was ordered, it may be more than forty years before the differential treatment of male and female employees in pension programs is totally eliminated.

Sexual Harassment

Charges of sexual harassment have presented particular problems for the judiciary. The term sexual harassment is generally used to refer to "repeated and unwelcomed advances, derogatory statements based on . . . sex, or sexually demeaning gestures or acts."[51] While sexual harassment is not a recent phenomenon, case law in this area is in its infant stage. Most of the litigation has been brought under Title VII's anti-sex discrimination provisions.

Initially, courts concluded that claims of sexual harassment were beyond the purview of Title VII. However, in the mid-1970s courts began interpreting Title VII as providing a remedy to victims of sexual harassment that results in adverse employment consequences such as termination, demotion, or denial of other benefits. Back pay and accompanying employment benefits have been awarded in several instances where employers have not successfully rebutted charges that an employee has been terminated or otherwise discriminated against because of rejection of sexual advances. Employers also have been found in violation of Title VII if they have failed to investigate employee's complaints of sexual harassment by supervisors, even if the supervisor's acts have violated company policy.[52]

In a significant 1981 case, the Washington, D.C., Circuit Court of Appeals ruled that sexual harassment per se violates Title VII; an employee need not prove that the harassment resulted in penalty or loss of tangible job benefits.[53] The appellate court found that improper sexual behavior toward female employees was a standard operating procedure in the plaintiff's office and that her complaints of harassment were not taken seriously. The court reasoned that proof that the harassing behavior had occurred was sufficient to establish a Title VII violation. This case suggests that the judiciary may become more willing to consider intangible as well as tangible losses in reviewing charges of sexual harassment.

In 1980 the EEOC issued guidelines stipulating that sexual harassment violates Title VII if it is an explicit or implicit term or condition of employment, is used as a basis for employment decisions, or has the "effect of unreasonably interfering with an individual's work performance or creating an intimidating, hostile, or offensive working environment."[54] Thus the guidelines also indicate that the effect of sexual harassment on working conditions as well as on an employee's status can be considered in Title VII cases. Under the guidelines, employers are responsible for sexual harassment of employees by supervisors, but not for acts among co-workers unless the employer knew or "should have known" of the harassing behavior and failed to take "immediate and appropriate corrective action." Hundreds of sexual harassment charges have been filed with EEOC since the guidelines were adopted, and it seems likely that the number of Title VII lawsuits involving this issue will escalate during the coming decade.

National Origin Discrimination

Similar to claims of racial bias, allegations of discrimination based on national origin most often have been initiated under the equal protection clause of the 14th Amendment or Title VII. Facially discriminatory policies generally have not been at issue. Instead, plaintiffs usually have challenged their alleged disparate treatment based on national origin, and thus have carried the burden of proving discriminatory intent. In an illustrative case, the Ninth Circuit Court of Appeals ruled that even if a Mexican-American curriculum supervisor had been able to establish an inference of discrimination, the school board's evidence that the supervisor was not able to work well with other employees was sufficient to satisfy its burden of articulating a legitimate nondiscriminatory reason for nonrenewal of her contract.[55] A Michigan federal district court similarly found that there must be evidence of intentional discriminatory acts to establish a prima facie case of disparate treatment under Title VII; the lack of personnel policies and an affirmative action plan pertaining to the hiring of national origin minorities would not suffice.[56]

Although most suits involving national origin discrimination have involved allegations of disparate treatment, the disparate impact criteria have been applied in some cases. For example, the Tenth Circuit Court of Appeals found that a prima facie case of national origin discrimination was established by evidence that the employer had never promoted a Spanish-American employee coupled with the vague and subjective promotion criteria used.[57] The employer did not rebut the prima facie case with adequate proof of a business necessity for the discriminatory promotion practices. However, the court did not find that the employer deliberately rendered the employee's working conditions so intolerable as to force the claimant to quit his job (constructive discharge). The plaintiff was thus entitled only to the difference between actual pay and the amount he would have made if selected as a foreman during the two-year period before he quit.

While courts have strictly interpreted the procedural requirements for filing a Title VII claim, under certain circumstances a plaintiff might be entitled to an extension of the time limitation for filing a suit. Such an extension was considered appropriate where a foreign-born plaintiff was not aware of the potential discrimination accompanying his discharge until several months later when his "abolished" position was again filled.[58] However, a plaintiff cannot bring a federal discrimination suit regarding an issue that has already been litigated by the state judiciary. In 1982 the Supreme Court ruled that since a state court had found a claim of national origin discrimination meritless under state law, the plaintiff was barred from litigating the same issue under Title VII.[59]

Related to allegations of discrimination based on national origin are challenges to citizenship requirements. In 1978 the Supreme Court rejected a constitutional challenge to a New York education law denying teacher certification to individuals who are eligible for citizenship but refuse to apply for naturalization. Recognizing that classifications based on citizenship status (unlike those based solely on national origin) are not suspect, the Court applied the rational basis equal protection test. It concluded that the state's interest in attaining its educational goals was rationally related to the citizenship requirement for teacher certification; individuals who do not wish to apply for U.S. citizenship cannot adequately convey appropriate citizenship values to students. The Court declared that certain functions are "so bound up with the operation of the State as a governmental entity as to permit the exclusion from those functions of all persons who have not become part of the process of self-government."[60] However, the Court has invalidated a law stipulating that only U.S. citizens can be hired in any competitive classified civil service positions.[61]

Religious Discrimination

Individuals enjoy explicit constitutional protection against governmental interference with their religious freedom. The First Amendment to the U.S. Constitution prohibits Congress from enacting a law *respecting the establishment* of religion or interfering with the *free exercise* of religious beliefs. These provisions have been made applicable to state action through the 14th Amendment (see chapter 3).

The Supreme Court has recognized on numerous occasions that while the freedom to believe is absolute, the freedom to act on those beliefs is subject to reasonable governmental regulations. Accordingly, public educators cannot assert a free exercise right to conduct devotional activities in public schools or to proselytize students; the establishment clause prohibits such activities. Similarly, the free exercise clause does not entitle teachers to disregard a portion of the state-prescribed curriculum that conflicts with their religious views.[62]

Although school personnel cannot use the public school classroom as a forum to spread their faith, neither must they relinquish their religious beliefs as a condition of employment. Prerequisites to public employment that entail a profession of religious faith abridge the First Amendment. Also, teachers have a free exercise right to abstain from certain school observances and activities that conflict with their religious beliefs as long as such abstention does not impede the instructional program or the efficient operation of the school. For example, teachers have a First Amendment right to refrain from saluting the American flag and pledging their allegiance, even though they cannot deny students the opportunity to engage in these observances.

Employees are also protected from religious discrimination under Title VII. In the 1972 amendments to Title VII, Congress stipulated that the protection against religious discrimination includes "all aspects of religious observance and practice, as well as belief, unless an employer demonstrates that he is unable to reasonably accommodate an employee's or prospective employee's religious observance or practice without undue hardship on the conduct of the employer's business."[64] The EEOC has promulgated guidelines with suggested religious accommodations such as accepting voluntary substitutes and work-shift exchanges, using flexible scheduling, and changing job assignments.

Many controversies have arisen over the degree of religious accommodations in work schedules required under Title VII. Although employers are not required to make costly accommodations, in several cases educational employees have proven that requests for religious absences would not place undue burdens on the public school. For example, in 1981 the Fourth Circuit Court of Appeals affirmed a federal district court's conclusion that the discharge of a teacher's aide for absences to observe the seven-day convocation of the Worldwide Church of God violated Title VII.[65] However, the appellate court disagreed with the district court's holding that the aide was entitled only to back pay from the time of her discharge to the end of her one-year contract. Reasoning that Title VII creates a substantive right to non-discriminatory treatment, the appeals court held that the plaintiff was entitled to back pay (mitigated by interim earnings) from the time of the discharge until a valid offer of reinstatement was made. The case was remanded with instructions for the district court to provide the school board the opportunity to demonstrate that the aide did not make reasonable efforts to obtain suitable employment to mitigate damages.

In 1980 a New Jersey federal district court also concluded that religious absences were a "substantial motivating factor" in the dismissal of a teacher in violation of Title VII.[66] Finding that the absences created no hardship for the school or students, the court ordered the teacher's reinstatement with back pay. But the court denied the teacher's request for compensatory and punitive damages. The court was not persuaded that the teacher suffered mental and emotional distress or that the superintendent and board acted with a malicious and wanton disregard for his constitutional rights.

In addition to federal requirements, most states also have constitutional or statutory provisions protecting individuals from religious discrimination. Interpreting such a provision, the California Supreme Court ordered reinstatement of a teacher who had been terminated for unauthorized absences for religious reasons.[67] The court held that the teacher was entitled to unpaid leave for religious observances since no evidence was presented that the teacher's absences had a detrimental effect on the educational program. However, a Colorado appeals court upheld the dismissal of a tenured teacher for similar unauthorized religious absences, reasoning that his teaching duties had been neglected.[68] The court ruled that the termination was justified and did not violate Colorado's antidiscrimination law because testimony indicated that the teacher's four unauthorized absences had interfered with the academic progress of his students and disrupted the management of the school.

While public school boards generally attempt to accommodate reasonable absences for religious reasons, paid leave need not be provided for this purpose. Indeed, paid leave tied specifically to religious observances implicates the establishment clause. For example, in a New Jersey case, teachers were allowed to use personal leave days for religious as well as other purposes, but the teachers association sought specific paid leave for religious observances.[69] The state supreme court ruled that the establishment clause prohibits the school board from granting such religious leave, and therefore negotiations over this item would be unconstitutional. The court reasoned that if specific leave were designated for religious reasons, the nonreligious employee could never enjoy the proposed benefit.

From litigation to date it appears that school authorities are expected to make reasonable accommodations to enable employees to practice their faith as long as the accommodations do not create substantial hardships for the school, significantly impede students' academic progress, or serve to advance religion. However, courts have recognized that the establishment clause precludes school boards from conferring special benefits on employees for religious reasons such as paid leave available only for sectarian observances. Also, a minimal impairment of employee's free exercise rights may be required in public school settings to protect vulnerable children from religious inculcation.

Discrimination Based on Handicaps

Individuals are protected from discrimination based on handicapping conditions by the equal protection clause and various federal and state civil rights laws. The most extensive legal protections against employment discrimination in this regard are contained in Section 504 of the Rehabilitation Act of 1973; thus, most recent litigation involving claims of employment bias against the handicapped have been initiated under this law. Section 504 provides in part that "no otherwise qualified handicapped individual . . . shall, solely by reason of his handicap, be excluded from participation in, be denied the benefits of, or be subjected to discrimination under any program or activity receiving Federal financial assistance."[70]

The U.S. Supreme Court delivered its first opinion interpreting Section 504 in 1979. In this case a licensed practical nurse brought suit after she was denied admission to a college program to train registered nurses. Her application was rejected because of her serious hearing deficiency, which the college asserted would prohibit her from participating in all aspects of the program and would pose a danger to her future work with patients. The Supreme Court concluded that Section 504 does not compel an institution to ignore the disabilities of an individual or substantially to modify its program to enable a handicapped person to participate. Instead, Section 504 prohibits institutions from barring an otherwise qualified handicapped person "who is able to meet all of a program's requirements in spite of his handicap."[71]

In employment cases, courts have reiterated that Section 504 requires reasonable accommodations only for handicapped persons who are otherwise qualified. For example, a blind California teacher was unsuccessful in challenging the school board's failure to appoint him to an administrative position because the board produced evidence that the plaintiff did not possess the requisite administrative skills or leadership experience for an administrative job.[72] The court rejected both equal protection and Section 504 claims, finding that the individual was not otherwise qualified for an administrative position and that there was a rational basis for the board's decision. The court also rejected the assertion that the board's action violated due process guarantees by creating an irrebuttable presumption that blind persons were unqualified to serve as administrators; the board did not impose a blanket ban on hiring blind employees in leadership roles. Moreover, the court reasoned that it was permissible for the committee to inquire as to how the teacher would cope with his blindness in fulfilling administrative job responsibilities.

However, handicapped individuals have successfully challenged employment decisions with evidence that they are qualified for the job and have been discriminated against solely because of their handicaps. For example, the Third Circuit Court of Appeals held that a blind teacher was entitled to back pay and retroactive seniority from the time she would have been hired, absent the school district's unlawful policy barring disabled persons from taking an examination that was a prerequisite to employment.[73] Since the suit was initiated before the effective date of Section 504, it was resolved on federal constitutional grounds. The appeals court concluded that the school district had violated due process guarantees by creating an irrebuttable presumption that blindness per se was evidence of incompetence. But the court denied the teacher's request for tenure to be granted, reasoning that the award of tenure should be based on the school district's assessment of the teacher's performance. More recently, a federal district court ruled that a school district's pre-employment inquiries about an applicant's prior mental problems were impermissible under Section 504 because the questions were not related to his present fitness for the position of teacher's aide.[74]

Courts will review employment decisions carefully to ensure that handicapped persons are not discriminated against solely because of their disabilities. A handicapped person is considered qualified if capable of performing the job with reasonable accommodations that do not present an undue business hardship. In evaluating the hardship imposed, courts consider the extent of the necessary accommodation and its expense. Employers are not required to make substantial adjustments in working conditions to accommodate handicapped individuals or to hire disabled persons who are not qualified for the job.[75]

Age Discrimination

Age is distinct among attributes discussed in this chapter in that all individuals are subject to the aging process. Because of medical progress in prolonging life coupled with the post-World War II decline in birthrates, the mean age of the American population has steadily climbed in recent years. This phenomenon has been accompanied by increasing public concern for the problems associated with aging and by legislative enactments prohibiting age-based discrimination. Similar to allegations of race and sex bias, claims of employment discrimination on the basis of age have been initiated under both the equal protection clause and federal and state statutory protections.

While the U.S. Supreme Court has not addressed an age discrimination suit involving public school personnel, it has reviewed a constitutional challenge to a Massachusetts law requiring the retirement of uniformed police officers at age 50.[76] Noting that age is not a suspect class and public employment is not a fundamental right, the Court reasoned that the retirement policy need only be rationally related to a legitimate state objective to satisfy equal protection mandates. The Court found that the retirement of police officers at an early age has a rational relationship to the objective of protecting the public by ensuring a physically competent police force.

In the school context, the Second Circuit Court of Appeals upheld a New York statute mandating teacher retirement at age 70 as having a rational basis.[77] The court noted that teachers are under physical demands and further reasoned that the retirement statute advances the legitimate objectives of 1) allowing younger individuals and minorities to be hired, 2) bringing fresh ideas into the classrooms, and 3) facilitating the administration of pension plans by predictable retirement dates. Also, the Third Circuit Court of Appeals found that a teacher's 14th Amendment rights were not violated by requiring her to retire at age 65 because all persons similarly situated were treated the same under the law.[78]

However, the Seventh Circuit Court of Appeals departed from the prevailing view in using the equal protection clause to strike down a school board's policy mandating retirement for public school teachers at age 65.[79] The court concluded that the mandatory retirement provision was not rationally related to the objective of eliminating unfit teachers. According to the court, competence should be judged on an individual basis, and a teacher's fitness to teach should not be assessed solely on age.

Although legislative enactments that classify individuals on the basis of age can satisfy equal protection guarantees if rationally related to a legitimate governmental objective, in recent years plaintiffs have not had to rely on constitutional protections in challenging age-based employment discrimination. In 1967 Congress enacted the Age Discrimination in Employment Act (ADEA), which prohibits employers, employment agencies, and labor unions from discriminating against employees on the basis of age in hiring, promotion, and compensation. The Act was intended to eliminate arbitrary, irrational age barriers to employment so that employment opportunities can be based on merit and ability. The protected category of employees includes persons age 40 to 70. The upper limit was extended from 65 to 70 in an amendment to ADEA in 1978, but there is no upper limitation for federal employees.[80] Remedies for violations of ADEA include 1) injunctive relief, 2) offer of employment or reinstatement, 3) back pay, and 4) liquidated damages where it is established that age discrimination was unlawfully motivated. Successful plaintiffs can also be awarded attorneys' fees.

Age classifications can be justified under ADEA if age is a bona fide occupational qualification (BFOQ) necessary to the normal operation of a particular business: "An age-related BFOQ permits an employer to admit that he has discriminated on the basis of age, but to avoid any penalty."[81] Schools boards have successfully substantiated an age BFOQ for certain roles such as bus drivers. Because establishment of a BFOQ is an affirmative defense (in contrast to rebuttal of a prima facie case), the burden is on the employer to produce appropriate evidence.

The substantive provisions of ADEA are almost identical to those of Title VII of the Civil Rights Act of 1964, and the judicial criteria developed in Title VII cases are often applied to evaluate age-discrimination charges under ADEA. Most courts, including several federal appellate courts, have required a showing of discriminatory intent in ADEA cases, thus adopting the disparate treatment standard of review. Employers have been able to rebut a prima facie case of disparate treatment based on age by articulating nondiscriminatory reasons for dismissals, such as excessive tardiness, poor performance, or inability to relate to a supervisor.[82]

However, in 1980 the Second Circuit Court of Appeals ruled that plaintiffs could establish a violation of ADEA, regardless of motive, by establishing that employment practices have a disparate impact on older employees.[83] In this case the defendant school board adopted a cost-cutting policy of preferentially hiring teachers with fewer than five years of experience. Evidence substantiated that over 92% of the state's teachers over 40 years of age had at least five years of experience, whereas only 62% of teachers under 40 had this much experience. The court concluded that the policy with a disparate impact on teachers over 40 had to be justified as a job necessity to satisfy ADEA. A Missouri federal district court applied similar logic in evaluating a prima facie case of age discrimination in connection with a university's policy reserving a certain portion of faculty slots for nontenured professors.[84] The court rejected the economic rationale offered in defense of this practice as an insufficient business necessity to justify the adverse impact of the policy on older professors.

The U.S. Department of Labor and several courts have interpreted ADEA as prohibiting age discrimination among employees *within* the protected age group. In other words, an employer cannot discriminate against employees who are 60 years old by preferring those who are 45. For example, the First Circuit Court of Appeals ruled that an employee need not show that he was replaced by a younger person outside the protected age group to establish a prima facie case of discrimination under ADEA.[85]

The award of specified damages has been ordered where willful employment discrimination based on age has been proven. Conflicting opinions have been rendered regarding whether employers can assert a good faith defense to avoid liquidated damages.[86] Courts also have differed as to whether victims of willful violations of ADEA are entitled to compensatory damages in addition to other types of relief. While several federal district courts have allowed such damages to be assessed against employers, two federal circuit courts of appeal have disallowed damages for pain, suffering, and emotional distress.[87] Courts in general have not allowed punitive damages, reasoning that Congress preferred liquidated damages in lieu of a punitive award.

Several states have enacted antidiscrimination statutes that provide greater protections to employees than afforded by ADEA. For example, the Montana Human Rights Act has been interpreted as prohibiting employment decisions based on age unless age is directly related to job performance.[88] This Act was held to prevail over a school board's mandatory retirement policy in the absence of evidence that the policy was necessitated by the nature of the job. The Nevada Supreme Court similarly ruled that a state university could not make hiring and retention decisions on the basis of age because of the state statute requiring all personnel actions taken by state, county, or municipal departments, agencies, boards, or appointing officers to be based solely on merit and fitness.[89] Also, the Iowa Supreme Court struck down a school board's attempt to dismiss a teacher who had attained age 65 and refused to retire in compliance with the school board's policy. The court reasoned that "age has nothing to do with fault" and, therefore, the discharge was not based on good cause.[90]

With the "graying" of the American citizenry, lobbying efforts to secure additional protections and benefits for older employees seem destined to continue. And it seems likely that courts increasingly will be called upon to assess claims of age discrimination under state and federal laws.

Conclusion

Social scientists, legal scholars, public policymakers, and the American citizenry agree that employment discrimination is a serious problem in this nation, and educational institutions have not escaped the negative consequences. In spite of general consensus that the elimination of employment discrimination will benefit individuals and our society, finding acceptable means to attain this goal has been extremely problematic. Delineating the types of prohibited discrimination and devising remedies to compensate victims of employment discrimination have proven to be awesome tasks.[91] All three branches of government have been involved in efforts to clarify the individual's protections against discrimination in the work force and employers' obligations to eliminate biased practices. Yet, despite numerous legislative acts and an escalating body of complex judicial rulings, many questions pertaining to discrimination in employment remain unanswered.

Even though the law governing employment discrimination is still evolving, there are certain principles that public employers can use to guide their daily actions. For example, hiring policies that facially discriminate on the basis of sex, national origin, age, or religion should be used *only* if justified as essential for the particular jobs, and facially discriminatory classifications based on race should never be imposed. Prerequisites to employment that disproportionately discriminate against certain classes of employees should not be used unless such prerequisites are valid measures of ability to perform the job. Promotion, compensation, and job-assignment decisions should be based on objective assessments of employees' qualifications, performance, length of service, etc., and not on employees' class membership, beliefs, or other attributes unrelated to the job. If an employer cannot justify an employment decision on legitimate nondiscriminatory grounds, equitable relief should be provided to restore the employee who has been the victim of discrimination to his or her rightful place.

However, employers do not have to hire, promote, or give other special benefits to unqualified individuals merely because of their membership in a protected group. Indeed, it is a disservice to hire an unqualified black or female or to place a handicapped person in a role that cannot be performed adequately because of a disability. Such action is the antithesis of fundamental fairness, perpetuates erroneous stereotypes when the unqualified individuals ultimately fail, and may subject the employer to a "reverse" discrimination suit.

Some of the most troublesome issues arise in situations where employees are currently at a disadvantage because of prior discrimination. Mere membership in a class that has been historically discriminated against should not catapult an individual into a preferred position; but without some special consideration, the lingering effects of past discrimination may never be eradicated. Employers are faced with the difficult task of ensuring that victims of past employment bias are "made whole," while at the same time protecting legitimate business interests and safeguarding the rights of the majority to equitable treatment. Temporary preferential treatment of racial and ethnic minorities, women, and the handicapped in hiring and personnel reduction practices may be necessary in some situations to compensate for past discriminatory acts.

Educational employers would be wise to ask themselves the following questions in making employment decisions:

1. Are hiring restrictions based on sex, national origin, age, or religion bona fide occupational qualifications?
2. Are prerequisites to employment valid indicators of success in the specific jobs for which they are used?
3. Is there a legitimate business necessity for policies that adversely affect certain classes of employees?
4. Are questions used in job interviews directly related to the candidate's ability to perform the job?
5. Are hiring, promotion, compensation, and job-assignment decisions based on considerations that relate to qualifications, merit, and performance, rather than stereotypic assumptions?
6. Is pregnancy treated like any other temporary disability in terms of sick leave, seniority, and disability benefits?
7. Have reasonable accommodations been made to enable qualified handicapped employees to perform adequately?
8. Have reasonable accommodations been made to the religious beliefs of employees?
9. Have precautions been taken to ensure that current practices do not perpetuate the effects of past discrimination?
10. Are employment policies and internal grievance procedures well publicized to all employees?

If the above questions can be answered affirmatively, school districts and school officials are likely to avoid legal liability when particular employment practices are challenged. Moreover, by taking steps to reduce employment discrimination, the public's interest in ensuring a competent educational work force will be advanced.

Footnotes

1. This chapter is condensed in part from a monograph, Martha McCarthy, *Discrimination in Public Employment: The Evolving Law* (Topeka, Kans.: National Organization on Legal Problems of Education, 1983).
2. Allegations of discriminatory treatment in connection with staff reduction practices are addressed in chapter 8.
3. National Educ. Ass'n v. South Carolina, 445 F. Supp. 1094 (D.S.C. 1977), *aff'd* 434 U.S. 1026 (1978). Prior to 1976, several federal appellate courts had found a constitutional violation in public school districts' use of tests as a prerequisite to employment if the tests had a disparate impact on minorities and had not been validated as predicting success in the particular jobs for which they were used. *See* Walston v. County School Bd. of Nansemond Cty., Virginia, 492 F.2d 919 (4th Cir. 1974); Chance v. Board of Examiners, 458 F.2d 1167 (2d Cir. 1972); Armstead v. Starkville Municipal Separate School Dist., 461 F.2d 276 (5th Cir. 1972). However, in *Washington* v. *Davis,* 426 U.S. 229 (1976), the Supreme Court announced that plaintiffs must prove discriminatory intent to establish that facially neutral prerequisites to employment violate the equal protection clause. *See also* Personnel Administrator of Massachusetts v. Feeney, 442 U.S. 256 (1979).
4. 42 U.S.C. § 2000e *et seq.*
5. *See* Albemarle Paper Co. v. Moody, 422 U.S. 405 (1975); Griggs v. Duke Power Co., 401 U.S. 424 (1971). Guidelines of the Equal Employment Opportunity Commission stipulate that a selection rate for any group protected by Title VII that is less than 80 percent of the highest group's rate generally will be regarded as evidence of adverse impact.
6. Connecticut v. Teal, 102 S. Ct. 2525, 2530 (1982), citing 645 F.2d 138 (2d Cir. 1981).
7. Newman v. Crews, 651 F.2d 222 (4th Cir. 1981).
8. McDonnell Douglas v. Green, 411 U.S. 792, 802 (1973).
9. *See, e.g.,* Lewis v. Central Piedmont Community College, 689 F.2d 1207 (4th Cir. 1982) (white applicant was better qualified than black applicant who was rejected); Johnson v. Michigan State University, 547 F. Supp. 429 (W.D. Mich. 1982) (denial of promotion and tenure to minority professor was based on poor performance); Lee v. Ozark City Bd. of Educ., 517 F. Supp. 686 (M.D. Ala. 1981) (nonrenewal of minority coach's contract was justified by legitimate objectives of athletic program); Adams v. Gaudet, 515 F. Supp. 1086 (W.D. La. 1981) (rejection of minority applicant was justified by reliance on employment criteria established by state department of education); Fusi v. West Allis Pub. Schools, 514 F. Supp. 627 (E.D. Wis. 1981) (minority teacher lacked proper certification).

10. Pittman v. Hattiesburg Municipal Separate School Dist., 644 F.2d 1071 (5th Cir. 1981).

11. Rogers v. International Paper Co., 510 F.2d 1340, 1345 (8th Cir. 1975). *See also* Royal v. Missouri Highway and Transportation Comm'n, 655 F.2d 159, 164 (8th Cir. 1981); Barnett v. W. T. Grant Co., 518 F.2d 543, 550 (4th Cir. 1975).

12. Evans v. Harnett, 684 F.2d 304 (4th Cir. 1982); *see also* Williams v. Colorado Springs School Dist. #11, 641 F.2d 835 (10th Cir. 1981). While the judiciary often relies on statistical evidence in assessing discrimination charges, the Supreme Court has cautioned that courts should move with circumspection in evaluating statistics because their usefulness is contingent on each individual set of circumstances. *See* International Brotherhood of Teamsters v. United States, 431 U.S. 324, 336 (1977); Castaneda v. Partida, 430 U.S. 482 (1977); Hazelwood School Dist. v. United States, 433 U.S. 299 (1977).

13. *See, e.g.*, Franks v. Bowman Transportation Co., 424 U.S. 747 (1976); Local 189 United Papermakers and Paperworkers v. United States, 416 F.2d 980 (5th Cir. 1969).

14. *See* American Tobacco Co. v. Patterson, 102 S. Ct. 1534 (1982); Pullman-Standard, Inc. v. Swint, 102 S. Ct. 1781 (1982). Although Title VII has been the most popular statutory basis for employment discrimination suits, some suits have been initiated under Title VI of the Civil Rights Act of 1964. Title VI prohibits discrimination on the basis of race, color, or national origin in programs or activities receiving federal financial assistance, 42 U.S.C. § 2000d. In a significant 1983 decision, the severely splintered Supreme Court ruled that evidence of discriminatory intent is not necessary to establish a Title VI violation. The majority interpreted Title VI regulations as prohibiting practices with a discriminatory impact. However, a different majority of the justices concluded that in the absence of proof of discriminatory motive, prevailing plaintiffs in Title VI disparate impact suits are entitled only to injunctive, prospective relief and not to compensatory relief such as an award of constructive seniority. Guardians Ass'n v. Civil Service Comm'n of the City of New York, 51 U.S.L.W. 5105 (July 1, 1983).

15. Ford Motor Co. v. Equal Employment Opportunity Comm'n, 456 U.S. 923 (1982). This case involved alleged sex discrimination under Title VII, but the principle announced by the Court is equally applicable to allegations of racial discrimination in hiring practices.

16. Boston Teachers' Union v. Boston School Comm., 671 F.2d 23 (1st Cir. 1982), *cert. denied*, 103 S. Ct. 62 (1982). *See also* Boston Chapter of NAACP v. Beecher, 679 F.2d 965 (1st Cir. 1982), *vacated and remanded*, 51 U.S.L.W. 4566 (May 17, 1983).

17. Oliver v. Kalamazoo Bd. of Educ., 498 F. Supp. 732 (W.D. Mich. 1980), *vacated and remanded*, 706 F.2d 757 (6th Cir. 1983).

18. *Id.* at 764. *See also* Kromnick v. School Dist. of Philadelphia, 555 F. Supp. 249 (E.D. Pa. 1982).

19. *See* Zaslawsky v. Board of Educ. of Los Angeles, 610 F.2d 661 (9th Cir. 1979); Wygant v. Jackson Bd. of Educ., 456 F. Supp. 1196 (E.D. Mich. 1982).

20. *See* Valentine v. Smith, 654 F.2d 503 (8th Cir. 1981); Caulfield v. Board of Educ. of the City of New York, 583 F.2d 605 (2d Cir. 1978).

21. Frontiero v. Richardson, 411 U.S. 677, 684 (1973).

22. *See, e.g.*, Mississippi University for Women v. Hogan, 102 S. Ct. 3331 (1982); Craig v. Boren, 429 U.S. 190 (1976). Employers can facially discriminate on the basis of sex under Title VII if gender is a bona fide occupational qualification (BFOQ) necessary to the normal operation of the business. While this type of overt discrimination is not usually an issue in school cases, the BFOQ exception to Title VII has generated litigation in other contexts. *See* Martha McCarthy, "Recent Developments in Sex Discrimination Litigation," in *School Law Update — 1977*, ed. M.A. McGhehey (Topeka, Kans.: National Organization on Legal Problems of Education, 1978), pp. 53-56.

23. Personnel Administrator of Massachusetts v. Feeney, 442 U.S. 256 (1979).

24. *See* Wilkins v. University of Houston, 654 F.2d 388 (5th Cir. 1981), *rehearing*, 662 F.2d 1156 (5th Cir. 1981), *vacated and remanded*, 103 S. Ct. 34 (1982), *vacated and remanded in part*, 695 F.2d 134 (5th Cir. 1983).

25. Texas Department of Community Affairs v. Burdine, 450 U.S. 248 (1981).

26. *See, e.g.*, Patterson v. Greenwood School Dist. 50, 696 F.2d 293 (4th Cir. 1982); Cummings v. School Dist. of City of Lincoln, 638 F.2d 1168 (8th Cir. 1981); Danzl v. North St. Paul-Maplewood-Oakdale Indep. School Dist., 706 F.2d 813 (8th Cir. 1983).

27. *See, e.g.*, Coble v. Hot Springs School Dist. No. 6, 882 F.2d 721 (8th Cir. 1982); Rodriguez v. Board of Educ. of Eastchester Union Free School Dist., 620 F.2d 362 (2d Cir. 1980); Tyler v. Board of Educ. of New Castle Cty., 519 F. Supp. 834 (D. Del. 1981); Schoneberg v. Grundy Cty. Special Educ. Cooperative, 385 N.E.2d 351 (Ill. App. 1979).

28. Sweeney v. Board of Trustees of Keene State College, 604 F.2d 106 (1st Cir. 1979), *cert. denied*, 444 U.S. 1045 (1980). *But see* Canham v. Oberlin College, 666 F.2d 1057 (6th Cir. 1981), in which the appellate court held that a college's asserted nondiscriminatory reasons for denying a permanent position to a male in favor of a female were not pretexts for sex bias. The college produced sufficient evidence that the decision was based on the male candidate's inadequate performance during a trial period.

29. North Haven Bd. of Educ. v. Bell, 102 S. Ct. 1912 (1982). Title IX, 20 U.S.C. § 1681(a), provides that "no person in the United States shall, on the basis of sex, be excluded from participation in, be denied the benefits of, or be subjected to discrimination under any education program or activity receiving Federal financial assistance." For a discussion of lower court litigation pertaining to this employment issue, *see* Martha McCarthy, "Title IX: A Decade Later," *Journal of Educational Equity and Leadership* 2 (1982): 215.

30. *See* Grove City College v. Bell, 687 F.2d 684 (3d Cir. 1982), *cert. granted*, 103 S. Ct. 1181 (1983); Hillsdale College v. Department of Health, Education and Welfare, 696 F.2d 418 (6th Cir. 1982); Haffer v. Temple University, 688 F.2d 14 (3d Cir. 1982); Rice v. President and Fellows of Harvard College, 663 F.2d 336 (1st Cir. 1981), *cert. denied*, 102 S. Ct. 1976 (1982); University of Richmond v. Bell, 543 F. Supp. 321 (E.D. Va. 1982); Othen v. Ann Arbor School Bd., 507 F. Supp. 1376 (E.D. Mich. 1981); Bennett v. West Texas State University, 525 F. Supp. 77 (N.D. Tex. 1981).

31. Lieberman v. University of Chicago, 660 F.2d 1185 (7th Cir. 1981), *cert. denied*, 456 U.S. 937 (1982) (no damages remedy); Cannon v. University of Chicago, 648 F.2d 1104 (7th Cir. 1981), *cert. denied*, 454 U.S. 1128 (1981) (proof of intentional discrimination required.)

32. Geduldig v. Aiello, 417 U.S. 484 (1974) (no constitutional violation); General Electric Co. v. Gilbert, 429 U.S. 125 (1976) (no Title VII violation).

33. Pregnancy Disability Act, 42 U.S.C.A. 2000e(k) (1978). A current controversy involves the application of this law to spouses of male employees. The Supreme Court recently affirmed a decision in which the Fourth Circuit Court of Appeals ruled that a health plan covering pregnancy for employees, but limiting spouses' coverage for pregnancy, violates Title VII by discriminating against married male employees, *Newport News Shipbuilding and Dry Dock Co.* v. *Equal Employment Opportunity Comm'n*, 667 F.2d 448 (4th Cir. 1982), *aff'd* 51 U.S.L.W. 4837 (June 20, 1983).

34. Cleveland Bd. of Educ. v. LaFleur, 414 U.S. 632 (1974); *see also* Paxman v. Campbell, 612 F.2d 848 (4th Cir. 1980).

35. Clanton v. Orleans Parish School Bd., 649 F.2d 1084 (5th Cir. 1981).

36. deLaurier v. San Diego Unified School Dist., 588 F.2d 674 (9th Cir. 1978). During the course of the litigation, California law was amended to prohibit both the ninth-month mandatory leave and the denial of sick leave for pregnancy-related absences.

37. *See* Thompson v. Board of Educ., 526 F. Supp. 1035 (W.D. Mich. 1981); Strong v. Demopolis City Bd. of Educ., 515 F. Supp. 730 (S.D. Ala. 1981).

38. Nashville Gas Co. v. Satty, 434 U.S. 136 (1977). However, pregnancy leave is not entitled to preferred treatment. In 1982 a Massachusetts appeals court upheld a collective bargaining agreement that disallowed seniority credit for medical disability leave including pregnancy leave, *Burton* v. *School Comm.*, 432 N.E.2d 725 (Mass. App. 1982).

39. *See* Board of Educ. of Farmingdale Union Free Pub. School Dist. v. New York State Division of Human Rights, 451 N.Y.S.2d 700 (1982); Schwabenbauer v. Board of Educ., 498 F. Supp. 119 (W.D.N.Y. 1980). *But see* White v. Columbus Bd. of Educ., 441 N.E.2d 303 (Ohio App. 1982), in which an Ohio appeals court found that a Title VII suit was not timely filed in connection with denial of a teacher's seniority for a prior year in which she did not teach the required 120 days because of a mandatory maternity leave.

40. Mitchell v. Board of Trustees of Pickens Cty. School Dist., 599 F.2d 583 (4th Cir. 1979).

41. Andrews v. Drew Municipal Separate School Dist., 507 F.2d 611 (5th Cir. 1975), *cert. denied*, 425 U.S. 559 (1976). *See also* Martin Sweets Co. v. Jacobs, 550 F.2d 364 (6th Cir. 1977), *cert. denied*, 431 U.S. 917 (1977).

42. Avery v. Homewood City Bd. of Educ., 674 F.2d 337 (5th Cir. 1982). The court cited *Mt. Healthy City School Dist. Bd. of Educ.* v. *Doyle*, 429 U.S. 274 (1977), in which the Supreme Court recognized that if a protected right is a substantial reason for a dismissal action, the school board must establish that it would have reached the same decision in the absence of the protected conduct.

43. *See, e.g.*, Coble v. Hot Springs School Dist. No. 6, 682 F.2d 721 (8th Cir. 1982); Marshall v. A & M Consol. School Dist., 605 F.2d 186 (5th Cir. 1979); Brennan v. Woodbridge School Dist., 74 LC 33, 121 (D. Del. 1974). Although courts have considered statistical evidence regarding wage disparities, such evidence has been rejected if all factors that might influence compensation differentials (e.g., education, experience) have not been considered.

44. *See* Melanson v. Rantoul, 536 F. Supp. 271 (D.R.I. 1982). Most cases under EPA have been initiated by females, but male plaintiffs in the Colleges of Agriculture and Home Economics at the University of Nebraska were successful in challenging pay differentials under the Act, *Board of Regents of the University of Nebraska* v. *Dawes*, 522 F.2d 380 (8th Cir. 1975).

45. *See* "Comparability: An Issue for the '80s," *California Women* (January, 1981), publication of the California Commission on the Status of Women, Sacramento, California; *see* Ruth Blumrosen, "Wage Discrimination, Job Segregation, and Women Workers," *Employee Relations Law Journal* (1980): 77, 79.

46. *See, e.g.*, International Union of Electrical, Radio, and Machine Workers, AFL-CIO-CLC v. Westinghouse Electric Corp., 631 F.2d 1094 (3d Cir. 1980); Gunther v. County of Washington, 602 F.2d 882 (9th Cir. 1979); Molthan v. Liberty Mutual Insurance Co., 449 F. Supp. 397 (W.D. Pa. 1978); Wetzel v. Liberty Mutual Insurance Co., 442 F. Supp. 448 (E.D. Pa. 1977).

47. Gunther v. County of Washington, 452 U.S. 161, 178 (1981).

48. 435 U.S. 702 (1978).

49. Norris v. Arizona Governing Committee, 671 F.2d 330 (9th Cir. 1982), *aff'd in part, rev'd in part* 51 U.S.L.W. 5243 (July 6, 1983).

50. Prior to the *Norris* decision, federal appellate courts had rendered conflicting opinions on the legality of TIAA-CREF's use of sex-segregated tables in calculating retirement benefits. *See* TIAA-CREF v. Spirt, 691 F.2d 1054 (2d Cir. 1982); Peters v. Wayne State University, 691 F.2d 235 (6th Cir. 1982).

51. Dayle Nolan, "Sexual Harassment in Public and Private Employment," *Education Law Reporter* 3 (1982): 227.

52. *See, e.g.*, Miller v. Bank of America, 600 F.2d 211, 213 (9th Cir. 1979); Tomkins v. Public Service Electric and Gas Co., 568 F.2d 1044 (3d Cir. 1977); Barnes v. Costle, 561 F.2d 983 (D.C. Cir. 1977); Heelan v. Johns-Manville Corp., 451 F. Supp. 1382 (D. Colo. 1978); Munford v. Barnes & Co., 441 F. Supp. 459 (E.D. Mich. 1977).

53. Bundy v. Jackson, 641 F.2d 934 (D.C. Cir. 1981). However, some courts since this decision have continued to require evidence of adverse employment consequences resulting from the harassment. *See, e.g.*, Walter v. KFGO Radio, 518 F. Supp. 1309 (D.N.D. 1981); Meyers v. I.T.T. Diversified Credit Corp., 527 F. Supp. 1064 (D. Mo. 1981).

54. 29 CFR § 1604.11(a)(1980). The Department of Education's Office for Civil Rights also is authorized to investigate complaints of sexual harassment in federally funded educational programs under Title IX of the Education Amendments of 1972. *See* Lee Berthel, "Sexual Harassment in Education

Institutions," *Capital University Law Review* 10 (1981): 585-90.

55. Correa v. Nampa School Dist. No. 131, 645 F.2d 814 (9th Cir. 1981); *see also* Panlilio v. Dallas Indep. School Dist., 643 F.2d 315 (5th Cir. 1981).

56. Skelnar v. Central Bd. of Educ., 497 F. Supp. 1154 (E.D. Mich. 1980).

57. Muller v. United States Steel Co., 500 F.2d 923 (10th Cir. 1975).

58. Baruah v. Young, 536 F. Supp. 356 (D. Md. 1982).

59. Kremer v. Chemical Construction Corp., 102 S. Ct. 1883 (1982). Also, in 1982 the Supreme Court dealt with the issue of class certification in connection with an allegation of national origin discrimination. The Court held that the respondent must do more than prove the validity of his own claim to bridge the gap between his charge of discrimination in the denial of promotion and the existence of a class of persons who have suffered similar injury in connection with hiring practices, *General Telephone Co. of the Southwest* v. *Falcon*, 102 S. Ct. 2364 (1982).

60. Ambach v. Norwick, 441 U.S. 68, 73-74 (1979).

61. Sugarman v. Dougall, 413 U.S. 634 (1973).

62. *See* Palmer v. Board of Educ. of the City of Chicago, 603 F.2d 1271 (7th Cir. 1979), *cert. denied*, 444 U.S. 1026 (1980).

63. *See* Russo v. Central School Dist. No. 1, 469 F.2d 623 (2d Cir. 1972); Opinions of the Justices to the Governor, 363 N.E.2d 251 (Mass. 1977); Hanover v. Northrup, 325 F. Supp. 170 (D. Conn. 1970).

64. 42 U.S.C. § 2000e(j)(1976).

65. Edwards v. School Bd. of Norton, Virginia, 483 F. Supp. 620 (W.D. Va. 1980), *vacated and remanded*, 658 F.2d 951 (4th Cir. 1981). In 1977 the Supreme Court recognized that Title VII does not require employers to bear more than minimal costs in accommodating the religious beliefs of employees, *Trans World Airlines* v. *Hardison*, 432 U.S. 63 (1977).

66. Niederhuber v. Camden Cty. Vocational and Technical School Dist. Bd. of Educ., 495 F. Supp. 273 (D.N.J. 1980).

67. Rankins v. Commission on Professional Competence, 593 P.2d 852 (Cal. 1979), *appeal dismissed*, 444 U.S. 986 (1979).

68. School Dist. #11, Joint Counties of Archuleta and LaPlata v. Umberfield, 512 P.2d 1166 (Colo. App. 1973).

69. Hunterdon Central High School Bd. of Educ. v. Hunterdon Central High School Teachers Ass'n, 416 A.2d 980 (N.J. Super. 1980).

70. 29 U.S.C. § 794 (1976).

71. Southeastern Community College v. Davis, 442 U.S. 397, 406 (1979).

72. Upshur v. Love, 474 F. Supp. 332 (N.D. Cal. 1979); *see also* Coleman v. Darden, 595 F.2d 533 (10th Cir. 1979), *cert. denied*, 444 U.S. 927 (1979); Sabol v. Board of Educ. of Twp. of Willingboro Cty., 510 F. Supp. 892 (D.N.J. 1981).

73. Gurmankin v. Costanzo, 411 F. Supp. 982 (E.D. Pa. 1976), *aff'd* 556 F.2d 184 (3d Cir. 1977), *aff'd in part, vacated and remanded in part*, 626 F. 2d 1115 (3d Cir. 1980), *cert. denied*, 450 U.S. 923 (1981).

74. Doe v. Syracuse School Dist., 508 F. Supp. 333 (N.D.N.Y. 1981). Several courts have ordered the reinstatement of handicapped school bus drivers based on evidence that the individuals can perform the job without unreasonable accommodations. *See* Coleman v. Casey Cty. Bd. of Educ.,

510 F. Supp. 301 (W.D. Ky. 1980); State Division of Human Rights v. Averill Park Central School Dist., 388 N.E.2d 729 (N.Y. 1979); Commonwealth of Pennsylvania Dept. of Transportation v. Byrd, 399 A.2d 425 (Pa. Commw. 1979).

75. In several recent cases courts have ruled that Section 504, like Title IX, prohibits discrimination based on handicaps only in programs that benefit directly from federal aid. *See, e.g.*, Doyle v. University of Alabama in Birmingham, 680 F.2d 1323 (11th Cir. 1982); Brown v. Sibley, 650 F.2d 760 (5th Cir. 1981); Pittsburgh Fed'n of Teachers, Local 400 v. Langer, 546 F. Supp. 434 (W.D. Pa. 1982). However, the Pennsylvania federal district court observed that a board of education might be subject to a Section 504 suit where federal funds are not directly implicated if the board's federal financial assistance is so substantial "that the entire operation of the school system may be treated as a 'program' for the purpose of Section 504," 546 F. Supp. at 437.

76. Massachusetts Bd. of Retirement v. Murgia, 427 U.S. 307 (1976). The Court subsequently applied similar reasoning in ruling that mandatory retirement at age 60 in the United States Foreign Service is rationally related to the legitimate objective of conducting foreign relations with a competent and physically fit staff, *Vance* v. *Bradley*, 440 U.S. 93 (1979).

77. Palmer v. Ticcione, 576 F.2d 459 (2d Cir. 1978).

78. Kuhar v. Greensburg-Salem School Dist., 616 F.2d 676 (3d Cir. 1980).

79. Gault v. Garrison, 569 F.2d 993 (7th Cir. 1977), *cert. denied*, 440 U.S. 945 (1979).

80. 29 U.S.C. § 621. The amendment extending the upper age limit to 70 allowed colleges and universities to compel tenured faculty members to retire at age 65 until 1 July 1982. In March 1983 the U.S. Supreme Court ruled that the application of ADEA to state and local government employees does not impinge on an attribute of state sovereignty essential for carrying out traditional governmental functions in violation of the 10th Amendment, *Equal Employment Opportunity Comm'n* v. *Wyoming*, 514 F. Supp. 595 (D. Wyo. 1982), *rev'd* 103 S. Ct. 1054 (1983).

81. Marshall v. Westinghouse Electric Corp., 576 F.2d 588, 591 (5th Cir. 1978). Individuals have a private right to bring suit under ADEA, but available state administrative remedies must first be pursued, although not exhausted. For a discussion of procedural requirements under ADEA, *see* Baruah v. Young, 536 F. Supp. 356 (D. Md. 1982); Sanders v. Duke University, 538 F. Supp. 1143 (M.D.N.C. 1982).

82. *See, e.g.*, Schwager v. Sun Oil Co., 591 F.2d 58 (10th Cir. 1979) (poor performance); Price v. Maryland Casualty Co., 561 F.2d 609 (5th Cir. 1977) (poor performance); Kerwood v. Mortgage Bankers Ass'n, 494 F. Supp. 1298 (D.D.C. 1980) (inability to relate to supervisor); Brennan v. Reynolds and Co., 367 F. Supp. 440 (N.D. Ill. 1973) (excessive tardiness).

83. Geller v. Mackham, 635 F.2d 1027, 1032 (2d Cir. 1980).

84. Leftwich v. Harris-Stowe State College, 540 F. Supp. 37 (E.D. Mo. 1982).

85. Loeb v. Textron, Inc., 600 F.2d 1003 (1st Cir. 1979); *see also* Polstorff v. Fletcher, 452 F. Supp. 17 (N.D. Ala. 1978); 29 C.F.R. § 860.91(a).

86. *Compare* Combes v. Griffin Television, Inc., 421 F. Supp. 841 (W.D. Okla.

1976), *with* Loeb v. Textron, 600 F.2d 1003 (1st Cir. 1979).

87. Federal district courts allowing compensatory damages include Buckholz v. Symons Manufacturing Co., 445 F. Supp. 706 (E.D. Wis. 1978); Coates v. National Cash Register Co., 433 F. Supp. 655 (W.D. Va. 1977); Bertrand v. Orkin Exterminating Co., 432 F. Supp. 952 (N.D. Ill. 1977). Damages for pain, suffering, and emotional distress have been disallowed in Rogers v. Exxon Research and Engineering Co., 550 F.2d 834 (3d Cir. 1977); Dean v. American Security Insurance Co., 559 F.2d 1036 (5th Cir. 1977).

88. Dolan v. School Dist. No. 10, 636 P.2d 825 (Mont. 1981).

89. Board of Regents of the University of Nevada System v. Oakley, 637 P.2d 1199 (Nev. 1981).

90. Johnston v. Marion Indep. School Dist., 275 N.W.2d 215, 216 (Iowa 1979). *See also* Selland v. Fargo Pub. School Dist. No. 1, 302 N.W.2d 391 (N.D. 1981).

91. In addition to specific remedies included in various civil rights laws, such as reinstatement and back pay, victims of public employment discrimination often have attempted to secure compensatory and punitive damages under 42 U.S.C. § 1983. For a discussion of judicial interpretations of this provision, *see* McCarthy, *Discrimination in Employment: The Evolving Law*, pp. 57-59.

3
Substantive Constitutional Rights: The First Amendment and Privacy

Arval A. Morris

The First Amendment to the Constitution, adopted in 1791, provides:

> Congress shall make no law respecting an establishment of religion, or prohibiting the free exercise thereof; or abridging the freedom of speech or of the press; or the right of the people peaceably to assemble, and to petition the Government for a redress of grievances.

On its face this Amendment appears to apply only to Congress. But the 14th Amendment, adopted 77 years later, prohibits a state from abridging "the privileges or immunities of citizens" and from depriving any person of liberty without due process of law. One of the provisions of the Bill of Rights that has been incorporated into the due process clause of the 14th Amendment is the First Amendment.[1] It now applies fully to the states, and thus to the entire public education establishment.[2]

Not all personal rights fundamental to a free people and implicit in the concept of an ordered liberty have specifically been set forth in either the Bill of Rights or the 14th Amendment. Recognizing this situation, the Ninth Amendment to the U.S. Constitution provides that "the enumeration in the Constitution of certain rights shall not be construed to deny or disparage others retained by the people." Although it based its earlier rulings on an implicit right to privacy, the Supreme Court explicitly recognized a constitutional right to privacy in 1965.[3] It, too, is

---

Arval Morris is a professor of law at the University of Washington.

part of the 14th Amendment, and it, too, is binding on the states and the public education establishment.

With these legal developments in mind, the focus of this chapter will be on the substantive constitutional protections of the public school employment relationship guaranteed by the First Amendment, particularly freedom of speech, and by the 14th Amendment's right to privacy. Woven into this chapter are the burden-of-proof standards required for establishing a prima facie case of denial of these constitutional rights and also the requirements an employer must meet when seeking to rebut the evidence submitted in the case.

First Amendment Rights of Teachers

Any notion that public school teachers and students are bereft of First Amendment as well as other constitutional rights was laid to rest in 1969 in *Tinker v. Des Moines Independent Community School District*,[4] where the U.S. Supreme court ruled:

> First Amendment rights, applied in light of the special characteristics of the school environment, are available to teachers and students. It can hardly be argued that either students or teachers shed their constitutional rights to freedom of speech or expression at the schoolhouse gate.

The question for courts, school attorneys, and school administrators since the *Tinker* case has been to determine what rights teachers and students take with them beyond the schoolhouse gate and just how far these rights might be taken "in light of the special characteristics of the school environment." Although some cases are definitive within their factual circumstances, the Supreme Court has yet to decide a case that sets all the boundaries of First Amendment rights of elementary and secondary school teachers in the school environment. Thus this discussion should not be considered exhaustive or definitive.

A Teacher's Freedom to Speak Out

Pickering v. *Board of Education*,[5] a leading case, partially clarified a teacher's right to freedom of speech under the First and 14th Amendments. As background for understanding the case, an Illinois school board had asked voters to approve a bond issue to build two new schools. The proposal passed on its second submission and the schools were built. The board then began a campaign to increase tax rates and to use the additional funds for educational programs. This campaign failed twice. During the second campaign to increase tax rates, Pickering, a teacher in the district, wrote a letter to the editor of the local newspaper in which he attacked: 1) the way in which the board handled the earlier school bond issues, 2) the way in which the board allocated funds between the educational and athletic programs, and, in addition, 3) charged the superintendent of schools with attempting to silence teachers, preventing them from opposing or criticizing the proposed tax increases.

The board dismissed Pickering for writing and publishing the letter. But Illinois law required the board to hold a hearing on Pickering's dismissal. At the hearing the board sought to justify its actions by charging that numerous statements in Pickering's letter were false and to the detriment of members of the board and the administration. After hearing testimony, the board found Pickering's statements to be false as charged. However, the board made no finding on the effects of Pickering's published letter, whether on the community as a whole, on the administration of the school system, or particularly on his effectiveness in the classroom.

The Supreme Court recognized "the special characteristics of the school environment," stating that "the State has interests as an employer in regulating the speech of its employees that differ significantly from those it possesses in connection with regulation of the speech of the citizenry in general." Thus the problem in Pickering's case came down to arriving at a balance between the interest of the teacher, as an ordinary citizen, in commenting on matters of public concern and the interests of the state, as an employer, in promoting the efficiency and effectiveness of the public services it performs through its employees. The question facing the Court was whether a teacher's exercise of freedom of speech impairs institutional effectiveness, and, if so, whether that impairment is so great as to justify restricting a teacher's freedom of speech.

The Court weighed those statements of Pickering that, it agreed, were unintentionally false. After careful consideration the Court concluded that the false statements, although critical of the board, were "neither shown nor could be presumed to have in any way either impeded the teacher's performance of his daily duties in the classroom or to have interfered with the regular operation of the schools generally."

Given the overall conclusion that Pickering's letter did not affect school discipline, effectiveness, or harmony among his co-workers, the state's interest in limiting Pickering's freedom of speech was held to be "not significantly greater than its interest in limiting a similar contribution by any member of the general public." Thus the state's interest weighed little in the overall balance. On the other hand, Pickering's right to free speech was, indeed, given considerable weight. The Court noted that a teacher may have a special vantage point from which to formulate an "informed and definite" opinion about the allocation of school funds, making it essential that teachers be able to speak out without fear of retaliation.

Consequently, the Court ruled for Pickering, and in doing so, it laid down a rule of constitutional law that applies to other cases like his where the fact of public employment is only tangentially involved in the subject matter of a teacher's public communication: "In sum, we hold that, in a case such as this, absent proof of false statements knowingly or recklessly made by him, a teacher's exercise of his right to speak on issues of public importance may not furnish the basis for his dismissal from public employment."

A critical element of the Supreme Court ruling in *Pickering* is the nature of the state's interest. That interest was described as "promoting the efficiency of the public services it performs through its employees." Thus when a teacher speaks out publicly, it is generally the effects of the content of his statements that must be assessed to determine whether they impede "the teacher's proper performance of his daily duties in the classroom or . . . interfere with the regular operation of the schools generally."[6] If they do not, then the decision is obvious: Pickering's precedent governs, even if some of the teacher's statements are false or marginally impair school effectiveness.

If, on the other hand, the teacher's public expression significantly impairs his effectiveness or interferes significantly with the regular operation of the schools, the decision is no longer obvious. The decision does not automatically favor the state in such a situation, but the balance is closer, and a court now must weigh the amount and duration of the teacher's ineffectiveness or interference with school operations due to his exercise of freedom of speech against his right to freedom of speech and its role in our society. In each context of close balancing, striking the right balance may involve differing considerations and produce different legal conclusions depending on the weights of the relevant considerations in each specific case.

In a recent case the Supreme Court reaffirmed and extended the *Pickering* precedent to apply to private communications between a teacher of English and her school principal, which were described by the principal as "insulting," "hostile," "loud," and "arrogant."[7] Freedom of speech, the Court ruled, is not "lost to the public employee who arranges to communicate privately with his employer rather than to spread his views before the public." Clearly, however, private expression in such circumstances may bring into balance factors that were not present in Pickering's case. When a teacher personally and insultingly confronts his immediate administrative superior, the employing school district's institutional efficiency may be threatened not only by the effects of the content of the teacher's message, as in *Pickering*, but also by the time, place, and manner in which the teacher delivers his message. On the other hand, this extension of *Pickering* probably means that a teacher may not be removed for "insubordination" solely because of private hostile or arrogant communications made to a principal about school policies or programs at a time, place, and in a manner that do not impair the teacher's or the institution's efficiency.

The *Pickering* "balancing approach" must be used by lower courts in this kind of case, and their decisions have further defined a teacher's right to freedom of speech. For example, in 1974 the Eighth Circuit Court of Appeals decided a case in which a mathematics teacher had been dismissed because, during his algebra class, he emotionally stated that the students were "4,000 strong"; that they could throw military recruiters, who were then present and recruiting, off the school's campus; and that the students and faculty should decide who should visit the school.[8] Some students testified that the teacher told them to throw their apples at the recruiters and "to get them in a crowd, and push them and kick them, make them feel like they weren't wanted." Later, the teacher personally confronted the recruiters and told them "We don't want you here."

The court ruled that the *Pickering* balance tipped against the teacher because his statements were "infused with the spirit of violent action" to the degree that school authorities could find a situation of disruption. In addition, the teacher's remarks were unrelated to his class and interfered with the operations of the school, which had granted permission for military recruitment. The state's interest in institutional efficiency outweighed the teacher's interest in free speech.

On the other hand, a teacher's dismissal after he twice refused the orders of two principals to remove a black armband was reversed by another federal appeals court.[9] The teacher wore the black armband "as an expression of his religious aversion to war in any form and as a sign of his regret over the loss of life in Vietnam." He made no attempt to proselytize his students. The court agreed that free speech was involved. There was no evidence that wearing the black armband impaired the teacher's effectiveness or the institutional effectiveness of the school. Consequently, the balance tipped in favor of the teacher's right to freedom of speech.

In yet another case, California's Supreme Court applied the *Pickering* balancing approach to disallow a transfer of a teacher from one school to another because the teacher had exercised his freedom of speech.[10] At a school-sponsored public forum meeting, he vigorously and persistently criticized the school's policy on dress and grooming, its policy on outside speakers, and the administration's refusal to permit publication of a second newspaper. His remarks produced some subsequent disharmony and friction with fellow teachers and with his principal. But there was no evidence that his teaching effectiveness was impaired or that institutional inefficiency resulted from his speech. Ruling that "mere fear of disruption due to the expression of unpopular views will not justify interference with the free expression of opinion," California's Supreme Court held in favor of the teacher, thereby precluding his transfer as retaliation for speaking out.

One can expect courts to reach the same result if a teacher is demoted, rather than transferred or dismissed, as retaliation for exercising his freedom of speech in a way that does not significantly impair his or the institution's effectiveness. The question is whether the transfer or demotion was punitive retaliation or was necessary for the effective operation of the school district.[11]

Finally, the Supreme Court has ruled that a local school board may not prohibit teachers who are not union representatives from speaking at open meetings where a proposed collective bargaining contract is under discussion, even if the state law directs the local board to prohibit teachers, other than union representatives, from participating.[12] The Court reasoned that "[t]eachers not only constitute the overwhelming bulk of employees of the school system, but they are the very core of that system; restraining teachers' expressions to the board on matters involving the operation of the schools would seriously impair the board's ability to govern the district."

A Teacher's Freedom To Associate

A right to freedom of association is not expressly set forth in the Constitution, but it has been implied from the First and 14th Amendments, and it applies to teachers as well as all other citizens.

During the 1950s the Arkansas legislature passed a statute compelling all teachers, as a condition of employment in a state-supported school, annually to file an affidavit listing without limitation every organization to which they have belonged or regularly contributed within the preceding five years. The law was challenged in the U.S. Supreme Court on the ground that it deprived Arkansas teachers of their rights to personal, associational, and academic liberty protected by the due process clause of the 14th Amendment. Agreeing with the teachers and ruling the law unconstitutional in *Shelton* v. *Tucker*,[13] the Supreme Court declared that "to compel a teacher to disclose his every associational tie is to impair that teacher's right to free association." It then ruled that the "unlimited and indiscriminate sweep of the statute now before us [and its] comprehensive interference with associational freedom goes far beyond what might be justified in the exercise of the State's legitimate inquiry into the fitness and competency of its teachers."

The Supreme Court did not rule out completely the power of the state to compel a teacher to disclose some of his associations under appropriate circumstances involving "the fitness and competency" of a teacher. During and after the McCarthy period, arguments were made that the circumstances were appropriate and that teachers should be compelled to declare whether they were members of the Communist

Party; if they were, they could be terminated. This argument represents a guilt-by-association view. Teachers were confronted with variously worded loyalty oaths. For example, a Florida oath required teachers to swear that they had never "knowingly lent their aid, support, advice, counsel or influence to the Communist Party." In 1961 the Supreme Court declared this law unconstitutionally vague because a law "which either forbids or requires the doing of an act in terms so vague that men of common intelligence must necessarily guess at its meaning and differ as to its application violates the first essential of due process of law."[14] Three years later the Court declared a Washington oath that required teachers to declare that they were not members of "subversive organizations" unconstitutionally vague.[15]

But suppose the oath is not vague: Can teachers be compelled to state that they are not members of the Communist Party, and be terminated if they refuse to disclaim? The answer is no, because the requirement is ultimately based on guilt by association when it makes membership alone grounds for dismissal. Individual membership in any organization can be innocent, constructive, or destructive. For a loyalty oath involving membership in a suspect organization to be constitutionally valid, it must be individualized, relating to the specific nature of an individual's membership. Thus the Supreme Court has ruled: "Mere knowing membership without specific intent to further the unlawful aims of an organization is not a constitutionally adequate basis for exclusion."[16] Guilt by association must be eliminated in such a situation.

Although loyalty oaths, especially disclaimer oaths, have been severely curtailed by the Supreme Court, it has not invalidated all oaths as such. To the contrary, the Supreme Court has upheld loyalty oaths for teachers that do not involve disclaimers. Generally, these oaths require teachers to swear that they will uphold federal and state constitutions. Colorado's oath is an example:

> I solemnly (swear) (affirm) that I will uphold the constitution of the United States and the constitution of the State of Colorado, and I will faithfully perform the duties of the position upon which I am about to enter.

The Supreme Court upheld this oath, ruling that it was within the constitutional power of Colorado's legislature to prescribe.[17]

Finally, it should be noted that, whether tenured or not, a teacher's constitutional right to free association includes the right to form and join a union. No teacher can constitutionally be terminated for union activities per se. A federal court of appeals declared that "it is beyond debate that freedom to engage in association for the advancement of beliefs and ideas is an inseparable aspect of the 'liberty' assured by the Due Process clause of the 14th Amendment, which embraces freedom of speech."[18] In as much as *Shelton* v. *Tucker* settled that "teachers have the right of free association," this court ruled that "an individual's right to form and join a union is protected by the First Amendment."

A Teacher's Right To Academic Freedom

Academic freedom implies immunity to some natural consequences of freedom of speech and association that ordinary citizens do not enjoy because they do not share the peculiar character and function of the scholar-educator. As such, academic freedom protects the right of faculty members to conduct whatever instruction and research they have been hired to perform consistent with standards of professional integrity. And, as the Supreme Court has declared in a higher education case, academic freedom is protected by the First Amendment.

> Our nation is deeply committed to safeguarding academic freedom, which is of transcendent value to all of us and not merely to the teachers concerned. That freedom is therefore a special concern of the First Amendment, which does not tolerate laws that cast a pall of orthodoxy over the classroom. . . . The classroom is peculiarly the "marketplace of ideas."[19]

The Supreme Court has decided no case based directly on a K-12 teacher's academic freedom with respect to classroom activities. It has, however, decided cases in which it indicated that K-12 teachers had rights to academic freedom, but the Court did not define those rights.[20] On the other hand, cases from lower federal and state courts provide some guidelines for academic freedom issues involving assignment of materials and teaching methods. The problems generally arise in contexts where there is no school district policy that expressly prohibits assignment of certain materials or use of certain methods, with such decisions left open to teacher discretion. In this context courts tend to use a balancing test weighing a teacher's interest in academic freedom against the state's need for some measure of control and discipline over public school classrooms.

In one case a teacher of high school English gave each member of his senior class a copy of the *Atlantic Monthly* containing an article by a professor at Yale's medical school.[21] The word "motherfucker" appeared in the article; and the school board attempted to dismiss the English teacher because this "dirty" word was, in the opinion of complaining parents, too shocking for high school seniors to deal with during class discussions of the article. Although the court stated it had "the greatest of respect" for parents, it went on to say that "their sensibilities are not the full measure of what is proper education." The court did acknowledge the state's interest in that "some measure of public regulation of classroom speech is inherent in every provision of public education." But, the court continued:

When we consider the facts . . . we find it difficult not to think that its application [public regulation] to the present case demeans any proper concept of education [because] the general chilling effect of permitting such rigorous censorship is even more serious. . . . With regard to the word itself, we cannot think that it is unknown to many students in the last year of high school. . . . No doubt its use genuinely offends the parents of some of the students — therein, in part, lay its relevancy to the article. . . . If . . . students must be protected from such exposure, we would fear for their future.[22]

In another case an eleventh-grade English teacher was dismissed by the board because she had assigned materials that allegedly had a "disruptive" effect on the school, and she had refused "the counselling and advice of the school principal."[23] She assigned as outside reading Kurt Vonnegut's story, "Welcome to the Monkey House." The court found that "rather than there being a threatened or actual disruption to the educational processes of the school, the evidence reflects that assigning the story was greeted with apathy by most of the students" and that the assignment "was not such that would materially and substantially interfere with reasonable requirements of discipline." One wonders what assignment would! Moreover, the court found that the story was appropriate for high school age students and that the school board had to carry the burden of showing that the story was inappropriate. It failed.

Ordering reinstatement of the teacher, the court concluded that her "dismissal constituted an unwarranted invasion of her First Amendment right to academic freedom."[24] Presumably, the opposite result would have been reached by the court if the school board had shown the material was "inappropriate," or if assigning the materials was disruptive of reasonable school discipline.

The usual way of proving that assigned materials are "appropriate" or "inappropriate" is by testimony stating the professional judgment of experts in the field, or from other professional standards. Sometimes certain materials are irrelevant to the subject area in the judgment of experts in the field and are, therefore, "inappropriate" and constitutionally unprotected by the First Amendment. For example, a federal appellate court upheld the dismissal of teachers of French, industrial arts, and language arts because they distributed brochures on the joyous pleasures of drug use and sex to their eighth-grade classes even though they did not discuss the subjects in their classes.[25] Academic freedom does not protect this type of teacher behavior.

Academic freedom protects appropriate teaching methods used in situations where no constitutionally reasonable rule of the school district prohibits their use. For example, in one case an eleventh-grade English teacher assigned a novel about a teacher who had taken over a rural one-room school in which the boys sat on one side and girls on the other.[26]

The teacher in the novel intermingled the sexes for classroom seating, and parents vigorously objected. During class discussion of the novel and of cultural taboos, the English teacher wrote the word "fuck" on the blackboard and contrasted it with another word, seeking to demonstrate its taboo quality. After a few minutes of discussion he went on to other matters. He was dismissed by the board for "conduct unbecoming a teacher." The court of appeals upheld a lower federal court's order requiring reinstatement of the teacher, ruling that the lower "court found that the [teacher's] conduct was within standards responsibly, although not universally recognized, and that he acted in good faith and without notice that [the board] as his superiors, were not of that view. Sanctions in this circumstance would be a denial of due process." The board "cannot justify a post facto decision by school authorities that the use of a particular teaching method is ground for discharge, or other serious sanction, simply because some educators disapprove of it."

In another case a high school political science teacher sought to present his class with four points of view from the mouths of their adherents — a Republican, a Democrat, a John Birch Society member, and a communist.[27] Just before the last of these four individuals was scheduled to speak, community pressure was brought to bear, and the board revoked its permission. It orally issued an order banning "all political speakers" from the high school. The teacher sued, claiming the board's action infringed his academic freedom. In deciding this case, the federal district court observed that the "medium is the message"; that the use of speakers was the teacher's medium for teaching; that the "act of teaching is a form of expression and the methods used in teaching are media." Ruling for the teacher, the court stated that the school board's order was unreasonable and that it had unreasonably "suppressed expression which the First Amendment protects."

In a case from Texas a teacher disclosed to his civics class his personal opinion that he was not opposed to interracial marriage.[28] After several parents complained, school officials urged him to confine his teaching exclusively to the assigned textbook, without injecting his opinions. He ignored this advice and several times departed from the text during the next five months. Shortly after administering an allegedly "propagandistic" test on race relations, the school board discharged him on the ground of "insubordination." The court ordered his reinstatement, declaring that a teacher has a right to choose teaching methods that serve a demonstrated educational purpose. "A responsible teacher," the court concluded, "must have freedom to use the tools of his profession as he sees fit."

In another case from Texas a teacher rated as "outstanding" used a method known as "Sunshine simulation" to teach American history of the post-Civil War Reconstruction period.[29] The students recreated the history of the period by playing roles. This method evoked strong student feelings on racial issues and complaints from their parents. A school official told the teacher "not to discuss blacks in American history" and that "nothing controversial should be discussed in the classroom." No one told her not to continue the project, and she continued it to completion. Later, her contract was not renewed, and she sued. The court of appeals ruled "that classroom discussion is protected activity" and that a teacher's discharge for classroom discussions "cannot be upheld unless the discussions clearly overbalance her usefulness as an instructor."

In summary, when dealing with disputes involving materials or teaching methods that are left to the discretion of the teacher, courts balance the teacher's interest of academic freedom against the state's interest of maintaining control over the public school so it might achieve its objectives. If no constitutionally reasonable school district policy prohibits the use of materials or teaching methods, courts have clearly recognized that public school teachers in situations left to their discretion have rights to academic freedom in the classroom when assigning materials or selecting teaching methods. Courts are not disposed to create general guidelines, and each case is judged individually on its facts.

In the absence of disruption of the school's program, it appears that teachers' claims of academic freedom will prevail when they have discretion and assign materials or use a teaching method approved by a majority of the expert professional opinion in their field. If a significant amount but less than a majority of expert professional opinion supports the teachers' view that the materials or methods serve a serious educational purpose, the teachers probably will still prevail so long as they acted sincerely, professionally, and their school's program was not disrupted. Thus a teacher has a qualified right to assign materials or to use teaching methods that are relevant and, in the opinion of experts of significant standing, have a serious educational purpose. "Relevancy" here refers not only to the subject matter of the course but also to the age and maturity of the students. This much is central to the rationale of academic freedom that is enjoyed by public school teachers.

A Teacher's Right To Be Politically Active

As the *Pickering* case demonstrates, the First Amendment protects a teacher's freedom to speak out on public issues. The First Amendment also protects teachers who actively campaign for political office for themselves or others. School officials cannot infringe on such political activities through demotions, transfers, or dismissals of teachers. Moreover, in *Elrod* v. *Burns* the Supreme Court ruled that employees, such as public school teachers, who hold non-policy making and non-confidential positions, cannot be terminated because their political beliefs and associations are opposed to the policy makers who gain control of the administrative structures.[30] In other words, "patronage dismissals" of non-policy making employees are unconstitutional. If a teacher should be discharged in such circumstance, the initial burden is on the teacher to present evidence showing that he or she was a non-policy maker and was transferred, demoted, or terminated because of his or her political beliefs, associations, or political activities. The burden then shifts to the board or superintendent to show that its action was justified; and if that cannot be shown, the court will set aside the board's action.

A teacher's right to be active politically is subject to the balancing test and can be limited in order to protect the proper functioning of a school. For example, proselytizing in class will not be allowed. In one case a teacher spoke to a class about a candidate for school superintendent as follows: "Many of you know Mr. Golway, what a fine man he is, and that he hopes to be elected soon; I think he would be more helpful to our department than a lady, and we need more men in our schools. . . . Sometimes your parents do not know one candidate from another." The teacher was suspended for ten weeks. The suspension was upheld because the teacher's remarks were "wholly foreign" to the teacher's subject matter and tended to introduce needless strife into school programs.[31] On the other hand, California's Supreme Court upheld the right of teachers in a teachers union to circulate a petition about education financing to other teachers in a school lounge.[32] The California court used a balancing test, declaring that a teacher's right to be active politically is constitutionally protected unless such political activity presents a "clear and substantial threat" to the proper operation of the school.

Teachers can constitutionally be prohibited from being politically active within their classrooms and from engaging in political activities that interfere with the proper operation of schools. All other peaceful political activities are constitutionally protected. For example, a Kentucky superintendent transferred and demoted seven teachers and administrators "for the betterment of the schools." They had publicly promoted and campaigned for a school board candidate opposed by the superintendent. Characterizing the superintendent's action as retaliatory, arbitrary, and therefore void, Kentucky's Supreme Court ruled in behalf of the teachers.[33]

School district rules can be imposed so long as they are reasonable and do not deny a teacher's right to be politically active. But an intermediate Kentucky court struck down a school board policy requiring that all employees seeking public office take a one-month leave of absence immediately prior to the election.[34] There was no evidence in the case showing that such political activity would lead teachers to neglect their duties or would have an adverse effect on their teaching.

Such evidence, regarding certain types of political activities, does not appear unduly difficult to collect. Thus it appears likely that a reasonable school board rule formulated on the basis of accumulated evidence, and no broader than the evidence, would be upheld in the proper case.

A Teacher's Freedom of Religion

The First Amendment states that "Congress shall make no law respecting an establishment of religion, or prohibiting the free exercise thereof." The establishment clause is the basis for litigation involving Bible reading, prayers, and other religious instruction in public schools, and financial aid to parochial schools.[35] The Supreme Court has ruled several times that constitutionally protected freedom from established religion means at least that:

> Neither a state nor the federal government can set up a church. Neither can pass laws which aid one religion, aid all religions, or prefer one religion over another. Neither can force or influence a person to go to or to remain away from church against his will or force him to profess a belief or disbelief in any religion. No person can be punished for entertaining or professing religious belief or disbelief, for church attendance or non-attendance. No tax in any amount, large or small, can be levied to support any religious activities or institutions, whatever they may be called, or whatever form they may adopt to teach or practice religion. Neither a state nor the Federal Government can, openly or secretly, participate in the affairs of any religious organizations or groups and *vice versa*. In the words of Jefferson, the clause against establishment of religion by law was intended to erect "a wall of separation between church and State."[36]

The establishment clause can also protect academic freedom. In *Epperson* v. *Arkansas* the Supreme Court had to rule on an Arkansas criminal statute prohibiting the teaching of evolution.[37] A biology teacher had used a textbook that contained a chapter setting forth "the theory about the origin . . . of man from a lower form of animal." Thus under Arkansas law, to teach the chapter would be a criminal offense, but not to do so could be interpreted as insubordination and neglect of duty. Noting that the Arkansas statute "was a product of the upsurge of 'fundamentalist' religious fervor of the Twenties," the Supreme Court ruled the law unconstitutional because it established religion by selecting "from the body of knowledge a particular segment which it proscribes for the sole reason that it is deemed to conflict with a particular religious doctrine; that is, with a particular interpretation of the Book of Genesis by a particular religious group."

The same decision was decreed by a court where, instead of prohibiting something from the curriculum, a school board required a teacher to teach so-called Creation Science, based on a particular interpretation of the Book of Genesis by a particular religious group.[38] It also follows from these precedents that teachers cannot proselytize in public schools because, as the Iowa Supreme Court has declared, "our public school system . . . shall not be used directly or indirectly for religious instruction, and above all it shall not be made an instrumentality of proselytizing influence in favor of any religious organization, sect, creed or belief."[39] A teacher's clearly improper use of authority — say to recruit students into a particular religion — can result in dismissal because of the teacher's attempt to establish religion.[40]

The second guarantee of religious freedom contained in the First Amendment is the free exercise clause. It is usually invoked by a teacher when a school board requires the teacher to do something directly conflicting with that teacher's freedom of religion. In this situation the Supreme Court invokes a balancing test weighing the teacher's interest in free exercise of religion against a state's interest in having the teacher comply with state law. For example, some Catholic nuns have been hired to teach in public schools but forbidden to wear religious garb while teaching. The Pennsylvania Supreme Court upheld the constitutionality of a law specifically prohibiting teachers in public schools from wearing religious garments when teaching, in the interest of promoting the religious neutrality of schools.[41] The court reasoned that the statute was aimed at "acts, not beliefs, and only against acts of the teacher whilst engaged in the performance of his or her duties as such teacher." However, other courts have ruled that dress is irrelevant to instruction and have allowed public school teachers to wear religious garb.

In *West Virginia* v. *Barnette* the Supreme Court declared that "if there is any fixed star in our constitutional constellation, it is that no official, high or petty, can prescribe what shall be orthodox in politics, nationalism, religion or other matters of opinion or force citizens to confess by word or act their faith therein."[42] It then ruled a compelled flag salute for students to be unconstitutional. Later, a federal court of appeals relied on this approach in upholding the right of a teacher to refuse as a matter of "conscience" to participate in the Pledge of Allegiance, stating "the right to remain silent in the face of an illegitimate demand for speech is as much a part of First Amendment protections as the right to speak out in the face of an illegitimate demand for silence."[43]

On the other hand, a teacher's dismissal was upheld when she refused to teach patriotic materials that a school board reasonably could require.[44] As a Jehovah's Witness, the teacher believed in the biblical injunction not to worship graven images and concluded that to teach about patriotism, love of country, or Abraham Lincoln was tantamount to idolatry. The federal appeals court declared that if her religious beliefs were allowed to control, they would result in a "distorted and unbalanced view" of history. The court ruled that "she has no constitutional right to require others to submit to her views and to forego a portion of their education they would otherwise be entitled to enjoy."

Thus it can be seen that when free exercise claims are involved in a case, courts look to see whether an accommodation between a state's and a teacher's interest is possible, and if not, they balance and uphold the interest having the greatest weight within the specific context of an individual case.[45]

Privacy Rights of Teachers

Teachers, like all other citizens, have constitutional rights to privacy. The Supreme Court has ruled that this right to privacy encompasses a woman's decision whether or not to terminate her pregnancy during its first two terms, and it applies in many other areas. For example, it also includes the constitutional right of persons to read and observe whatever they please, including hard-core pornography, within the privacy of their own homes.[46]

The issue of the constitutional right to privacy is raised when school administrators and local boards attempt to control the activities of teachers outside the classroom and off the school campus. Teachers properly complain that attempts to control their lives away from school violate their rights to privacy and freedom of association. Thus constitutional rights to privacy and free association can conflict with the axiom that teachers be exemplary models in the community. This is especially true in situations where teachers are involved in homosexuality, unwed pregnancies, or nonconforming lifestyles. Typically, teachers are dismissed or their contracts are not renewed for "immorality" or for "unfitness to teach," and they sue for reinstatement. In such cases, courts first require that any administrative attempt to regulate a teacher's off-campus life must be based on evidence and must bear a rational relationship to that teacher's effectiveness in the classroom, and second they judge whether the overall balance of the interests weigh in favor of the state. Administrators and school boards seeking to control teachers' off-campus lives as a way to instill conventional values in students present neither the necessary rational relationship nor a sufficiently weighty interest to overcome teachers' constitutional right to privacy. Courts, recognizing the dynamic and changing character of American society, approach these problems on a case-by-case basis and do not lay down broad general guidelines about teacher conduct.

The Supreme Court has decided no case pitting the rights to privacy and association of a homosexual teacher against the state's interest in the teacher as exemplar. This unresolved issue continues to create controversy, but other courts provide some guidance. One leading case comes from the California Supreme Court where the board of education revoked a teacher's certificate for private homosexual acts, which the board said "constituted immoral and unprofessional conduct, and an act involving moral turpitude."[47] The teacher sued to have the board's decision set aside. Ruling in favor of the teacher, the court declared:

> The private conduct of a man, who is also a teacher, is a proper concern to those who employ him only to the extent it mars him as a teacher. . . . Where his professional achievement is unaffected, where the school community is placed in no jeopardy, his private acts are his own business and may not be the basis of discipline.[48]

In short, the question is whether the teacher's off-campus conduct indicates that his or her on-campus teaching effectiveness is impaired. This question must be decided solely on the evidence, which can include the proximity or remoteness in time of the conduct, whether the conduct actually adversely affected students or fellow teachers' teaching effectiveness, the extenuating or aggravating circumstances, and the extent to which disciplinary action may inflict an adverse impact or chilling effect on the constitutional rights of the teacher involved or other teachers. The California Supreme Court stated that "the Board failed to show that [the teacher's] conduct in any manner affected his performance as a teacher." The court was emphatic: "Before the Board can conclude that a teacher's continued retention . . . presents a significant danger of harm to students or fellow teachers, essential factual premises in its reasoning should be supported by evidence or official notice."

Consistent with the California Supreme Court decision, a lower federal court has declared that "the time has come today for private, consenting, adult homosexuality to enter the sphere of constitutionally protected interests" and that "intolerance of the unconventional halts the growth of liberty." When the case was appealed, the appellate court affirmed, declaring that a homosexual can come out of the closet without fearing a loss of his position so long as his "interviews [do not] disrupt the school, substantially impair his capacity as a teacher, or give school officials reasonable grounds to forecast that these results would flow from what he said."[49]

Another case from a lower federal court dealt with whether an elementary school teacher could be dismissed for "immorality in that the Board has been presented with a physician's certificate stating that [she] became pregnant during the current school year at which time [she was] a single unmarried person."[50] The board made no finding that the teacher's alleged "immorality" had affected her competency or effectiveness as a teacher; and no evidence showed any connection between her pregnancy and her teaching effectiveness. The court ruled for the teacher, holding that the state's "immorality" provision had been applied to the teacher "in a manner which invaded her constitutional right to privacy."

In another case from the New Mexico Supreme Court, a teacher, rated better than satisfactory, requested maternity leave and then was terminated for immoral conduct "because she was single and had engaged in premarital intercourse, as evidenced by the fact that she was pregnant."[51] Ruling for the teacher, the court declared the burden was on the board and that since "the failure of the Board to make a prima facie showing that good cause existed" for terminating the teacher's employment, the board's action "was arbitrary, unreasonable and not supported by substantial evidence."

Community disapproval of a teacher's lifestyle cannot justify termination as long as the teacher's classroom performance is effective and satisfactory. For example, in a case in which a teacher was not renewed, the official reasons given were that her program was too idealistic; her classrooms had been disorderly; and "there was a lack of dynamics . . . in motivating students."[52] But her principal revealed that the real reasons were recurring rumors that she was having an affair with another resident in the trailer park where she lived; that there was dissatisfaction in the community with the fact that she played cards and that she did not attend church regularly; and that she did not have an attractive physical appearance, which the school required of its physical education teachers. The "lack of dynamics" to which the principal had referred in his letter was her obesity. The jury found that the teacher's contract was not renewed "for constitutionally impermissible reasons" and that "the Board and school principal were acting in bad faith." The federal court entered judgment for the teacher, saying that it was "disinclined to overturn the jury's determination."

Lower courts have split on whether grooming and dress codes for teachers violate their constitutional rights. No Supreme Court decision exists on the subject for teachers, but the Court has upheld the validity of a county's hair grooming regulation for its male police officers. In *Kelley* v. *Johnson*,[53] Justice Rehnquist placed the burden on the police officer challenging the regulation to show it bore no reasonable relation to safety of persons and property. He stated that the issue on the hair code was whether the regulation was "so irrational that it may be branded 'arbitrary'." He found "that similarity in appearance of police officers" is rational and justified because it "may be based on a desire to make police officers readily recognizable to members of the public, or a desire for the *esprit de corps* which such similarity is felt to inculcate within the police force itself." Thus the Court ruled a rational connection could exist between the hair code and "the promotion of safety of persons and property."

Neither of these two justifying reasons applies easily to public school teachers. Nevertheless, shortly after *Kelley*, a federal court of appeals, relying on *Kelley*, upheld a school regulation requiring all males to wear ties.[54] The court ruled that a board's "dress code is presumptively constitutional" and that the teacher had to carry the burden "of demonstrating that the dress code is so irrational that it may be branded arbitrary." Since the teacher failed to carry his burden, the court upheld the dress code, saying that in "view of the uniquely influential role of the public school teacher in the classroom, the board is justified in imposing this regulation" and that "teachers may properly be subjected to many restrictions in their professional lives which would be invalid if generally applied."

On the other hand, a different federal court ruled in favor of three males when they challenged a Mississippi school board rule that eliminated long hair and restricted beards and moustaches.[55] The court's reasoning in this case was different from *Kelley* in that a regulation prescribing "grooming habits of adults as condition of public employment, unrelated to one's ability to perform his work, can only be viewed with close judicial scrutiny." This court put the burden on the board to justify its grooming code. The court could find no valid reason for applying a grooming code to teachers and, without proof of disruption, concluded that the board lacked power to require it.

Grooming codes can also be challenged when they treat men and women differently under Title VII of the Civil Rights Act of 1964, which prohibits gender discrimination with respect to "compensation, terms, conditions or privileges of employment."[56] One court has already ruled under this law that a savings and loan association may be able to require all its employees to wear uniforms, but it could not require females to wear uniforms and males to wear business suits.[57] Thus grooming codes for teachers would have to apply equally. Obviously, some variations in grooming will be permitted between the sexes as long as they reasonably are based on acceptable norms and related to educational needs.

Burdens of Proof in First Amendment and Privacy Cases

The first burden of proof teachers must meet when litigating is proving their claim. With the possible exception of grooming code cases, the burden of proof standards for establishing a prima facie case of denial of a teacher's constitutional rights is the same in First Amendment and right-to-privacy suits. The burden on the teacher is to show 1) that the specific activity engaged in came within the First Amendment or privacy guarantees, and 2) that the protected activity was a factor — one factor — motivating the board or a school administrator to take action against the teacher, whether it be reprimand, transfer, demotion, or dismissal. If the teacher can carry this burden, then the administrative action may rest on an unconstitutional foundation. If the administration introduces no evidence, the teacher will win. However, the board or administrator is permitted to show that the state has the weightier interest. It has the burden of introducing evidence on the state's interest. For example, in a

Pickering-type case the board might introduce evidence showing that the teacher's communication destroyed his working relationships with his colleagues and immediate supervisors and impaired his classroom effectiveness with his students. This evidence would show that the state's interest in the efficient operation of its schools had been impaired. Since the board introduced evidence, the court now must invoke the balancing test, weighing the evidence and the interest on each side and ruling in favor of the party with the weightier case.

A second type of burden can apply to all First Amendment and privacy cases when the board fails to carry its burden under the *Pickering* balancing test and loses under that test. This second burden stems from the 1977 Supreme Court ruling in *Mt. Healthy City School District Board of Education* v. *Doyle*.[58] The teacher had been dismissed from his teaching position for complex reasons, some relating to his exercise of free speech rights and some relating to other, valid considerations. He sued. At this point Doyle had the burden of establishing a prima facie case of unconstitutional motivation. This is the same burden that a teacher must carry under the *Pickering* balancing test. Doyle proved his termination was based on at least one unconstitutional factor — retaliation for exercising his right to free speech. The Supreme Court accepted that Doyle had proved unconstitutional motivation on the school district's part but, nevertheless, reversed and remanded the case. A teacher's showing of unconstitutional motivation, said Justice Rehnquist, merely shifts a second, and different, burden to the school district. While it could introduce evidence on the state's interest, the school district could introduce additional evidence showing that it would have reached the same decision, i.e., to terminate Doyle, based solely on other valid (not unconstitutional) factors. If it carries this burden and shows that the teacher would have been terminated on valid grounds, then an invasion of a teacher's constitutional rights is not the "real" basis for the administrative action, and the school board wins.

The Supreme Court's approach in *Mt. Healthy* obviously creates problems. It invites a school board to engage in post hoc rationalizations of what it might have done. The court must examine the various reasons that are proffered and decide which of them are valid. The dilemma facing the court is how to distinguish between what a defendant school board actually would have done absent unconstitutional motivation and a mere post hoc rationalization.

Conclusions

Courts decide individual lawsuits on a case-by-case basis and do not enact general or sweeping guidelines regarding teacher or administrative conduct. Case law seems to support the following statements:

1. Teachers have a constitutional right to communicate their opinions to the public, or to school administrators, about all aspects of the school system. However, if their communication disrupts school programs or substantially interferes with school effectiveness, their right to free speech can be limited.

2. Reprimands, demotions, transfers, dismissals, or any kind of retaliatory action based solely on exercise of First Amendment or privacy rights are unconstitutional and will be set aside.

3. Even if a school district's disciplinary action against a teacher was originally based, in part, on an unconstitutional motivating factor, it will be upheld if the school district can show by a preponderance of the evidence that it would have reached the same decision anyway on valid (not unconstitutional) factors.

4. Where discretion is vested in the teacher, assigned classroom materials and teaching methods must be relevant to the objectives of the course and sincerely used with a serious educational purpose. Age and the intellectual and emotional maturity of students are important factors when experts judge "relevancy."

5. Generally, teachers cannot be required as a condition of employment to sign a disclaimer oath, but they can be required to pledge support to the U.S. and state constitutions. Membership in an organization having some unlawful purposes is an unconstitutional basis for disciplining or terminating a teacher. Questions related to a teacher's fitness to teach must be answered if put to the teacher by the appropriate administrator.

6. A school district cannot discipline or terminate teachers for political activities carried on off-campus, but their activities can be regulated by reasonable rules, based on evidence, that protect the state's interest in operating its schools effectively.

7. School districts must make reasonable accommodations for a teacher's religious beliefs, but neither a teacher nor the school district can promote any religious belief, or all religious beliefs, in classrooms or outside them in any way that affects a school's educational mission.

8. Private conduct of a teacher (e.g., unwed pregnancy or homosexuality) that does not impair a teacher's fitness to teach cannot be ground for dismissal, even if the activity is disapproved of by the community.

9. School districts can impose on teachers reasonable grooming codes that are relevant to achieving school effectiveness.

Footnotes

1. *See, e.g.*, Gitlow v. New York, 268 U.S. 652 (1925).
2. For further discussion, *see* Arval Morris, *The Constitution and American Education,* 2nd ed. (Racine, Wisc.: West Publishing Co., 1980), pp. 48-57.

3. Griswold v. Connecticut, 381 U.S. 479 (1965).

4. 393 U.S. 503 (1969).

5. 391 U.S. 563 (1968).

6. 391 U.S. at 572-73.

7. Givhan v. Western Line Consol. School Dist., 439 U.S. 410 (1979); *see also* Ayers v. Western Line Consol. School Dist., 691 F.2d 766 (5th Cir. 1982).

8. Birdwell v. Hazelwood School Dist., 491 F.2d 490 (8th Cir. 1974); Whitsel v. Southeast Local School Dist., 484 F.2d 1222 (6th Cir. 1973) (upheld a dismissal of a teacher because he spoke publicly to a group of protesting students after the principal had ordered them back to their classrooms).

9. James v. Board of Educ., 461 F.2d 566 (2d Cir. 1972), *cert. denied*, 409 U.S. 1042 (1972).

10. Adcock v. Board of Educ., 513 P.2d 900 (Cal. 1973); *see also* McGill v. Board of Educ., 602 F.2d 744 (7th Cir. 1979).

11. Transfers have been upheld where the teacher's speech "interfere[d] with the management and operation of the school, and create[d] animosity and the possibility of physical violence between plaintiff [the teacher] and the assistant principals," and are not seen as punitive but as based on "legitimate managerial reasons." Austin v. Mehlville R-9 School Dist., 564 S.W.2d 884 (Mo. 1978).

12. City of Madison Joint School Dist. No. 8 v. Wisconsin Employment Relations Comm'n, 429 U.S. 167(1976).

13. Shelton v. Tucker, 364 U.S. 479 (1960).

14. Cramp v. Board of Pub. Instruction, 368 U.S. 278 (1961).

15. Baggett v. Bullitt, 377 U.S. 360 (1964).

16. Keyishian v. Board of Regents, 385 U.S. 589 (1967).

17. Ohlson v. Phillips, 397 U.S. 317 (1970); *see also* Connell v. Higginbotham, 403 U.S. 207 (1971).

18. McLaughlin v. Tilendis, 398 F.2d 287 (7th Cir. 1968).

19. Keyishian v. Board of Regents, 385 U.S. 589, 603 (1967).

20. *See, e.g.*, Shelton v. Tucker, 364 U.S. 479 (1960), and Justice Stewart's concurrence in Epperson v. Arkansas, 393 U.S. 97 (1968).

21. Keefe v. Geanakos, 418 F.2d 359 (1st Cir. 1969).

22. *Id.* at 362.

23. Parducci v. Rutland, 316 F. Supp. 352 (M.D. Ala. 1970).

24. *Id.* at 356.

25. Brubaker v. Board of Educ., 502 F.2d 973 (7th Cir. 1974), *cert. denied*, 421 U.S. 965 (1975); *see also*, Simon v. Jefferson Davis Parish School Bd., 289 So. 2d 511 (La. App. 1974).

26. Mailloux v. Kiley, 448 F.2d 1242 (1st Cir. 1971).

27. Wilson v. Chancellor, 418 F. Supp. 1358 (D. Ore. 1976).

28. Sterzing v. Fort Bend School Dist., 376 F. Supp. 657 (S.D. Tex. 1972).

29. Kingsville Indep. School Dist. v. Cooper, 611 F.2d 1109 (5th Cir. 1980). *But cf.* Adams v. Campbell School Dist., 511 F.2d 1242 (10th Cir. 1975).

30. 427 U.S. 347 (1976).

31. Goldsmith v. Board of Educ., 66 Cal. App. 157, 225 P. 783 (1924).

32. Los Angeles Teachers Union v. Los Angeles Bd. of Educ., 78 Cal. Rptr. 723, 455 P.2d 827 (1969).

33. Calhoun v. Cassady, 534 S.W.2d 806 (Ky. 1976).

34. Allen v. Board of Educ., 584 S.W.2d 408 (Ky. App. 1979). *See also* the Wyoming Supreme Court's dubious ruling that a teacher cannot be elected to a school board because of an inherent conflict of interest, *Haskins* v. *State*, 516 P.2d 1171 (Wyo. 1973).

35. *See, e.g.*, A. Morris, *supra* note 2, ch. V.

36. McCollum v. Board of Educ., 333 U.S. 203 (1948).

37. 393 U.S. 97 (1968).

38. McLean v. Arkansas Board of Educ., 529 F. Supp. 1255 (E.D. Ark. 1982).

39. Knowlton v. Baumhover, 166 N.W. 202 (Iowa 1918).

40. LaRocca v. Board of Educ., 406 N.Y.S.2d 348 (Sup. Ct. App. Div. 1978).

41. Commissioners v. Herr, 78 A. 68 (Pa. 1910).

42. 319 U.S. 624 (1943).

43. Russo v. Central School Dist., 469 F.2d 623, 634 (2d Cir. 1972); *accord*, Opinions of the Justices to the Governor, 363 N.E.2d 251 (Mass. 1977).

44. Palmer v. Board of Educ., 603 F.2d 1271 (7th Cir. 1979), *cert. denied*, 444 U.S. 1026 (1980).

45. Title VII of the Civil Rights Act of 1964 requires school districts to make "reasonable accommodations" of teachers' religious beliefs. *Cf., e.g.*, TWA v. Hardison, 432 U.S. 63 (1977); Rankin v. Commission on Professional Competence, 154 Cal. Rptr. 907, 593 P.2d 852 (1979), *cert. denied*, 444 U.S. 986 (1979).

46. Stanley v. Georgis, 394 U.S. 557 (1969).

47. Morrison v. Board of Educ., 1 Cal. 3d 214, 82 Cal. Rptr. 175, 461 P.2d 375 (1969). *But see*, Gaylord v. Tacoma School Dist., 559 P.2d 1340 (Wash. 1977), *cert. denied*, 434 U.S. 879 (1977).

48. 461 P.2d at 382.

49. Acanfora v. Board of Educ., 359 F. Supp. 843 (D. Md. 1973), *aff'd*, 491 F.2d 498 (4th Cir. 1974). *But see*, Gaylord v. Tacoma School Dist., 559 P.2d 1340 (Wash. 1977).

50. Drake v. Board of Educ., 371 F. Supp. 974 (M.D. Ala. 1974).

51. Board of Educ. v. Stoudt, 571 P.2d 1186 (N.M. 1977).

52. Stoddard v. School Dist., 590 F.2d 829 (10th Cir. 1979); *accord*, Board of Trustees v. Holso, 584 F.2d 1009 (Wyo. 1978); Fisher v. Snyder, 476 F.2d 375 (8th Cir. 1973); Thompson v. School Dist., 483 F. Supp. 1170 (W.D. Mo. 1980). *But see*, Sullivan v. Meade School Dist., 530 F.2d 799 (8th Cir. 1976).

53. 425 U.S. 238 (1976).

54. East Hartford Educ. Ass'n v. Board of Educ., 562 F.2d 838 (2d Cir. 1977); *accord*, Miller v. School Dist., 495 F. 2d 658 (7th Cir. 1974); Tardif v. Quinn, 545 F.2d 761 (1st Cir. 1976).

55. Conrad v. Goolsby, 350 F. Supp. 713 (N.D. Miss. 1972).

56. 42 U.S.C. § 2000e-2(a)(1) (1976).

57. Carroll v. Talman Federal Savings & Loan Ass'n, 604 F.2d 1028 (7th Cir. 1979).

58. 429 U.S. 274 (1977). For an application of *Mt. Healthy* in the context of a claim to freedom of speech and press under *Pickering, see*, Nicholson v. Board of Educ., 682 F.2d 858 (9th Cir. 1982). For an application of *Mt. Healthy* in a First Amendment case involving an unwed pregnant teacher, *see*, Avery v.

Board of Educ., 674 F.2d 337 (5th Cir. 1982). For a case applying *Mt. Healthy* in a privacy context involving an unwed pregnant teacher, *see*, Brown v. Bathke, 566 F.2d 588 (8th Cir. 1976).

4

Procedural Due Process

Nelda H. Cambron-McCabe

Adverse employment decisions affecting school personnel generate substantial litigation each year. One of the central issues in these cases is the adequacy of due process procedures provided by public school officials. The litigation shows a wide variety of procedural claims instituted against school systems, ranging from the infringement of particular aspects of due process guarantees to complete denial of due process. With both constitutional and statutory laws granting teachers procedural protections, it is important for school officials to become familiar with established due process principles and to apply them in rendering adverse employment decisions.

Basic due process rights are embodied in the 14th Amendment, which guarantees that no state shall "deprive any person of life, liberty, or property without due process of law." The nature of due process required is influenced by the individual and governmental interests at stake and the applicable state laws. Courts have established that a teacher's interest in public employment may entail significant property and liberty rights necessitating due process prior to employment termination. If protected constitutional rights are implicated, due process entitles the teacher at least to a notice of the reasons for the school board's action and an opportunity for a hearing.

In this chapter, two basic questions are explored: When is due process required? and What due process is required? Due process is required only if a teacher is able to establish a protected property or liberty interest. In the first section of the chapter, the dimensions of teachers'

Nelda H. Cambron-McCabe is an associate professor at Miami University, Oxford, Ohio.

property and liberty rights are examined in the context of employment terminations. In the second section, procedural requirements of due process are identified and discussed. The concluding sections include an overview of remedies available to teachers for the violation of due process rights and general guidelines for the development of teacher termination policies.

When Due Process is Required

Employment terminations can be classified as either dismissals or nonrenewals. The distinction between the two has significant implications for the procedural rights that must be accorded a teacher. Nonrenewal is the release of a probationary or nontenured teacher at the end of the contract period, and generally it requires only notice that the teacher will not be reappointed. On the other hand, dismissal is the termination of a tenured teacher, or a nontenured teacher within the contract period, and necessitates full procedural protection. In this section, the procedural rights that must be provided the tenured teacher and the nontenured teacher are distinguished. Specific attention is given to the conditions that may give rise to a nontenured teacher acquiring a protected liberty or property interest in employment and thereby establishing a claim to procedural due process.

Dismissal

The term dismissal refers to the termination for cause of any tenured teacher or a probationary teacher within the contract period. Both tenure statutes and employment contracts establish a property interest entitling teachers to full procedural protection. At a minimum, the federal Constitution guarantees that a property right will not be deprived without notice and an opportunity to be heard. Beyond the basic constitutional requirements, state laws and school board policies contain detailed procedures that must be followed. Statutory procedures vary as to specificity, with some states enumerating extensive steps and others identifying only broad parameters. In each instance, the requirements are binding on the school board. Furthermore, a school district must comply with its own procedures, even if they exceed state law. For example, if school board policy provides for a preliminary notice of teaching inadequacies and an opportunity to correct remediable deficiencies prior to dismissal, this step is essential in meeting due process.

A critical element in dismissal actions is to show justified cause for termination of employment. If causes are identified by state law, a school board must base dismissal on those grounds. Failure to relate the charges to statutory grounds can invalidate the termination decision.

Because typical statutes list broad causes such as incompetency, insubordination, immorality, unprofessional conduct, neglect of duty, and other good and just cause,[1] notice of discharge must clearly indicate conduct substantiating the legal charges. Procedural safeguards ensure that not only will a teacher be informed of the specific reasons and grounds for dismissal but that the school board must prove the grounds and base its decision on those grounds. Detailed aspects of procedural due process requirements are elaborated in subsequent sections of this chapter.

Nonrenewal

In most states, procedural protections are not accorded to the probationary teacher when employment is not renewed. At the end of the contract period, employment can be terminated simply for no reason or any reason, as long as the reason is not constitutionally impermissible (e.g., exercise of fundamental constitutional rights). Generally, the only statutory requirement is notification of nonrenewal on or before a specified date prior to the expiration of the contract. A few states provide for a written statement of reasons and, on the request of the teacher, an opportunity for a hearing; but such provisions usually do not imply the right to an evidentiary hearing requiring the school board to show cause for termination.

Although state laws may not provide the probationary teacher specific procedural protections, a teacher's interest in public employment may be constitutionally protected. Protected interests encompassed by the 14th Amendment were addressed by the U.S. Supreme Court in two significant decisions in 1972: *Board of Regents* v. *Roth*[2] and *Perry* v. *Sindermann*.[3] According to these decisions, the infringement of a liberty or property interest entitles a probationary teacher to due process rights similar to the rights of the tenured teacher.

In *Roth* the question presented to the Court was whether a nontenured teacher had a constitutional right to a statement of reasons and a hearing prior to nonreappointment. Roth was hired for one academic year; at the end of the year the university informed him he would not be appointed for a second year. As a nontenured teacher, he was not entitled to procedural due process under Wisconsin law. He challenged the nonrenewal, alleging that failure to provide notice of reasons and an opportunity for hearing infringed his due process rights.

The Supreme Court held that nonrenewal did not require procedural protection unless impairment of a protected liberty or property interest could be shown. To establish infringement of a liberty interest the Court said the teacher must show that the employer's action 1) resulted in damage to his or her reputation and standing in the community, or 2) imposed a stigma that foreclosed other employment opportunities. The evidence presented by Roth indicated there was no such damage to his reputation or future employment. Accordingly, the Supreme Court concluded that "it stretches the concept too far to suggest that a person is deprived of 'liberty' when he simply is not rehired in one job but remains as free as before to seek another."[4]

The Supreme Court also denied Roth's claim to a property interest in continued employment. To establish a property right, the Court said that an individual must have "a legitimate claim of entitlement" to a position. This entitlement does not flow from the federal Constitution but from state laws or employment contracts that secure specific benefits. An abstract desire or unilateral expectation of continued employment alone does not constitute a property right. The terms of Roth's appointment and the state law precluded absolutely any possible claim of entitlement.

In *Sindermann* the Supreme Court examined the circumstances that might create a legitimate expectancy of reemployment for a nontenured teacher. Sindermann was a nontenured teacher in his fourth year of teaching when he was notified, without a statement of reasons or an opportunity for a hearing, that his contract would not be renewed. He challenged the lack of due process, alleging that nonrenewal deprived him of a property interest protected by the 14th Amendment and violated his First Amendment right to freedom of speech.

In advancing a protected property right, Sindermann claimed that the college, which lacked a formal tenure system, had created an informal or de facto tenure system through various practices and policies. Specifically, Sindermann cited a provision in the faculty guide stating that "the College wishes the faculty member to feel that he has permanent tenure as long as his teaching services are satisfactory."[5] The Supreme Court found in this case, unlike *Roth*, that the teacher's claim may have been based on a legitimate expectancy of reemployment promulgated by the college. According to the Court, the lack of a formal tenure system did not foreclose the possibility of an institution fostering an entitlement to a position through its personnel policies.

In assessing Sindermann's free speech claim, the Supreme Court confirmed that a teacher's lack of tenure does not void a claim that nonrenewal was based on the exercise of constitutionally protected conduct. Due process must be afforded when a substantive constitutional right is violated. According to a more recent Supreme Court decision, if a constitutional right is implicated in a nonrenewal, the burden is placed on the teacher to show that protected conduct was a substantial or motivating factor in the school board's decision.[6] The establishment of this prima facie case then shifts the burden to the school board to show by a preponderance of evidence that it would have reached the same decision in the absence of the protected activity.

The *Roth* and *Sindermann* cases serve as the legal precedents for assessing the procedural rights of nontenured teachers. To summarize, the

Supreme Court held that a nontenured teacher does not have a constitutionally protected property right in employment requiring procedural due process before denial of reappointment. However, certain actions of the school board may create conditions entitling a nontenured teacher to notice and a hearing similar to the tenured teacher. Such actions would include:

1. nonrenewal decisions damaging an individual's reputation and integrity,
2. nonrenewal decisions foreclosing other employment opportunities,
3. policies and practices creating a valid claim to reemployment, and
4. nonrenewal decisions violating fundamental constitutional guarantees.

Subsequent litigation has provided further clarification of school board actions that may create property interests or impair liberty interests.[7]

Property Interest. In general, a nontenured employee does not have a property claim to reappointment unless state or local governmental action has clearly established such a right.[8] A federal district court found that a Delaware school board created a reasonable expectancy of reemployment requiring procedural protection when it advised a principal that his contract would be renewed if his performance was satisfactory. The court concluded that the principal was justified in believing that he would be reappointed after receiving a satisfactory performance rating.[9] On the other hand, issuing an employee a series of contracts over a number of years was not found to constitute a valid claim to continued employment in the absence of a guarantee in state law, local policy, or an employment contract.[10] Similarly, a statute providing a teacher, upon request, a hearing and statement of reasons for nonrenewal did not confer a property interest in employment requiring legally sufficient cause for termination.[11] Such a law simply gave the teacher an opportunity to present reasons why the contract should be renewed.

Establishing an expectancy of reemployment in a school district with a formal tenure system is difficult. If a tenure system exists, courts have refused to consider de facto tenure arguments except in "extraordinary circumstances."[12] An Arizona federal district court decision illustrates the unique conditions that must exist to present a valid property claim.[13] In that case, an individual was offered a faculty position with tenure, but because of personal considerations, he rejected the offer and secured assurance that tenure would be awarded at a later time. In fact, the dean of the college attached an addendum to the offer stating that "the initial appointment will not be with tenure, but you will receive tenure automatically beginning in the year 1982-83 [third year], or sooner at our mutual convenience." Prior to awarding the teacher tenure, the university decided, without a statement of reasons or a hearing, not to renew his contract. The teacher challenged the action as a violation of his property rights, and the federal court agreed. The court concluded that the offer of employment promising tenure was an exceptional situation that would lead the faculty member legitimately to expect continued employment. With such an expectation, the university was required to treat his termination in the same manner as a tenured teacher.

As noted, property rights are created by state law or contracts but also may emanate from policies, regulations, or implied contracts. However, the sufficiency of the claim must be interpreted in light of a state's laws, irrespective of the claim's origin. In some instances, reference to state law can narrowly restrict or limit alleged property interests. For example, the U.S. Supreme Court, in construing a North Carolina employee's property rights, relied on the state supreme court's opinion that "an enforceable expectation of continued public employment in that State can exist only if the employer, by statute or contract, has actually granted some form of guarantee."[14] Although in this case a city ordinance implied due process rights after six months of employment, the Supreme Court reasoned that, in the absence of statutory or contractual obligations, the employee worked at the will and pleasure of the city. To determine a property right, then, it is not only necessary to determine that the employer's actions led to an expectancy of employment but also that state law does not void the claim.

Liberty Interest. The Supreme Court established in *Roth* that damage to a teacher's reputation or employability could infringe 14th Amendment liberty interests. In subsequent decisions, the Court identified other factors that are prerequisite to constitute a denial of a liberty interest. According to the Supreme Court, procedural protections must be afforded only if stigma or damaging statements are:

1. related to a loss of employment,
2. publicly disclosed, and
3. alleged to be false.[15]

Governmental action damaging a teacher's reputation, standing alone, is insufficient to invoke the procedural safeguards of the 14th Amendment. The Supreme Court has held that a liberty interest must be raised in connection with a loss of a governmental benefit such as employment. Generally, under this test, a teacher who has been defamed by reassignment or a transfer cannot claim violation of a liberty interest. The Fifth Circuit Court of Appeals noted that "the internal transfer of an employee, unless it constitutes such a change of status as to be regarded essentially as a loss of employment, does not provide the additional loss of a tangible interest necessary to give rise to a liberty interest meriting protection under the due process clause of the Fourteenth Amendment."[16]

Likewise, liberty is unaffected unless damaging reasons are publicly communicated. The primary purpose of a hearing is to enable an individual to clear his or her name. Without public knowledge of the reasons for nonreappointment, such a hearing is not required. A school board is not constitutionally obligated to provide a hearing as long as reasons are conveyed in a confidential manner or at a closed meeting.[17] Neither is a protected liberty interest affected by statements that are disclosed in a public meeting requested by the teacher, since the board's action did not publicize the comments. Further, rumors or hearsay remarks surfacing as a result of nonrenewal do not impair liberty interests. The First Circuit Court of Appeals noted that "in terms of likely stigmatizing effect, there is a world of differences between official charges (say, of excessive drinking) made publicly and a campus rumor based upon hearsay."[18]

Even when a school board publicly announces stigmatizing reasons for its action, there must be a factual dispute regarding the truth of the allegations. If a teacher does not challenge the truth of the statements, a name-clearing hearing serves no purpose. At the same time, however, nonrenewal based on false, stigmatizing reasons that are not publicly aired does not injure a protected liberty interest.

The primary liberty issue in termination of contracts is what charges constitute stigmatization. Nonrenewal alone is insufficient. As the Ninth Circuit Court of Appeals noted, "nearly any reason assigned for dismissal is likely to be to some extent a negative reflection on an individual's ability, temperament, or character," but circumstances giving rise to a liberty interest are narrow.[19] Charges must be serious implications against character, such as immorality and dishonesty. Accusations found by lower federal courts to necessitate a hearing include: 1) a serious drinking problem, 2) apparent emotional instability, 3) mental illness, 4) immoral conduct, and 5) mid-year termination of contract.[20] Reasons held to pose no threat to a liberty interest include: 1) job-related comments such as personality differences and difficulty in getting along with others, 2) hostility toward authority, 3) incompetence, 4) aggressive behavior, and 5) poor performance.[21] Charges relating to job performance may have an impact on future employment but do not assume a constitutional magnitude.

Requirements of Procedural Due Process

Governmental actions impairing individual property and liberty rights secured by the 14th Amendment trigger procedural due process. The central question when procedural protection applies is *what process is due.* Courts have noted that there is no fixed set of procedures applicable under all circumstances. Rather, due process entails a balancing of the individual and governmental interests affected in each situation. According to the Supreme Court, a determination of the specific aspects of due process requires consideration of:

> First, the private interest that will be affected by the official action; second, the risk of an erroneous deprivation of such interest through the procedures used, and the probable value, if any, of additional or substitute procedural safeguards; and finally, the Government's interest, including the function involved and the fiscal and administrative burdens that the additional or substitute procedural requirement would entail.[22]

Application of these standards requires only minimum procedures in the suspension of a student but a more extensive, formal process in the dismissal of a teacher.

In assessing the adequacy of due process safeguards, the judiciary looks for the provision of certain basic elements to meet constitutional guarantees. Generally, courts have held that a teacher facing a severe loss such as termination of employment must be ensured procedures encompassing the following elements:[23]

1. The teacher must be notified of the list of charges.
2. Adequate time must be provided for the teacher to prepare a rebuttal to the charges.
3. The teacher must be given the names of witnesses and access to evidence.
4. The hearing must be conducted before an impartial tribunal.
5. The teacher has the right to representation by legal counsel.
6. The teacher (or legal counsel) can introduce evidence and cross-examine adverse witnesses.
7. The school board's decision must be based on the evidence and findings of the hearing.
8. A transcript or record must be maintained of the hearing.
9. The teacher has the right to appeal an adverse decision.

Beyond these constitutional considerations, courts also enforce procedural protections conferred by state laws and local policies. These procedures often are more extensive than constitutional guarantees and must be strictly followed. Examples of such requirements are: advising probationary teachers of reasons for nonrenewal, providing detailed performance evaluations prior to termination, notifying teachers of weaknesses and allowing an opportunity for improvement before dismissal, and providing nontenured teachers a hearing upon request.[24] Failure to comply with these state and local stipulations will invalidate the school board's action.

Various elements of school board due process proceedings may be contested as inadequate. Questions arise regarding issues such as the sufficiency of notice, impartiality of the board members, and the burden of proof. The aspects of procedural due process that courts frequently scrutinize in assessing the fundamental fairness of school board actions are examined below.

Notice

Notice of charges is a minimum requirement of procedural due process. In general, a constitutionally adequate notice is a timely notice that informs the teacher of specific charges and allows the teacher sufficient time to prepare a response. Beyond the constitutional guarantees, state laws and school board policies (local and state) usually impose very specific requirements relating to form, timeliness, and content of notice. In legal challenges, the adequacy of a notice is assessed in terms of whether it meets constitutional requirements as well as adheres to state laws and school board policies. Since failure to comply substantially with mandated requirements will void school board action, careful consideration must be given to specific elements of notice.

Timeliness of notice often is a contested element of due process. This particular aspect of notice is strictly construed by most courts. When a deadline for nonrenewal or dismissal is designated by statute, a school board *must* notify a teacher on or before the established date. The fact that the school board has set in motion notification (e.g., mailed the notice) generally does not satisfy the statutory requirement; actual receipt of the notice by the teacher is critical.[25] For example, in a situation where a statutory deadline was April 30 and the notice was mailed on April 29 but not received until May 2, notice was held to be inadequate.[26] A teacher, however, cannot purposively avoid or deliberately thwart delivery of notice and then claim insufficiency of notice.[27]

Issuance of a timely notice to probationary teachers is imperative. Although the probationary teacher is not constitutionally entitled to reasons for nonrenewal, most states require the school board to notify a teacher by a certain date of its decision to nonrenew. Failure to observe this deadline may result in reinstatement for an additional year or even the granting of tenure in some jurisdictions.[28] Generally, a school board cannot assert that the terms of a teacher's contract waive the statutory right to timely notice. However, in a Wyoming case, the state supreme court held that a "one year only" clause in a teacher's contract accompanied by a detailed, verbal explanation of the temporary nature of the position constituted sufficient notice of nonreappointment. The court did caution that general use of the clause to circumvent the statutory notice requirement would not be acceptable.[29]

The form or type of notice is usually delineated by state law. Courts generally have held substantial compliance with form requirements (as opposed to strict compliance required for notice deadline) to be sufficient. Under this review standard, the decisive factor is whether the notice adequately informs the teacher of the pending action rather than the actual form of the notice.[30] For example, if a statute requires notification by certified mail and the notice is mailed by registered mail or is personally delivered, it substantially complies with the state requirement. The wording of a notice is assessed similarly. In an Arkansas case, the state supreme court said that a notice to a teacher that stated "You will not be presented to the Board of Directors . . . for re-election for the 1980-81 school year" was adequate to notify the teacher of nonrenewal.[31] The teacher had claimed the notice was deficient because it did not directly indicate nonrenewal as required by state law. Although substantial compliance is the primary consideration regarding form, oral notification will not satisfy the requirement of written notification. However, if notice form is not identified in statute, any timely notice that informs a teacher is adequate.[32]

While form and timeliness are important concerns in issuing a notice, the primary consideration is the statement of reasons or charges for an action. Nonrenewal of teachers requires simply notification that the teaching contract will not be renewed for the following year unless state or local restrictions require otherwise.

With termination of a tenured or nonprobationary teacher's contract, however, school boards must bring specific charges against the teacher. If the state law identifies grounds for dismissal, charges must be based on the statutory causes. A teacher cannot be forced to defend against vague and indefinite charges such as incompetency or neglect of duty. Notice must include specific accusations to enable the teacher to prepare a proper defense. To illustrate, the Wyoming Supreme Court found a notice that a teacher was using teaching methods that conflicted with the philosophy of the school board and administration to be impermissibly vague.[33] Similarly, a federal district court found conclusory statements identifying the teacher's need to improve and ways to improve to be inadequate notice.[34] Finally, only charges identified in the notice can form the basis for dismissal.

Hearing

In addition to notice, procedural due process requires an opportunity to be heard. Some form of a hearing is required before an individual is deprived of a property or liberty interest. Courts have not prescribed in detail the procedures to be followed in administrative hearings. Basically, the fundamental constitutional requirement is fair play, that is, an opportunity to be heard at a meaningful time and in a meaningful manner. Beyond this general requirement, the specific aspects of a hearing are influenced by the circumstances of the case, with the potential for grievous losses necessitating more extensive safeguards. According to the Missouri Supreme Court, a hearing, in general, should include a meaningful opportunity to be heard, opportunity to state one's position, opportunity to present witnesses, right to counsel, opportunity to cross-examine witnesses, and access to written reports in advance of hearing.[35] Implicit in these rudimentary requirements is the assumption that the hearing will be conducted by an impartial decision maker and the decision will be based on the evidence presented. The following discussion examines issues that may arise in adversarial hearings before the school board.

Adequate Notice of Hearing. As noted, due process rights afford an individual an opportunity to be heard at a meaningful time. This implies that sufficient time is allowed between notice of the hearing and the scheduled meeting. Unless a time period is designated by state law, the school board can establish a reasonable time for the hearing. The length of time provided may vary from situation to situation, depending on the facts and circumstances. In a termination action, the school board would be expected to provide ample time for the teacher to prepare a defense. However, the burden is placed on the teacher to request additional time if the length of notice is insufficient to prepare an adequate response. A notice as short as two days was upheld as satisfying due process where the teacher participated in the hearing and did not object to the time or request a postponement.[36] Similarly, a one-day notice was found not to violate due process when the teacher did not attend the meeting to raise objections.[37] A teacher who participates fully in the hearing process or waives the right to a hearing by failure to attend cannot later raise lack of adequate time to invalidate the due process proceeding.

Waiver. Although a hearing is an essential element of due process, a teacher can waive this right by refusing to attend a hearing or walking out of a hearing.[38] If state law provides an opportunity for a hearing upon the request of a teacher, failure to request such a hearing also constitutes a waiver. In some states, a hearing before the school board may be waived by an employee's election of an alternative hearing procedure such as a grievance mechanism. A Pennsylvania school board was not required to provide a school employee a hearing in addition to the arbitration proceeding he had selected.[39] In this case the Third Circuit Court of Appeals held that either a hearing before the school board or arbitration under the collective bargaining agreement met the constitutional requirements of due process.

Impartiality of the School Board. One of the central questions raised regarding hearings is the impartiality of the school board as a hearing body. This issue arises because school boards often perform multiple functions in a hearing; they may investigate the allegations against a teacher, initiate the proceedings, and render the final judgment. Teachers have contended that such expansive involvement violates their right to an unbiased decision maker. Generally, case law has rejected the idea that combining the adjudication and investigation functions violates due process rights.[40] As such, prior knowledge of the facts does not disqualify school board members. Similarly, the fact that the board makes the initial decision to terminate employment does not render subsequent review impermissibly biased. Neither is a hearing prejudiced by a limited, preliminary inquiry to determine if there is a basis for terminating a teacher. The Colorado Supreme Court noted that since hearings are costly and time-consuming, a preliminary investigation to determine the need for school board action may save time as well as potential embarrassment.[41]

The U.S. Supreme Court firmly established that the school board is a proper review body to conduct dismissal hearings in *Hortonville Joint School District* v. *Hortonville Education Association*.[42] In the *Hortonville* case the Supreme Court held that a school board's involvement in collective negotiations did not disqualify it as an impartial hearing board in the subsequent dismissal of striking teachers. The Court noted:

> A showing that the Board was "involved" in the events preceding this decision, in light of the important interest in leaving with the Board the power given by the state legislature, is not enough to overcome the presumption of honesty and integrity in policymakers with decision-making power.[43]

Although the school board is the proper hearing body, specific bias on the part of the board or its members is constitutionally unacceptable. A high probability of bias can be shown to exist if a board member has a financial or personal interest in the outcome of the hearing or if a board member has suffered personal abuse or criticism from a teacher. Several recent cases illustrate instances of unacceptable bias. For example, the Alabama Supreme Court invalidated a teacher termination hearing for "intolerably high bias" created by a school board member's son testifying against the teacher.[44] The son had been the target of personal abuse by the teacher. In a Tenth Circuit case, bias was shown to exist when one of the board members had campaigned to remove the superintendent from his position, and two other board members had made unfavorable statements to the effect that the superintendent "had to go."[45] The Iowa Supreme Court concluded that a school board's role of "investigation, instigation, prosecution, and verdict rendering" denied a teacher an impartial hearing, since in reaching a decision, the only evidence the board had to call on was its own personal knowledge of the case because there were no witnesses.[46] Other instances of potential bias would include school board members testifying as witnesses, prior announcements by board members of views and positions showing closed minds, and board members assuming adversarial or prosecuting roles.[47]

Unless bias clearly can be demonstrated, as in the aforementioned cases, the school board will be deemed an impartial decision maker. To disqualify the board or a particular board member, a teacher has the burden of showing specific bias, not merely potential for bias. However, school boards are not required to submit their members to examination and interrogation for potential bias. This examination, which is an aspect of judicial proceedings, is usually not available to interrogate members of administrative hearing bodies. A Pennsylvania court, in rejecting such a request, stated that, "The administrative process should be speedy, cheap and simple, keeping the role of lawyers to a minimum necessary to achieve fairness."[48] Further, the court noted that even if it were shown that board members had prior knowledge or views, it would not affect the fairness of the hearing.

Evidence. Under teacher tenure laws, the burden of proof is placed on the school board to show cause for dismissal. This burden requires the board to produce substantial evidence to justify dismissal. Generally, the standard of proof applied to administrative bodies is to show a "preponderance of evidence." More stringent reviews such as the "clear and convincing standard" and the "beyond a reasonable doubt standard" are inappropriate. Proof by a preponderance of evidence simply indicates that the majority of the evidence supports the board's decision. If the board fails to meet this burden of proof, the decision will not be upheld by the judiciary. For example, the Nebraska Supreme Court, in overturning a school board's dismissal decision, concluded that dissatisfaction of parents and school board members was not sufficient evidence to substantiate claims of incompetency of a teacher who had received above-average performance evaluations during her entire term of employment.[49]

In nonrenewals, of course, the burden of proof is placed on the teacher challenging the board's decision to show that the board's action was based on impermissible reasons. As noted earlier, the teacher must establish that constitutionally protected conduct is a substantial or motivating factor in nonrenewal; and then the burden shifts to the board to show by a preponderance of evidence that it would have reached the same decision in the absence of the protected activity.[50]

The objective of school board hearings is to ascertain the relevant facts of the situation.[51] In the school setting, hearings are not encumbered by technical, judicial rules of evidence. However, evidence introduced should be relevant, related to the charges, and well documented. Only evidence presented at the hearing can be the basis for the board's decision. Unlike formal judicial proceedings, hearsay evidence is generally admissible in administrative hearings. Courts have held that such evidence provides the background necessary for understanding the situation.[52] While comments and complaints of parents have been considered relevant, hearsay statements of students have been given little weight.[53]

Findings and Decisions. At the conclusions of the hearing, the board must make specific findings of fact. A written report of the findings on which the board based its decision is essential. Many states require such a record, and most federal and state courts impose the requirement. Without a report of the findings of fact, appropriate administrative or judicial review would be impeded. The Minnesota Supreme Court identified several problems that might occur with judicial review in the absence of clear findings of fact: Specifically, the court noted:

> Without findings of fact, the trial court [has] no way of knowing upon which of the four charges the school board based its decision. If the trial court were to review the merits of the case without findings of fact, there would be no safeguard against judicial encroachment on the school board's function since the trial court might affirm on a charge rejected by the school board.[54]

Similarly, the Oklahoma Supreme Court held that a probationary teacher entitled to a hearing by state law also is entitled to be told why the board reached its decision.[55] The court admonished that "an absence of required findings is fatal to the validity of administrative decisions even if the record discloses evidence to support proper findings."[56] The findings of fact do not have to be issued in technical legal language but simply in a form that explains the reasons for the action.

Related to the necessity of enumerating findings of fact is the school board's duty to vote on the specific charges brought against the teacher. A teacher has the right to know the charges the board relied on in reaching an adverse employment decision.[57] Additionally, the board's record must indicate the evidence supporting its decision.

Post-Termination Hearings. Generally, a post-termination hearing does not satisfy constitutional due process requirements in dismissals for cause. An Arkansas federal district court summarized the inherent inequity of such hearings:

> The very purpose of procedural protection is the tempering of the decision process to help insure fairness, and fairness demands that competing interests be represented before the decision maker on as equal a footing as circumstance permits. The individual who is the object of the proposed governmental action should not have to bear the handicap of overcoming the inertia of the status quo; he should not bear the burden of persuading the decision maker to reverse a fait accompli unless the proponent of the action can show specific, valid, and appropriate reasons for precipitous, prehearing action.[58]

Unless extenuating circumstances justify immediate action, a hearing must occur prior to the termination decision. Circumstances involving severe disruption to the educational process or threat to the health and safety of students could necessitate prompt action. Ordinarily, even under these conditions, teachers should be suspended with pay pending the final decision to terminate.[59]

Remedies for Violation of Due Process Rights

An element of due process is the right to appeal an adverse decision of an administrative body to a higher authority such as a court of law. The legal cases cited in this chapter illustrate the variety of issues appealed to courts on procedural grounds. Several points are important to note regarding judicial review. First, courts generally will not interject themselves into school board review proceedings until all aspects of the administrative appeal process have been exhausted. A teacher alleging denial of due process must first use established administrative procedures prior to resorting to judicial review. Second, in reviewing teacher termination actions, the judiciary does not substitute its judgment for that of the school board. Rather, courts examine cases to determine if the school board failed to accord the teacher procedural protections, impaired substantive constitutional rights, or was arbitrary and capricious in its decision. If upon review it is found that protected rights have been violated, courts attempt to redress the wrong by framing an appropriate remedy.

Judicial remedies for the violation of procedural due process rights in employment terminations may include award of compensatory and punitive damages, reinstatement to the former position, and attorney's fees. The specific nature of the award depends on individual state statutory provisions and the discretion of courts. State laws often identify damages that may be recovered or place limitations on types of awards. Unless state provisions restrict specific remedies, courts have broad discretionary power to formulate equitable settlements.

Under Section 1983 of the Civil Rights Act of 1871, both school board members and school boards are liable for payment of damages to teachers when constitutional rights such as due process are violated. Individual school officials may claim qualified immunity for actions taken in "good faith"; however, disregard of constitutionally protected rights or impermissible motivation may demonstrate a lack of good faith. While board members possess a certain degree of immunity, school boards are not protected against liability, even if their employees have acted in good faith. The Supreme Court's interpretations of Section 1983 in recent years have expanded significantly the likelihood of teachers recovering damages from school systems, and therefore more and more teachers are turning to federal courts for restitution.[60]

Monetary damages may be extensive for procedural violations if a teacher is able to demonstrate substantial losses. A Delaware federal district court cited earlier illustrates the factors considered by courts in ordering relief.[61] The federal district court found that a principal, who had been assured of contract renewal if his performance was satisfactory, was entitled to due process before termination of employment. The failure of the school board to provide procedural protection resulted in a judgment against the board and its members. The court held that the injured individual should be compensated for lost salary, out-of-pocket expenses, physical and mental stress, and injury to reputation in the amount of $51,000. In addition to the compensatory damages to repay the principal for harm inflicted by the board, the court found that punitive damages were appropriate. The sole purpose of punitive awards is to deter school board members and others from committing similar offenses in the future; but unless evidence indicates gross disregard of protected rights, extraordinary awards will not be imposed.[62] In this case, a jury award of $77,500 was found to be excessive and was reduced to $7,750. Further, the court ordered reinstatement of the principal and expungement of personnel records.

Types of remedies awarded by courts will depend on the protected interest impaired. While reinstatement generally is ordered when property rights are at stake, it is not appropriate for the impairment of a liberty interest since no right to continued employment existed. Ordinarily a successful liberty claim would require only an opportunity to clear one's name. However, the Tenth Circuit Court of Appeals noted that reinstatement is not absolutely foreclosed if a teacher can prove that he or she would have been retained had full procedural due process been provided.[63] But the court did note that with the problems of proof, the probability of success was remote.

Attorneys' fees are not automatically granted the teacher who prevails in a lawsuit, unless authorized by state or federal laws. Although some state courts may exercise discretion in awarding attorneys' fees, generally fees are dependent on statutory authorization. At the federal level, however, Congress's enactment of the Civil Rights Attorneys' Fees Award Act in 1976 gives federal courts discretion to award fees in civil rights suits.[64] Receipt of fees at either state or federal level requires the teacher to be the prevailing party.

Guidelines for Developing Due Process Procedures

Termination of a teacher's employment may involve both state and federal rights. State tenure laws identify specific employment rights, while the federal Constitution ensures that a teacher will be provided

procedural due process if a property or liberty interest exists in employment. Below are some broad guidelines to assist school officials in the
development of due process procedures.

1. Due process procedures should be established locally for the
dismissal and nonrenewal of teachers. Procedures should delineate when
due process will be given, specific rights of teachers, and elements of due
process.

2. Procedural policies adopted by the school board must not conflict
with state requirements.

3. Although the school board is not required to provide reasons for
nonrenewal, the board policy should identify impermissible grounds for
nonrenewal. These grounds would include violation of substantive constitutional rights; arbitrariness or capriciousness of school officials; and
discrimination involving race, sex, and religion.

4. School board policies should not enumerate specific reasons for
nonrenewal or denial of tenure but should include general criteria for
evaluating teaching performance for reappointment and tenure.

5. A nontenured teacher may be terminated at the end of a contract
period without cause, as long as the termination is not for an impermissible reason.

6. Procedures should allow a teacher an opportunity for a conference
with the board when termination is based on allegedly impermissible
reasons.

7. If reasons for nonrenewal are given to a teacher, they should be
communicated in a confidential manner to avoid damage to the teacher's
reputation or future employment opportunities.

8. A tenured teacher may be dismissed only for causes specified in
state law and must be provided full procedural due process.

9. Procedural policies should address form and timeliness of notice,
scheduling of the hearing, and conduct of the hearing.

10. Full procedural rights in a dismissal hearing must include representation by counsel, presentation of evidence and witnesses, examination
and cross-examination of witnesses, report of findings of facts, decision
based on evidence, and a record of the proceeding.

Footnotes

1. For a discussion of dismissal grounds, *see* Martha M. McCarthy and Nelda
    H. Cambron, *Public School Law: Teachers' and Students' Rights*, Chapter 5.
    (Boston, Mass.: Allyn and Bacon, 1981).
2. 408 U.S. 564 (1972).
3. 408 U.S. 593 (1972).
4. 408 U.S. 564, 575 (1972).
5. 408 U.S. 593, 600 (1972).

6. Mt. Healthy City School Dist. Bd. of Educ. v. Doyle, 429 U.S. 274 (1977).
7. *See* Chapter 3 for a discussion of substantive due process rights.
8. *See, e.g.*, Longarzo v. Anker, 578 F.2d 469 (2d Cir. 1978); Buhr v. Buffalo Pub. School Dist. No. 38, 509 F.2d 1196 (8th Cir. 1974).
9. Schreffler v. Board of Educ. of Delmar School Dist., 506 F. Supp. 1300 (D. Del. 1981).
10. *See* Robertson v. Rogers, 679 F.2d 1090 (4th Cir. 1982).
11. *See* Perkins v. Board of Dir., 686 F.2d 49 (1st Cir. 1982).
12. Haimowitz v. University of Nevada, 579 F.2d 526, 528 (9th Cir. 1978).
13. Harris v. Arizona Bd. of Regents, 528 F. Supp. 987 (D. Ariz. 1981).
14. Bishop v. Wood, 426 U.S. 341, 345 (1976).
15. Codd v. Velger, 429 U.S. 624 (1977); Bishop v. Wood, 426 U.S. 341 (1976); Paul v. Davis, 424 U.S. 693 (1976).
16. Moore v. Otero, 557 F.2d 435 (5th Cir. 1977).
17. Robertson v. Rogers, 679 F.2d 1090 (4th Cir. 1982); Longarzo v. Anker, 578 F.2d 469 (2d Cir. 1978); Buhr v. Buffalo Pub. School Dist. No. 38, 509 F.2d 1196 (8th Cir. 1974).
18. Beitzell v. Jeffrey, 643 F.2d 870, 879 (1st Cir. 1981).
19. Gray v. Union Cty. Intermediate Educ. Dist., 520 F.2d 803, 806 (9th Cir. 1975).
20. Robertson v. Rogers, 679 F.2d 1090 (4th Cir. 1982); Vanelli v. Reynolds School Dist. No. 7, 667 F.2d 773 (9th Cir. 1982); Dennis v. S & S Consol. Rural High School Dist., 577 F.2d 338 (5th Cir. 1978); Lombard v. Board of Educ. of City of New York, 502 F.2d 631 (2d Cir. 1974); Bomhoff v. White, 526 F. Supp. 488 (D. Ariz. 1981).
21. Gray v. Union Cty. Intermediate Educ. Dist., 520 F.2d 803 (9th Cir. 1975); Bomhoff v. White, 526 F. Supp. 488 (D. Ariz. 1981); Harris v. Arizona Bd. of Regents, 528 F. Supp. 987 (D. Ariz. 1981).
22. Mathews v. Eldridge, 424 U.S. 319, 335 (1976).
23. This chapter focuses on procedural protection required in the termination of teacher employment. However, it should be noted that other school board decisions may impose similar constraints on decision making. For example, transfers, demotions, or mandatory leaves may violate a protected interest. For an example, an Ohio court found that the transfer of a tenured teacher from a regular classroom position to a position as a permanent itinerant substitute violated the teacher's due process rights. Mroczek v. Board of Educ. of Beachwood City School Dist., 400 N.E.2d 1362 (C.P. Ohio 1979); *see also* Dunsanek v. Hannon, 677 F.2d 538 (7th Cir. 1982), *cert. denied*, 103 S. Ct. 379 (1982); Stewart v. Pearce, 484 F.2d 1031 (9th Cir. 1973); Otto v. Davie, 110 Cal. Rptr. 114 (Cal. App. 1973).Adverse employment decisions involving nonrenewal and reduction in force (RIF) usually will not require the extensive procedures outlined. Nonrenewal issues are discussed in this chapter, but for a discussion of procedural due process required for RIF, *see* Chapter 9, and Robert E. Phay, *Reducation in Force: Legal Issues and Recommended Policy* (Topeka, Kans.: National Organization on Legal Problems of Education, 1980).
24. *See, e.g.*, Wilt v. Flanigan, 294 S.E.2d 189 (W. Va. 1982); Maxwell v. Southside School Dist., 618 S.W.2d 148 (Ark. 1981); Trimboli v. Board of

Educ. of Wayne Cty., 280 S.E.2d 686 (W. Va. 1981); Miller v. Indep. School Dist. No. 56, 609 P.2d 756 (Okla. 1980); Lehman v. Board of Educ. of City School Dist., 439 N.Y.S.2d 670 (Sup. Ct. App. Div. 1981).

25. This general rule of actual receipt of notice would not apply, of course, if a statutory provision indicated other means of satisfaction, such as requiring the notice to be postmarked by the U.S. mail by a certain date. *See* Andrews v. Howard, 291 S.E.2d 541 (Ga. 1982).

26. State *ex rel.* Peake v. Board of Educ. of South Point Local School Dist., 339 N.E.2d 249 (Ohio 1975); *see also* School Dist. RE-11J, Alamosa Cty. v. Norwood, 644 P.2d 13 (Colo. 1982).

27. Stollenwerck v. Talladega Cty. Bd. of Educ., 420 So. 2d 21 (Ala. 1982); Ledbetter v. School Dist. No. 8, 428 P.2d 912 (Colo. 1967).

28. Lipka v. Brown City Commun. Schools, 271 N.W.2d 771 (Mich. 1978); Board of Trustees of Nogales Elementary School Dist. v. Cartier, 559 P.2d 216 (Ariz. App. 1977).

29. Borman v. Sweetwater Cty. School Dist. No. 2, 627 P.2d 1364 (Wyo. 1981).

30. Andrews v. Howard, 291 S.E.2d 541 (Ga. 1982); People *ex rel.* Head v. Board of Educ. of Thornton Fractional Twp. South High School Dist., 419 N.E.2d 505 (Ill. App. 1981). *But see* Hoyme v. ABC School Dist., 165 Cal. Rptr. 737 (Cal. App. 1980).

31. Allred v. Little Rock School Dist., 625 S.W.2d 487 (Ark. 1981).

32. Griffin v. Galena City School Dist., 640 P.2d 829 (Alaska 1982).

33. Board of Trustees, Laramie Cty. School Dist. No. 1 v. Spiegel, 549 P.2d 1161 (Wyo. 1976); *see also* State *ex rel.* Franceski v. Plaquemines Parish School Bd., 416 So. 2d 150 (La. App. 1982); Lee v. Board of Educ. of City of Bristol, 434 A.2d 333 (Conn. 1980).

34. Wagner v. Little Rock School Dist., 373 F. Supp. 876 (E.D. Ark. 1973).

35. Valter v. Orchard Farm School Dist., 541 S.W.2d 550 (Mo. 1976).

36. Ahern v. Board of Educ. of School Dist. of Grand Island, 456 F.2d 399 (8th Cir. 1972).

37. Birdwell v. Hazelwood School Dist., 491 F.2d 490 (8th Cir. 1974); *see also* Crane v. Mitchell Cty. Unified School Dist. No. 273, 652 P.2d 205 (Kan. 1982).

38. Birdwell v. Hazelwood School Dist., 491 F.2d 490 (8th Cir. 1974); Ferguson v. Board of Trustees of Bonner Cty. Unified School Dist. No. 82, 564 P.2d 971 (Idaho 1977); Crane v. Mitchell Cty. Unified School Dist. No. 273, 652 P.2d 205 (Kan. 1982). But refusal of a teacher to participate in a post-termination or "after the fact" hearing did not constitute a waiver of due process rights. *See* Wertz v. Southern Cloud Unified School Dist., 542 P.2d 339 (Kan. 1975).

39. Pederson v. South Williamsport Area School Dist., 677 F.2d 312 (3d Cir. 1982), *cert. denied*, 103 S. Ct. 305 (1982); *see also* Jones v. Morris, 541 F. Supp. 11 (S.D. Ohio 1981), *aff'd*, 102 S. Ct. 1699 (1982).

40. *See* Withrow v. Larkin, 421 U.S. 35 (1975).

41. Weissman v. Board of Educ. of Jefferson Cty., 547 P.2d 1267 (Colo. 1976); *see also* Ferguson v. Board of Trustees, 564 P.2d 971 (Idaho 1977); Griggs v. Board of Trustees of Merced Union High School Dist., 389 P.2d 722 (Cal. 1964).

42. 426 U.S. 482 (1975).

43. *Id.* at 496-97.

44. Greenberg v. Alabama State Tenure Comm'n, 395 So. 2d 1000 (Ala. 1981). However, another court said that a board member's wife being a principal objector to the teacher did not deny the teacher a fair and proper hearing. Danroth v. Mandaree Pub. School Dist. No. 36, 320 N.W.2d 780 (N.D. 1982).

45. Staton v. Mayes, 552 F.2d 908 (10th Cir. 1977), *cert. denied,* 434 U.S. 907 (1977). *But see* Welch v. Barham, 635 F.2d 1322 (8th Cir. 1980).

46. Keith v. Community School Dist. of Wilton, 262 N.W.2d 249, 260 (Iowa 1978).

47. *See generally* Withrow v. Larkin, 421 U.S. 35 (1975).

48. Graham v. Mars Area School Dist., 415 A.2d 924, 926 (Pa. Commw. 1980).

49. Schulz v. Board of Educ. of the School Dist. of Freemont, 315 N.W.2d 633 (Neb. 1982).

50. See text accompanying Note 6 *supra.*

51. *See generally* Alabama State Tenure Comm'n v. Tuscaloosa Cty. Bd. of Educ., 401 So. 2d 84 (Ala. App. 1981); Doran v. Board of Educ. of Western Boone Cty. Commun. Schools, 285 N.E.2d 825 (Ind. App. 1972).

52. Fay v. Board of Dir. of North-Linn Commun. School Dist., 298 N.W.2d 345 (Iowa App. 1980); Vorm v. David Douglas School Dist., 608 P.2d 193 (Ore. App. 1980); Baxter v. Poe, 257 S.E.2d 71 (N.C. App. 1979), *cert. denied,* 259 S.E.2d 298 (N.C. 1979).

53. Hollingsworth v. Board of Educ., 303 N.W.2d 506 (Neb 1981).

54. Morey v. School Bd. of Indep. School Dist. No. 492, 128 N.W.2d 302, 307 (Minn. 1964).

55. Jackson v. Independent School Dist. No. 16, 648 P.2d 26 (Okla. 1982).

56. *Id.* at 31.

57. *See* State *ex rel.* Franceski v. Plaquemines Parish School Bd., 416 So. 2d 150 (La. App. 1982).

58. Wagner v. Little Rock School Dist., 373 F. Supp. 876, 882 (E.D. Ark. 1973).

59. Vanelli v. Reynolds School Dist. No. 7, 667 F.2d 773 (9th Cir. 1982); Crane v. Mitchell Cty. Unified School Dist. No. 273, 652 P.2d 205 (Kan. 1982); Wertz v. Southern Cloud Unified School Dist. No. 334, 542 P.2d 339 (Kan. 1975).

60. *See* Maine v. Thiboutot, 448 U.S.1 (1980); Owen v. City of Independence, 445 U.S. 622 (1980); Monell v. Department of Social Services of the City of New York, 436 U.S. 658 (1978).

61. Schreffler v. Board of Educ. of Delmar School Dist., 506 F. Supp. 1300 (D. Del. 1981).

62. The Supreme Court held in *City of Newport* v. *Fact Concerts,* 453 U.S. 247 (1981), that punitive awards cannot be assessed against bodies such as school boards.

63. McGhee v. Draper, 639 F.2d 639 (10th Cir. 1981).

64. 42 U.S.C. § 1988 (1976).

5

Collective Bargaining Issues in Public School Employment

Hugh D. Jascourt

It is difficult to generalize about collective bargaining in public education because it is such a dynamic process. Its focus changes as relationships change and as different priorities arise. Currently, for example, fiscal crises in school districts and declining enrollments permeate most collective bargaining relationships. Because of the depressed economy, the political climate is unfavorable to unions in general; and because school systems are the largest category of local expenditures of public funds, the political climate is unfavorable to teacher unions in particular. As a result of these and other factors, public attitudes will affect the goals and positions of public employers. In turn collective bargaining is directly affected.

It is also difficult to make generalizations about collective bargaining in public school employment. Only 31 states have laws authorizing collective bargaining, and few of these laws are alike.[1] Some cover all public employees; some cover just teachers. A further complication is the variety of administrative and legal structures that enforce collective bargaining rights and obligations. Nevertheless, collective bargaining by teachers does exist in every state regardless of the euphemism applied to it. In states such as Ohio, which has no statute sanctioning collective bargaining, those unions with exclusive recognition sometimes exercise more power and obtain stronger enforcement of their rights by the courts than their counterparts in states that have statutes authorizing

Hugh D. Jascourt is director of the Public Employment Relations Research Institute, Washington, D.C.

collective negotiations. Despite these differences, a considerable degree of consensus has evolved throughout the states. Nevertheless, one should be familiar with local law and decisions pertaining to it in order to apply accurately any generalization to specific local circumstances. Also, keep in mind that decisions from other states are frequently argued as precedent and often may have that effect in cases of initial impression or even modification of previously judge-made law in a particular state.

This chapter will highlight the major features of the law as it has evolved to this point, identify trends, and speculate on future issues.

Constitutional Issues

Until recently the primary issues in public sector labor relations involved constitutional rights. In fact, more often than not a lead case involved public education, with school boards invariably one of the parties.

The seminal cases were both decided in 1968. In *McLaughlin* v. *Tilendis* the Seventh Circuit Court of Appeals held that the First Amendment protected the right of teachers to engage in union organizing activity;[2] and in *Pickering* v. *Board of Education* the Supreme Court delineated the narrow limits a school board as an employer could place on its employees, particularly with regard to public criticism of the employer.[3] For many years the major cases and major issues were expressed in constitutional terms, culminating in 1979 with *Abood* v. *Detroit Board of Education* in which the Supreme Court upheld the constitutionality of the agency shop in school districts, giving the union exclusive recognition as in the private sector model.[4] Specifically, the Court ruled that the union could collect service fees from teachers who were not members of the union.

Thereafter, the courts became increasingly reluctant to deal with constitutional issues involved in labor relations cases. For example, in a 1978 case in Ohio the federal district court complained:

> [t]his case presents the all-too-familiar situation in which a dispute, commonplace in the private sector, becomes constitutional litigation by virtue of the fact that a public employer [the school board] is involved, rather than private entities, and the [plaintiff is] therefore, able to turn a problem of labor relations into a constitutional issue.[5]

Today, the "larger" issues are seldom raised. Instead, attention tends to be directed at the collective bargaining process itself, with the exception of cases involving affirmative action, the impact of seniority on reductions in force, contractual provisions affecting maternity leave, or the looming issue of "comparable worth." Plaintiffs are no longer trying to create due process or other constitutional rights applicable to labor relations.[6] Perhaps this is so because of a perception by unions that there is not presently a receptive judicial climate. It may also be due to the general acceptance of the doctrine that the state as an employer cannot ask an employee to surrender a right he or she would otherwise be entitled to as a private citizen. Individual rights are most likely to be diminished by attacking the principle that constitutional rights are involved when the government takes action with respect to an employee. Taking its place will be the theory that "governmental action" is not involved when government, as an employer, deals with its employees in a manner that does not affect their rights as private citizens and allows a public employer rights comparable to a private employer dealing with its employees.

The issues in labor relations in the near future will deal with specific problems and are less likely to have effect on the entire body of constitutional law. One recent battleground has been the role of the exclusive representative with regards to free speech, as in the right to use a school's internal mail system. Commonly, the exclusive representative negotiates a contractual provision to preclude competing unions from such use. The Sixth Circuit Court upheld the constitutionality of such a policy as rationally related to the goal of preserving labor peace within the school system.[7] However, the Seventh Circuit Court viewed such a policy as unconstitutional, explaining that, because limitation of speech on the basis of its content or on the basis of the identity of the speaker usually requires rigorous judicial scrutiny, there must be a compelling state interest for such limitation. In other words, it was not enough for the limitation to be merely rationally related to a legitimate state interest. The court found no clear proof that the incumbent union's execution of its duties would be significantly impaired by permitting access to the school's mail system, and that claims of substantial disruption amounted to mere speculation; therefore, disparate access to communication channels (as distinguished from other rights such as dues checkoff) could not be justified.[8] The Supreme Court overturned the Seventh Circuit Court on the basis that the school mail system is not a public forum and that the access policy, based on the union's status as exclusive representative, is constitutionally permissible since it is a reasonable means of ensuring labor peace. In short, exclusive recognition was a sufficient distinction.[9]

The issue of whether a union may waive the constitutional rights of those it represents is another issue on the horizon. In one case a federal district court ruled that teachers could waive their academic freedom through a collective bargaining agreement and, as a consequence, the school board could ban books it otherwise could not prohibit.[10] However, on appeal the Tenth Circuit Court held that the waiver was not clear and express enough and that the school board could exclude the books in contest on other grounds.[11] There have been a few other cases establishing such a waiver, but the union's authority to do so is less than clear and is likely to be challenged.[12]

In a case involving termination of a teacher, the plaintiff claimed that *one* of the employer's reasons for termination was the plaintiff's exercise of free speech, which is protected under the First Amendment. In ruling on this case, *Mt. Healthy City School District Board of Education* v. *Doyle*,[13] the Supreme Court held that the teacher could not be reinstated unless it was shown that his discharge would not have occurred unless the board desired to penalize the teacher for his exercise of free speech. The Court explained that an employee should not be able to shield himself from discipline by raising as a defense that one of the employer's reasons was improper. Borrowing from the *Mt. Healthy* context, the National Labor Relations Board subsequently applied a like test to unfair labor practices, changing its past policy of allowing one bad reason to taint all other reasons or defenses.[14] The latter test had been commonly used by state public employment relations boards. Now there is a question whether states will follow the NLRB's new policy, and also the question — which has yet to be settled in the private sector — of where the burden of proof resides once the existence of mixed motives has been established.

If the future brings no significant additions to the number of states sanctioning collective bargaining for public employees and if some of the current states with skeletal sanctioning laws do not amplify their statutes, with a change in political climate the Supreme Court's decision in *National League of Cities* v. *Usery*[15] undoubtedly will be reexamined and will become a pressing legal issue. The Supreme Court scuttled what had appeared to be almost a certainty: the passage of a national public sector law. Its decision held that Congress lacked the constitutional power to apply the Fair Labor Standards Act to state and local governments. However, the case was decided by a narrow 5-4 majority, and the decision may be subject to review and modification in later cases. The basic proposition in *Usery* was that Congress "may not force directly on the states its choices as to how essential decisions regarding the conduct of integral government functions are to be made."[16]

The key word in the above quote is "force." The word takes on added meaning when it is realized that in order for municipalities to take over private transit companies and to receive federal funds under the Federal Urban Mass Transportation Act, the municipality must comply with certain labor law requirements. Thus far, the courts have held that such a requirement is not unconstitutional since a locality is not compelled to seek federal funds and, therefore, participates at its own option.[17] The obvious question is whether it would be constitutional to condition receipt of revenue sharing upon public sector labor relations requirements or whether the reliance on federal funds *de facto* forces a choice on state governments with regard to the conduct of integral government functions. The answer may be one of the most hotly debated topics of the decade and may indicate how the future of nationally established labor relations standards will affect public education.

Authority to Bargain in Absence of Statute

For many years there had been debate as to whether a state or municipal jurisdiction could engage in collective bargaining with a representative of its employees when there was no express statutory authority to do so. Now, in most states without statutory authorization, the courts have accepted that by virtue of the power to "do business" or the power to hire teachers and to fix their salaries, a school board has the authority to engage in a collective bargaining relationship.[18]

In these states there is no compulsion to negotiate; there are only voluntary arrangements. As a corollary, there is no enforcement machinery, since, in effect, there are no obligatory rights. However, courts in these states are prone to fill the void. For example, in Ohio there is no statute authorizing negotiations, but there is a law prohibiting public employee strikes. A court enjoined a strike by teachers, but went beyond and required the school board to enter into an oral contract it reached with the union but later refused to sign and execute.[19]

Where collective bargaining exists due to union power rather than statutory right, only the strongest unions have obtained recognition. Due to such strength, they often possess power and contractual rights beyond what a statute would accord. Difficulties are likely to be faced in the future when new state laws preserve such bargaining and contract rights and privileges but do not grant such rights and privileges to others. In fact, the existence of such prior rights and privileges sometimes results in broader rights for unions than otherwise would have been probable.

Recognition of Unions and Representation Questions

Generally, in the private sector unions have been accorded recognition to represent smaller employee units than is permitted in the public sector. Although larger units are characteristic of the public sector, the extent to which fragmentation should be allowed to exist continues to be an issue. Because a governmental employer usually has larger and more diversified groups of employees, it would be faced with both cost and administrative problems if it had to bargain with separate units of employees represented by different unions. However, homogeneity of a bargaining unit may help to promote stability, and a union may have difficulty in representing workers who do not share the same goals or aspirations. Also, when a smaller group of workers is swallowed up by a larger group, the smaller group may have difficulty in obtaining meaningful representation.

In most school districts professional education employees are in a single unit, even if they are noninstructional. Similarly, most nonprofessionals are lumped into one or two units. In addition, there has been a tendency to add other employee groups to these already large units. Two recent cases in Pennsylvania are illustrative. In one case the state's intermediate court upheld the addition of substitutes, who were certified teachers employed on a full-time basis, to the existing bargaining unit of teachers.[20] In another case the court sustained the inclusion of support personnel from the school's adult education program in the unit of support personnel serving the regular secondary program.[21] Questions to be faced in the future include how far these accretions will be permitted to go and will the courts reexamine the inclusion of occupational groups such as librarians, guidance counselors, or nurses in teacher units.

A far larger problem looms as the result of hybrid arrangements between private and public employers, multiple public employers, or different levels of governmental employers designed to achieve efficiency as a result of fiscal constraints. For example, a Maine bus company was held to be acting on the behalf of the school district because of the degree of control the district maintained over the details of the work to be performed. The school district supplied the buses to the company, which could be used only for transportation of city school children. Further, the school district remained responsible for compliance with state and federal regulations pertaining to equipment on buses, retained veto power over the hiring of any school bus driver, and supplied all gasoline to operate the buses.[22] The NLRB appears to be applying a similar degree-of-control test. However, in noneducation cases, other factors, such as monetary control, have been used to determine who is the public employer. The result sometimes has been a finding that there are co-employers.[23] If state governments or state boards of education continue to assume a greater role in financing public education or in imposing requirements on local education, the identity of the employer can be a critical issue to unions that wish to negotiate on major decisions not controlled by the local school board.

An off-shoot of these hybrid arrangements is the difficulty of determining who are employees. For example, are interns, who teach in a school district for no more than one term and receive a stipend of $2,000, employees when they continue to be registered as college students and pay tuition, although their sole academic responsibility is their internship? Such a case occurred in Wisconsin where the court held that the interns were employees of the school district under the state's collective bargaining statute, but were placed in a bargaining unit apart from the regular teachers due to their short-term appointments and their expectations to be hired elsewhere.[24] As job sharing and other arrangements, such as private sector employees teaching in public schools for specified durations, continue to develop, the determination of who is an employee will become even more critical.

Another issue in public sector collective bargaining is differences of opinion concerning who is a supervisor or a management official. In the private sector, managerial employees have no statutory rights, although an employer can voluntarily accord recognition to a union that represents them. In the public sector, employers seldom are given any choice. Either supervisors are excluded, are mandatorily included in an existing unit, or are represented in a separate unit. There is a further division of opinion as to whether administrators are also supervisors. Frequently, the state statute supplies these answers, or sometimes a state public employee relations board (PERB) makes the decisions. In one case the New Hampshire Supreme Court upheld a PERB decision granting recognition to a unit of 13 elementary school principals and eight secondary school assistant principals, while excluding three junior high school principals, the high school principal, and his two associate principals. The determination that certain principals were agents of management was based on their actual involvement in managerial functions rather than on the title they held.[25]

The potential for conflict of interest in such situations is illustrated by an agreement that preceded the statute that now exists in Iowa. By this agreement the school district included principals and supervisors in the bargaining unit and provided that it would not discriminate against any unit member for membership or participation in union activities. Nevertheless, the school district refused to renew the contract of a principal who acted as the chief negotiator for the union, citing this activity as an "extraordinary example of his . . . failures in judgment." The Eighth Circuit Court upheld the constitutionality of the nonrenewal on the basis that the principal's acting as chief negotiator constituted a conflict of interest.[26]

Rights and Obligations of the Exclusive Bargaining Representative

In the private sector an exclusive representative has a duty to represent all employees in the unit. This duty of fair representation is complicated in the public sector when the same union may represent both supervisory personnel and subordinates. The duty may be tested any time a unit employee complains that another unit employee received a promotion or some other preferential treatment. Such a situation faced the Rhode Island Supreme Court when a successful applicant for department head claimed that the teachers union had breached its duty to him when the union pressed the grievance of an unsuccessful applicant who had more seniority. The court applied the private sector standard that the union "must choose its side in a nonarbitrary manner based on its good faith judgment as to the competing claims." The union does not have to remain neutral since to do so would weaken its ability to represent employees and to enforce the contract. In this case the union was found to have breached its duty because it never contacted the successful applicant and never investigated the qualifications of two other teacher candidates.[27]

The private sector rule is now the general rule in the public sector, although the wide range of reasonableness that must be accorded to a bargaining representative recently was allowed to be judged by a jury.[28] The same duty also applies in the bargaining process, even though a specific agreement may give one component of membership an advantage over another.[29] However, a collective bargaining agreement cannot waive equal employment opportunities, such as those related to sex or race, since to do otherwise would be to defeat the legislative purpose of nondiscrimination in employment.[30]

Under exclusive representation, an employee cannot personally negotiate with the employer. This doctrine was further extended in the case of a Pennsylvania nonunion teacher who did not want to participate in a negotiated dental plan.[31] However, in *City of Madison School District No. 8* v. *Wisconsin Employment Relations Commission* the Supreme Court ruled that a teacher did have the right at an open school board meeting to present a petition opposing the agency shop provision that his exclusive representative was advocating.[32] The Court viewed the teacher as a citizen in the community and ruled that the school board was precluded from barring speakers on the basis of employment or the content of their speech. The dual role of a person as an employee and as a citizen creates difficulties for traditional concepts of labor relations, which are likely to continue in the future.

The Pennsylvania decision referred to may lead to a significant decision on a different issue of minority rights, i.e., nonunion members. A case presently on appeal to the Supreme Court involves a decision that upheld a ratification election in which nonunion members were not allowed to vote but were notified and invited to come to the ratification meeting to ask questions and express their opinions. The Pennsylvania court interpreted these actions as showing that the union members did not disregard the "interests of their nonunion fellows."[33]

Another conflict between the rights of the minority and the rights of the exclusive representative in acting for the entire unit involves the traditional concept of the "agency shop." An earlier issue associated with the agency shop was the union dues "checkoff," which is no longer in dispute except in Wisconsin where the high court of that state found "no reasonable relationship between granting of an exclusive checkoff and the functioning of the majority organization in its representative capacity."[34] Another controversial issue was the mandatory payment of a service fee to the union by nonmembers in the bargaining unit. The Supreme Court, in *Abood* v. *Detroit Board of Education*,[35] upheld the agency shop provisions and proclaimed that such provisions do not deny nonunion teachers their First Amendment rights to freedom of association to the extent that agency shop fees are used to pay for the expenses of collective bargaining, contract administration, and grievance adjustment. The Court further declared that agency shop fees may not be used to support ideological causes opposed by unit members or for functions not germane to the union's representative role. The Court explained that the considerations of labor stability in the private sector have no less weight in the public sector.

The Court ruling in *Abood* has created a favorable legislative climate for the agency shop. In fact, the Ohio Supreme Court has enforced an agency shop agreement even in the absence of a law authorizing it.[36] However, two legal controversies persist. One issue is whether the discharge of a teacher for nonpayment of the required union service fee conflicts with the state teacher tenure act. There is no consensus on this point.[37] The other battle is over the formula used to assess the fees to be paid by the nonmember that are used solely for bargaining purposes and not for so-called "ideological" purposes. Such a case did reach the U.S. Supreme Court but was dismissed for want of a substantial federal question.[38] The same issue has surfaced when unions have properly identified the portion of the dues used for political or ideological purposes but collected them using a "reverse checkoff," which requires the nonmember to object to payment by filling out a form in advance or by specifically requesting a refund.[39]

Scope of Bargaining

Traditionally, in collective bargaining in the private sector the obligation of the parties is to make a good faith attempt to reach an agreement with respect to wages, hours, and other conditions of employment. This is also true in those public sector jurisdictions with comprehensive bargaining laws, although the scope of subjects open to bargaining may differ among jurisdictions. Some states specify those subjects that are open to negotiation and/or those that are not.

In most jurisdictions timing is a critical aspect of the bargaining process, particularly in the context of impending legislative action. The fact that laws or regulations are changed may not relieve the public employer of a prior bargaining obligation. A case occurred when a Connecticut city held public hearings to consider a residency requirement for future employees. The court held that the union did not waive its rights by appearing at the hearings and by later failing to present a bargaining proposal, since the union was not obliged to anticipate that the ordinance would survive the political process and become law, especially when that process took 21 months. To require bargaining on every proposal affecting negotiable matters, the court explained, would place too onerous a burden on both employers and employees. Therefore, the union did not have to demand negotiations while the measure was under legislative consideration.[40] Similarly, the Minnesota Supreme Court enjoined the contracting out of bus services even though the buses had been sold, since the school board had violated an obligation to negotiate.[41]

The aspect of the obligation to negotiate that remains largely unsettled revolves around which subjects a school board must refrain from changing without first dealing with the exclusive representative. A Kansas court, which has narrowly construed the scope of bargaining, held that this obligation applied to changing a six-period class day to a seven-period class day.[42] A New Jersey court held the obligation was not applicable to changes in teaching modules that did not lengthen the school day. The court explained, "without some measure of flexibility constant battles would be urged over every change in format, with each change viewed as an opportunity to extract more concessions."[43] A New York court held that this obligation did not extend to changes that are not mandatory subjects of bargaining, which in this case was the length of individual employment contracts. The court's rationale was that since the subject was not negotiable the employees were not deprived of any rights by the change.[44]

Another aspect of the obligation to bargain not usually specified in a state law is the interrelationship with other laws. The trend has been to allow collective bargaining supremacy over laws, unless there is a specific prohibition against this in the collective bargaining statute. In Illinois, which does not have a comprehensive bargaining statute, a statute that gave the school board power to transfer principals was not construed to preclude a negotiated agreement that before a principal is transferred to a lower administrative grade, he or she had certain negotiated procedural rights.[45] In another Illinois case, where the Workmen's Compensation Act provides an employee with a statutory remedy for accidents associated with employment, the court held the act did not preclude parties from negotiating supplemental benefits.[46]

A future area of conflict is in the relationship of collective bargaining to affirmative action and tenure requirements. In Michigan a collective bargaining agreement required a school board to lay off first those teachers most recently hired. When layoffs were prompted by a fiscal crisis, the percentage of black teachers was reduced to 8.9% despite an earlier court order to desegregate the school system by attempting to raise the black faculty percentage to 20%. A federal district court invalidated the layoff of black teachers, explaining that "the absence of

discriminatory motive makes little difference since the remedy was needed to provide role models to the black community and to prove to its
black students that blacks are not always the ones who will bear the
brunt of layoffs during times of financial hardship."[47] In another case a
Minnesota court upheld the right of a union to waive tenure rights but
not to override a legislative scheme to deal with the problem of declining
enrollments.[48] The task facing courts in the future will be to determine
what special requirements are not superseded by collective bargaining
agreements.

The precise scope of bargaining will continue to depend on the definitions and limitations under state statutes. Some statutes exclude specific
subjects dealing with working conditions on the theory that management
should not have the discretion to bargain away functions for which it is
accountable to the public. Other statutes prohibit bargaining on "matters of inherent managerial policy" or on "educational policy." Since
many matters affect both the working conditions of teachers and the exercise of management prerogatives, most state courts have arrived at a
balancing test rather than ruling that a subject must be negotiated
because working conditions are affected or that a subject is prohibited
from negotiation because management policy is affected. The balancing
test has become prevalent regardless of the wording of the statute, even if
the statute contains no management rights provision. Illustrative of this
test, the Oregon Employment Relations Board found mandatorily negotiable a union proposal that a teacher be allowed to remove from the
classroom a student whom the teacher identified as a "discipline problem." The threat of immediate physical danger to the teacher was held to
outweigh the educational policy concerns involved.[49]

Another widely recognized rule has been the requirement that management negotiate on the impact or implementation of a policy that is
itself outside the scope of bargaining. The Minnesota Supreme Court
held teacher-transfer policy to be a matter of inherent managerial policy
but found negotiable a proposal to make disputes over the school
district's adherence to transfer criteria subject to binding grievance arbitration, since the proposal affected only the application of management's right.[50]

Recently, there has been an increasing number of bargaining demands made by management. At the same time, there has been a rising
number of issues related to layoffs and reductions in force. For example,
when an Iowa school board proposed that school administrators retain
their bargaining unit seniority in their major teaching area, the Iowa
Supreme Court ruled that the union could not be compelled to negotiate
on benefits to employees currently outside the unit.[51]

It is not now known how far courts and PERBs will go in holding
negotiable union proposals that limit a school board's ability to react to

economic constraints. The Maine Supreme Court upheld the negotiability of a proposal that contracting out work "shall not cause the discharge or layoff of any member of the bargaining unit."[52] A New York court upheld a negotiated agreement prohibiting the termination of unit employees for budgetary reasons and forbidding the abolition of programs during the life of the agreement.[53]

Another issue to watch is whether the scope of bargaining will be expanded where there is no legal right to strike, following the example of the Michigan Supreme Court's view that the less power the union has should be counterbalanced by a broader legal right at the bargaining table.[54] At the same time, the prohibited area has become enlarged where changing public attitudes have been translated into "policy." One example is a decision of a Pennsylvania court, similar to court decisions in several other states, finding that a school board had no obligation to bargain on the school's extension of a ban on smoking in school buildings to teachers, as well as students. The court viewed the board's decision as educational policy, which outweighed the interests of teachers.[55]

Grievances

The grievance procedure incorporated in collective bargaining agreements is a mechanism that provides for interpretation of contract provisions when disputes arise over improvident wording or unforeseen situations. The grievance procedure also allows a union to contest an alleged abuse of management discretion in areas in which a union did not wish to negotiate, or was prohibited from negotiating, on the management's right to make a decision. When a grievance is unable to be resolved by the parties, an arbitrator is called in to render a judgment.

The competency of an arbitrator, rather than the school board, to judge employee complaints has long been recognized.[56] Nevertheless, the largest single area of labor relations litigation has involved arbitration, whether in terms of contesting whether a grievance is subject to arbitration or in terms of challenging the decision rendered by an arbitrator. Most jurisdictions adhere to the private sector presumption that grievances are subject to arbitration; and most, such as the Connecticut Supreme Court,[57] have specifically embraced the "positive assurance" test. Under this test, judicial inquiry is limited strictly to the question of whether the party challenging arbitrability did agree to arbitrate such a grievance. In this context, an order to stay arbitration is granted only when it may be said with "positive assurance" that the arbitration clause is not susceptible to being interpreted as covering the asserted dispute. If there are doubts, then the decision is resolved in favor of coverage under arbitration. In addition, if there are several appeal channels, the grievance arbitration route will be preferred, as illustrated by a Pennsylvania case of an employee who was denied the right to sue in court for interest on salary that was paid late, since the grievance procedure was held to be exclusive under the terms of his contract.[58]

The only major departure from the doctrine of presumption of arbitrability was a New York Supreme Court case in which the court believed there were equally persuasive arguments for and against a teacher's grievance being construed as subject to the arbitration provision in the negotiated contract. The court held that it could not imply arbitration and that there had to be a clear and unequivocal agreement that the employer intended to refer the issue to arbitration "inasmuch as the responsibilities of the elected representatives of the taxpaying public are overreaching and fundamentally nondelegable."[59] Despite the respect generally given to the New York court, the decision has yet to serve as a precedent for other cases. In fact, the same court ruled shortly thereafter in favor of arbitrability in cases that did not appear to meet its clear and unequivocal standard.[60]

The public sector differs from the private sector with respect to negotiability. In the private sector, an employer may bargain on a matter upon which it is not obligated to negotiate. In the public sector, a prohibited subject is just that. The employer may not bargain on such a subject; and if it does, the provision is unenforceable. In cases where a union initiates action to arbitrate a provision in a contract, it is in reality an action to enforce that provision. In these cases a court will preclude arbitrability despite the clear intent of the contract, as did the Maine Supreme Court in refusing to enforce a provision prohibiting a school board from hiring a teacher from outside the school system when there were applicants from within the system.[61]

Normally, the arbitrator decides whether a grievance is unrelated to the grievance provision or is clearly frivolous or spurious. New York has strayed from this practice and has denied arbitrability where "the lack of specificity in the wording of the grievance makes it impossible to determine intelligently whether or not the grievance relates" to the contractual provision claimed to be the basis for arbitrability.[62] A major issue of the future may be whether this interpretation will be adopted in other jurisdictions.

Another basis for claiming that a grievance is not subject to arbitration is that the remedy requested is impermissible. The Massachusetts Supreme Court rejected this defense as applied to a tenure situation on the basis that, if a violation were found, the school committee might voluntarily accede to the arbitrator's recommendation or the arbitrator might be able to fashion a remedy that would fall short of intruding on the school committee's exclusive domain.[63]

Similar to the presumption of arbitrability, courts have confined the review of arbitrators' decisions to very narrow grounds. Nevertheless, a large portion of the caseload in public sector labor relations involves appeals of the arbitrator's decision. The degree of deference to the arbitrator is revealed by this statement of the Rhode Island Supreme Court: "As a general rule, when a party claims that the arbitrators have exceeded their authority, the claimant bears the burden of proving this contention, and every reasonable presumption in favor of the award will be made. . . . the mere fact that the arbitrator misconstrues the contract or the law affords no basis for striking the award."[64]

The Iowa Supreme Court explained the restrictive view of judicial involvement in the arbitration process in this manner:

> Arbitration is a faster process, draws on the expertise of persons in the field and is less expensive. To allow a court to "second guess" an arbitrator by granting a broad scope of review would nullify those advantages. Most important, limited judicial review gives the parties what they have bargained for — binding arbitration, not merely arbitration binding if a court agrees with the arbitrator's conclusion.[65]

In affirming that in the absence of complete irrationality an arbitration award would not be subject to judicial revision, the New York Supreme Court revealed frustration with the frequency with which public policy is raised as a school board defense and used these words to stem the flood of appeals:

> Every collective bargaining agreement involves some relinquishment of educational control by a school district. Only when the award contravenes a strong public policy, almost invariably an important constitutional or statutory duty or responsibility, may it be set aside.[66]

Effect of the Legislative Process

The most significant difference between the public and private sector is that in the public sector the funding of an agreement is subject to a public process, and frequently a major portion or all of the funding is in the control of a body not a party to a negotiated agreement. Problems arising when negotiated agreements cannot be fulfilled because of inadequate funding have not reached the courts in sufficient numbers to establish broad legal precedents. However, questions arising out of legislative refusal to fund contracts will likely be a significant issue in court cases over the next several years, out of which will come important decisions affecting other aspects of labor relations.

In the few cases heard thus far, the courts have generally upheld contracts previously in existence. When the citizens of California limited tax revenues through the passage of Proposition 13, the state legislature responded by enacting a law to void any collective bargaining agreement by a local agency that called for a salary increase in excess of that granted to state employees. Consequently, when the state employees received a zero increase, some agencies refused to grant increases required by contracts already in effect. Noting that "an increase in wages is frequently the very heart of an employment contract" and that the union may have traded off other benefits to secure such wages, the state supreme court held that collective bargaining agreements had the same protections as any other contract and could not be so impaired.[67]

The Massachusetts Supreme Court rendered the extraordinary remedy of affirming an injunction to compel the mayor of Boston to submit to the city council a request for a supplemental appropriation of $12.1 million to fund an executed agreement between the teachers union and the school committee and not to veto the city council's appropriation. The court viewed the mayor as having no bargaining or appropriation function and, therefore, only a ministerial role with no authority to frustrate or delay the appropriation process. The court also enjoined the city council from setting the tax rate for the city until the supplemental appropriations were properly acted on, because of the irreparable harm that would have occurred had the tax rate been set prematurely.[68]

In contrast, the Illinois Supreme Court reversed an appellate court decision and held, over a vigorous dissent, that a school board did not violate its contractual obligation to the union when it closed school a day early and did not pay school employees for that day in response to a projected $52 million operating deficit. The court construed the state school code as empowering the school board to control budgetary considerations and, therefore, the agreement could not preclude the school board from exercising such powers.[69] Similarly, a Tennessee court held that an agreement fixing a schedule of wage increases over a five-year period of time was dependent each year on funding by the county commissioners and, therefore, was not binding for that year until such approval. The union's only remedy was to renegotiate the contract when funding was insufficient.[70]

Negotiations Impasse

Most states compel a negotiations impasse to go to mediation and fact finding and/or arbitration. Some statutes provide that such procedures must be used if agreement has not been reached at a specified time prior to the budget submission date. There have been many challenges to the constitutionality of laws compelling a school board to comply with the order of an arbitrator as to the terms of a new collective bargaining agreement. In Maine, where an earlier constitutional challenge had failed, a school committee claimed that the law provided inadequate safeguards to protect against unfair and arbitrary decisions. The state supreme court denied the challenge on the basis that the ever-widening use of arbitration had resulted in the evolution of criteria that have become inherent in "today's arbitration process." Citing cases from Minnesota, New Jersey, and Pennsylvania that were not related to education, the court added:

> Formulation of rigid standards for the guidance of arbitrators in dealing with complex and often volatile issues would be impractical, and might destroy the flexibility necessary for arbitrators to carry out the legislative policy of promoting the improvement of the relationship between public employers and their employees.[71]

In effect, the arbitration process is viewed as a substitute for the strike. Because most jurisdictions do not grant the legal power to strike, a growing number of decisions have held that this limitation on the union's power should be offset by limitations on the school board's rights to engage in "self-help." For example, the Florida Public Employment Relations Commission has held that although a collective bargaining agreement has expired, the school board must maintain the status quo with regard to continuing wages, hours, terms and conditions of employment, and grievance procedures, since "to conclude otherwise would be to promote disharmony at a time when harmony is most needed."[72] The New Jersey Supreme Court viewed such a unilateral change as frustrating the statutory objective of mandating collective bargaining; and the Pennsylvania Supreme Court held that such a change was intended to be coercive and, therefore, was unlawful.[73]

Another issue likely to spark future controversy is the question of when a party can take off the bargaining table a permissive subject (i.e., one for which there is no obligation to negotiate but which the party receiving the proposal may at its own option agree to negotiate). Normally, permissive subjects may not be pressed to impasse. However, the Massachusetts Supreme Court held that once parties had agreed voluntarily to go to impasse arbitration, proposals in the permissive area could properly be considered by the arbitrator, at least if they are not so central to educational policy that the school committee could not relinquish control over them.[74]

Another emerging trend has been intervention by judges who, instead of acting on the legal issue before them, have assumed the role of mediators or dispute resolvers. A Missouri court, fearful that the granting of an injunction would only exacerbate a negotiation impasse, added to a restraining order against striking teachers an order to the school board to "meet and confer" in good faith, although there was no statutory requirement for the school board to do so.[75]

Strikes

The right to engage in picketing, without interfering with access, etc., has become so accepted that there have been no reported cases on this issue in the past three or four years. Also, the once raging controversy over the right to strike has all but disappeared from the legal scene as proponents of the right to strike have failed to win any final court battles. Should the issue emerge again, the theory opposing the view that there is no common law right to strike might be shaped from a dissent in an Idaho Supreme Court decision that viewed common law rules as evolving and flexible. On that basis, the dissent explained it would not impose the old common law rule on the legal rights of married women in our present society and, similarly, the right to strike would have to take into account the reality of the times.[76]

However, seven states do have statutes that permit strikes under certain circumstances: Alaska (only nonteaching employees of school districts), Hawaii, Minnesota, Oregon, Pennsylvania, Wisconsin, and Vermont. The Pennsylvania Supreme Court rejected a constitutional challenge to its limited right to strike law in which it was contended that strikes deprived children of their constitutional right to a public education.[77]

The area in which there may continue to be litigation is over what constitutes a strike. Subterfuges have long been revealed for what they are, as in the case of resignations by teachers, which the Florida Supreme Court viewed as not really intended to be permanent.[78] Recently, the issues have been more subtle, as in the case of teachers who did not receive pay for extracurricular activities and who refused to continue to perform such duties. A New Jersey court enjoined the "strike" because "extracurricular activities are a fundamental part of a child's education, making the supervision of such activities an integral part of a teacher's duty toward his or her students."[79]

Perhaps the right to strike is no longer a momentous issue because public managers increasingly favor giving unions the right to strike in preference to giving unions the right to take impasses to binding arbitration. This attitude may be attributable to a perception that unions will feel freer to press issues to impasse arbitration without having to take the risks that a strike poses. It may also be attributable to the growing number of states that have followed a 1968 Michigan Supreme Court decision that a strike injunction should be considered on the usual equity grounds: whether irreparable harm would occur and whether the party requesting the injunction has "clean hands," that is, in the case of a school board, whether it is free from unfair labor practices and has exhausted impasse procedures.[80] The Rhode Island Supreme Court, in embracing this theory, stated the automatic issuance of an injunction based merely on the illegality of the strike could make "the judiciary an unwitting third party at the bargaining table and potential coercive force in the collective bargaining process."[81]

The Michigan Supreme Court added another facet by holding that those striking against unfair labor practices, even if they started by striking for economic reasons, may be excused from strike sanctions.[82] Consequently, under such judge-made rules, "illegal" strikers have greater rights than strikers in states that statutorily permit strikes because most state statutes allowing strikes prohibit strikes based on an employer's unfair labor practices. Instead of equity grounds, "clean hands," or other such concepts, a strike is permitted only when there is no harm to the public health or safety (although states differ in their precise formulations).

Another subject once controversial but now dormant is the enforceability of a strike settlement regardless of the legality of the strike. Generally, such a settlement will be construed and enforced in accordance with customary contract law.[83]

Two issues that may receive judicial attention include civil action damages caused by an illegal strike and contractual provisions prohibiting strike actions. The Michigan Supreme Court has refused to recognize a course of action in damages for an illegal strike, holding that a new cause of action would unsettle an already precarious labor-management balance in the public sector.[84] A school board's attempts to legally protect itself from strikes through contractual arrangements fared better. Recently, the Illinois Supreme Court upheld the validity of individual teacher contracts that provided higher salaries for those who signed a provision that they would refrain from participation in any work stoppage, sit-in, or strike. The court explained that since the public policy against strikes "has been frequently and blatantly ignored," a contractual no-strike clause is a reasonable and practical consideration to reduce the risk of untoward expenses caused by strikes.[85]

Sunshine or Open Meeting Laws

"Sunshine" laws or "open meeting" laws have spawned much litigation and it is likely to continue. The problem arises out of the conflict between the requirement that local public bodies in open public meetings act on bargaining proposals and the highly private nature of the collective bargaining process. A variety of rulings have resulted. A North Dakota school board, which engaged in private but judicially supervised negotiation sessions, was excused from its failure to allow public attendance because it publicly disclosed the content of the negotiation sessions.[86] The Delaware Supreme Court upheld the action of a school board in seeking a temporary restraining order against a threatened teacher strike, although the board meeting was closed to the public.[87] However, a Kentucky court held that reports or status briefings to the school board by an assistant superintendent on his dealings with two competing unions were not entitled to privacy.[88]

Reflective of the incompatability between sunshine laws and collective bargaining is the case in which a Minnesota lower court, viewing open meeting laws literally, held that mediation had to be conducted in public. The state supreme court reversed that decision because it was impossible to conduct mediation under such circumstances.[89]

Concluding Note

The cases used as illustrations involve education employees. However, courts and PERBs rely heavily and frequently on cases involving non-education employees, on cases from the private sector, and even on cases from other jurisdictions in deciding issues raised by public school employers or their employees.

Illustrative of the reliance on other states, a Pennsylvania court had to rule on whether an arbitrator properly sustained grievances by teachers who were denied renewals of contracts to be advisors to student extracurricular activities. Based on rulings in cases decided in Delaware, Minnesota, and Washington that teachers when acting in the capacity of advisors are not professional employees and as such are not covered by the collective bargaining agreement, the court did not defer to the arbitrator.[90] Similarly, the Washington Court of Appeals looked to decisions in Florida, Oregon, and Wisconsin in concluding that an order of the state PERC directing an election is not a "final decision" subject to review under the state administrative procedures act.[91] In other words, in both cases the issues were ones of specific construction and not of broad generality, and yet decisions of other states were instructive.

New York law requires, when the state PERB makes a decision about unfair labor practice, that

> fundamental distinctions between public and private employment should be recognized, and no body of federal or state law applicable wholly or in part to private employment, shall be regarded as binding or controlling precedent.

Nevertheless, the PERB relied heavily on NLRB precedent and was attacked by a school board for the disregard of the quoted provision. A New York court upheld the PERB decision, stating "the wealth of experience in the private sector need not be completely disregarded" and that such decisions may properly be used as a guide.[92]

Footnotes

1. The states with laws that sanction collective bargaining are: Alaska, California, Connecticut, Delaware, Florida, Hawaii, Idaho, Indiana, Illinois, Iowa, Kansas, Maine, Maryland, Massachusetts, Michigan, Minnesota, Montana, Nebraska, Nevada, New Hampshire, New Jersey, New York, North Dakota, Oklahoma, Oregon, Pennsylvania, Rhode Island, South Dakota, Tennessee, Vermont, Washington, and Wisconsin. Some of these

jurisdictions have laws that grant minimal rights with loose or no enforcement mechanisms. Others are comprehensive and even permit the right to strike. Ohio has enacted a law that will go into effect 1 April 1984.

2. 398 F.2d 287 (7th Cir. 1968).
3. 391 U.S. 563 (1968).
4. 431 U.S. 209 (1977) (*infra* note 34 and accompanying text).
5. Newark Teachers Ass'n v. Newark City Bd. of Educ., 444 F. Supp. 1283, 1285 (D. Ohio 1978).
6. Due process rights are discussed in chapter 4.
7. Memphis American Fed'n of Teachers, Local 2032 v. Board of Educ., 534 F.2d 699 (6th Cir. 1976).
8. Perry Local Educators' Ass'n v. Hohlt, 652 F.2d 1286 (7th Cir. 1981).
9. Perry Educ. Ass'n v. Perry Local Educators' Ass'n, 103 S. Ct. 743 (1983).
10. Cary v. Board of Educ., 425 F. Supp. 945 (D. Colo. 1977).
11. 598 F.2d 535 (10th Cir. 1979).
12. *See, e.g.*, Board of Educ. v. Nyquist, 404 N.Y.S.2d 710 (App. Div. 1978), in which the constitutional right of a tenured teacher to receive pay pending the resolution of disciplinary proceedings was waived by a collective bargaining agreement.
13. 429 U.S. 274 (1977).
14. Wright Line Inc., 251 NLRB 150, 105 LRRM 1169 (1980).
15. 426 U.S. 833 (1976).
16. *Id.* at 855.
17. *See, e.g.*, City of Macon v. Marshall, 439 F. Supp. 1209 (M.D. Ga. 1977).
18. The lead case, although only by a lower state court, is *Chicago Division of the Illinois Education Association* v. *Board of Education*, 222 N.E.2d 243 (Ill. App. 1966).
19. Cleveland City School Dist. v. Cleveland Teachers Union, 427 N.E.2d 540 (Ohio App. 1980).
20. Richland Educ. Ass'n v. Richland School Dist., 418 A.2d 787 (Pa. Commw. 1980).
21. Erie Cty. Area Voc.-Tech. School v. Pennsylvania Labor Relations Bd., 417 A.2d 796 (Pa. Commw. 1980).
22. Baker Bus Serv. v. Keith, 416 A.2d 727 (Me. 1980).
23. Soy City Bus Serv., 249 NLRB No. 167, 104 LRRM 1269 (1980).
24. Arrowhead United Teachers Org. v. Wisconsin Employment Relations Comm'n, 1981-83 PBC ¶37,359 (Wis. Cir. Ct. 1981).
25. In re Nashua Ass'n of School Principals, 398 A.2d 832 (N.H. 1979).
26. Norbeck v. Community School Dist., 545 F.2d 63 (8th Cir. 1976).
27. Belanger v. Matteson, 346 A.2d 124 (R.I. 1975), *cert. denied*, 424 U.S. 968 (1976).
28. Trinque v. Mount Wachusett Commun. Faculty Ass'n, 437 N.E.2d 564 (Mass. App. 1982).
29. *See, e.g.*, Offutt v. Montgomery Cty. Bd. of Educ., 404 A.2d 281 (Md. App. 1979).
30. School Comm. of Brockton v. Massachusetts Comm'n Against Discrimination, 386 N.E.2d 1240 (Mass. 1979).
31. Pennsylvania Labor Relations Bd. v. Eastern Lancaster Cty. Educ. Ass'n, 427 A.2d 305 (Pa. Commw. 1981).

32. 429 U.S. 167 (1976).

33. 427 A.2d at 309.

34. Milwaukee Fed'n of Teachers, Local No. 252 v. Wisconsin Employment Relations Comm'n, 266 N.W.2d 314 (Wis. 1978).

35. 431 U.S. 209 (1977).

36. Jefferson Area Teachers Ass'n v. Lockwood, 433 N.E.2d 604 (Ohio 1982).

37. *Compare* Anderson Fed'n of Teachers, Local 519 v. Alexander, 416 N.E.2d 1327 (Ind. App. 1981), *with* White Cloud Educ. Ass'n v. Board of Educ., 300 N.W.2d 551 (Mich. App. 1981).

38. Threlkeld v. Robbinsdale Fed'n of Teachers, 74 L.Ed.2d 40, 111 LRRM 2528 (1982).

39. *See, e.g.*, Kentucky Educators Pub. Affairs Council v. Kentucky Registry of Election Finance, 110 LRRM 2398, 677 F.2d 1125 (6th Cir. 1982) (finding that such a system did not coerce teachers).

40. City of New Haven v. Connecticut State Bd. of Labor Relations, 410 A.2d 140 (Conn. Super. Ct. 1979); *see also* Evansville-Vanderburgh School Corp. v. Roberts, 405 N.E.2d 895 (Ind. 1980) (teachers' knowledge of a new evaluation plan being formulated did not trigger the union's obligation to request negotiations).

41. General Drivers Union Local 346 v. Independent School Dist. No. 704, Proctor School Bd., 283 N.W.2d 524 (Minn. 1979); *see also* Van Buren Pub. School Dist. v. Wayne Cty. Circuit Judge, 232 N.W.2d 278 (Mich. App. 1975) (rejecting as a defense the economic plight of the school district).

42. Dodge City NEA v. Unified School Dist. No. 443, 635 P.2d 1263 (Kan. App. 1981).

43. Caldwell-West Caldwell Educ. Ass'n v. Caldwell-West Caldwell Bd. of Educ., 435 A.2d 562, 566 (N.J. Super. Ct. App. Div. 1981).

44. Spencerport Transportation Ass'n v. New York PERB, 436 N.Y.S.2d 43 (Sup. Ct. App. Div. 1981).

45. Chicago Principals Ass'n v. Board of Educ. of City of Chicago, 406 N.E.2d 82 (Ill. App. 1980).

46. Board of Educ. v. Chicago Teachers Union, Local No. 1, 402 N.E.2d 641 (Ill. App. 1980).

47. Oliver v. Kalamazoo Bd. of Educ., 498 F. Supp. 732 (W.D. Mich. 1980).

48. Jerviss v. Independent School Dist. No. 294, 273 N.W.2d 638 (Minn. 1978).

49. Lincoln Cty. Educ. Ass'n v. Lincoln Cty. School Dist. No. C-64-78 (Ore. Employment Relations Bd. 1979).

50. Minneapolis Fed'n of Teachers Local 50 v. Minneapolis Special School Dist. No. 1, 258 N.W.2d 802 (Minn. 1977).

51. Marshalltown Educ. Ass'n v. Iowa PERB, 299 N.W.2d 469 (Ia. 1980).

52. Superintending School Comm. v. Bangor Educ. Ass'n, 433 A.2d 383 (Me. 1981).

53. Yonkers City School Dist. v. Yonkers Fed'n of Teachers, 353 N.E.2d 569 (N.Y. 1976).

54. Van Buren Pub. School Dist. v. Wayne Cty. Circuit Judge, 232 N.W.2d 278 (Mich. 1975).

55. Chambersburg Area School Dist. v. Pennsylvania Labor Relations Bd., 430 A.2d 740 (Pa. Commw. 1981).

56. Board of Educ. v. Associated Teachers of Huntington, 30 N.Y.S.2d 122 (N.Y. 1972).
57. Board of Educ. v. Frey, 392 A.2d 466 (Conn. 1978).
58. Donnellan v. Mt. Lebanon School Dist., 377 A.2d 1054 (Pa. Commw. 1977).
59. Acting Supt. of Liverpool Cty. School Dist. v. Unified Liverpool Faculty Ass'n, 399 N.Y.S.2d 189, 192 (N.Y. 1977).
60. *See, e.g.*, South Colonie School Dist. v. Longo, 43 N.Y.2d 136 (1977).
61. Board of School Dir. v. Maine School Admin. Dist. No. 36 Teachers Ass'n, 428 A.2d 419 (Me. 1981).
62. *See, e.g.*, Enlarged City School Dist. v. Troy Teachers Ass'n, 434 N.Y.S.2d 761 (App. Div. 1980).
63. School Comm. of Danvers v. Tyman, 360 N.E.2d 877 (Mass. 1977); *see also* Board of Educ. v. Middle Island Teachers Ass'n, 407 N.E.2d 411 (N.Y. 1980).
64. Coventry Teachers Alliance v. Coventry School Comm., 417 A.2d 886 (R.I. 1980); *see also* Trinity Area School Dist. v. Trinity Area Educ. Ass'n, 412 A.2d 167 (Pa. Commw. 1980).
65. Sergeant Bluff-Luton Educ. Ass'n v. Sergeant Bluff-Luton Commun. School Dist., 282 N.W.2d 144 (Ia. 1979).
66. Port Jefferson Station Teachers Ass'n v. Brookhaven Comsewogue Union Free School Dist., 383 N.E.2d 553, 554 (N.Y. 1978).
67. Sonoma Org. of Pub. Employees v. County of Sonoma, 152 Cal. Rptr. 903, 909 (Cal. 1979).
68. Boston Teachers Union Local 66 v. City of Boston, 416 N.E.2d 1363 (Mass. 1981).
69. Board of Educ. of City of Chicago v. Chicago Teachers Union Local 1, 430 N.E.2d 1111 (Ill. 1981).
70. Carter Cty. Bd. of Educ. Comm'rs v. American Fed'n of Teachers, 609 S.W.2d 512 (Tenn. App. 1980). *But see*, Town of Scituate v. Scituate Teachers Ass'n, 296 A.2d 466 (R.I. 1972).
71. Superintending School Comm. of City of Bangor v. Bangor Educ. Ass'n, 433 A.2d 383, 387 (Me. 1981).
72. In re Levy Cty. School Bd., Florida PERC Order No. 79-D-188 (1979).
73. *See* Galloway Twp. Bd. of Educ. v. Galloway Twp. Educ. Ass'n, 393 A.2d 218 (N.J. 1978); In re Appeal of Cumberland Valley School Dist., 100 LRRM 2050 (Pa. 1978).
74. School Comm. v. Boston Teachers Union Local 66, 363 N.E.2d 485 (Mass. 1977).
75. Parkway School Dist. v. Provaznik, 617 S.W.2d 489 (Mo. App. 1981).
76. Oneida Cty. v. Oneida Educ. Ass'n, 567 P.2d 830, 836-37 (Idaho 1977) (Bakes, J., dissenting).
77. Butler Area School Dist. v. Butler Area Educ. Ass'n, 391 A.2d 1295 (Pa. 1978).
78. Pinnellas Cty. Classroom Teachers v. Board of Pub. Instruction, 214 So. 24 (Fla. 1968).
79. Board of Educ. v. Asbury Park Educ. Ass'n, 368 A.2d 396 (N.J. Super. 1976).
80. School Dist. v. Holland Educ. Ass'n, 157 N.W.2d 206 (Mich. 1968).

81. School Comm. v. Westerly Teachers Ass'n, 299 A.2d 441, 446 (R.I. 1973); *see also* Timberlane Regional School Dist. v. Timberlane Teachers, 317 A.2d 555 (N.H. 1974); Rockwell v. Board of Educ. of School Dist. of Crestwood, 227 N.W.2d 736 (Mich. 1975).

82. Rockwell v. Board of Educ. of School Dist. of Crestwood, 227 N.W.2d 736 (Mich. 1975).

83. *See* Hawaii State Teachers Ass'n v. Hawaii PERB, 590 P.2d 993 (Hawaii 1979).

84. Lamphere Schools v. Lamphere Fed'n of Teachers, 252 N.W.2d 818 (Mich. 1977).

85. Bond v. Board of Educ., 408 N.E.2d 714 (Ill. 1980).

86. Dickinson Educ. Ass'n v. Dickinson Pub. School Dist. No. 1, 252 N.W.2d 205 (N.D. 1977).

87. Wilmington Fed'n of Teachers v. Howell, 374 A.2d 832 (Del. 1977).

88. Jefferson Cty. Bd. of Educ. v. Courier-Journal, 551 S.W.2d 25 (Ky. App. 1977).

89. Minnesota Educ. Ass'n v. Bennett, 391 N.W.2d 395 (Minn. 1982).

90. Greater Johnstown Area Voc.-Tech. School v. Greater Johnstown Area Voc.-Tech. Educ. Ass'n, 426 A.2d 1203 (Pa. Commw. 1981).

91. Renton Educ. Ass'n v. Washington PERC, 603 P.2d 1271 (Wash. App. 1979).

92. Saratoga Springs City School Dist. v. New York State PERB, 416 N.Y.S.2d 415 (App. Div. 1979). *See also*, "Is Looking Up Case Precedent in Other Jurisdictions Worthwhile?" *Journal of Law and Education* 6 (April 1977): 205-228.

6

Documentation of Employee Performance

Kelly Frels and Timothy Cooper

The principal purpose of a school district's evaluation system is to improve employees' performance so they can become successful and contribute to achieving the objectives of the district. But if the evaluation procedures and the follow-up assistance do not result in the performance level desired, then the employee must be replaced, either by resignation or termination. Thus the district's evaluation procedures and its supporting documentation system serve a secondary purpose — the removal of the unsatisfactory employee.

Depending on the specifics of the employee's contract, a school district must observe various degrees of procedural due process when terminating a person. In many situations this process culminates with a hearing before the board of education or a hearing panel to determine whether there is cause to terminate the employee. Chapter 4 dealt with the procedural requirements necessary to effect a termination. This chapter will provide practical advice to school administrators concerning the documentation to be generated and used in the evaluation process and, if necessary, to present at a hearing to support a recommendation for termination.

Procedural due process affords significant protection for employees, but it does not shield them from termination. Incompetent or insubordinate employees can and should be terminated. Due process requirements simply prescribe procedures that must be followed in

Kelly Frels and Timothy Cooper are attorneys with the firm Bracewell and Patterson in Houston, Texas.

carrying out those terminations. Of course, the permissible grounds for termination will usually be enunciated in state law, the teacher's contract, board policy, and/or a collective bargaining agreement. Therefore, those sources must be examined to determine the criteria on which employees must be judged and evaluated.

In public school employee termination hearings, school administrators are often faced with the charge that there is not enough documentation to support the termination or that there is little evidence to show that the administrator has attempted to assist the employee in improving performance. In other cases the claim is made that the administrator has collected or produced so much documentation that it is obvious the employee is being harassed. At still other employee termination hearings the complaint is made that the process is unfair because the employee did not know what was expected. The specifics may differ, but the complaints run along the lines of "I never saw that memorandum or had any such conferences regarding this situation." "You have padded the file." "I never had any of these meetings, and you never gave me a chance to face my accuser or defend myself." "Your memos were not specific enough to give me direction." "Why didn't you talk with me?" As a result of these types of complaints, administrators often are reluctant to bring a recommendation for termination, because the administrator recognizes that he, rather than the employee, is likely to be put on trial.

To ensure fair treatment of employees who are evaluated, a simple but effective system of documentation is needed, which can be used in conjunction with any school district's evaluation system. The documentation system used should be in compliance with the contractual schemes in the district and with state statutes. While the ultimate objective of the documentation system is to provide a communication process to help improve an employee's performance, the system should also provide the necessary documentation for the administrator to have confidence in recommending the employee's voluntary resignation or termination.

An effective documentation system is essential for preparing an administrator for a hearing before the board of education; for appeals and lawsuits filed with a state commissioner of education, an arbitrator, or a court; and also for discrimination complaints filed with the Equal Employment Opportunity Commission or the U.S. Department of Education. If there is a systematic documentation of poor performance before a teacher engages in public inflammatory statements, the hearing can address the performance deficiency and not get involved in extraneous matters. However, without such careful documentation of poor performance, a teacher could bring charges of harassment for making public statements and might be legally untouchable under First Amendment free speech rights[1] (see the discussion of the *Mt. Healthy* decision in chapters 3 and 4).

Elements of an Effective Documentation System

An effective documentation system for employee evaluations involves at least five types of written memoranda. First are memoranda to the administrator's files. These should be used sparingly to record less significant infractions or deviations by an employee. Second are specific incident memoranda used to record conferences with a teacher concerning more significant events. Third are summary memoranda used to record conferences with a teacher in which several incidents, problems, or deficiencies are discussed. Fourth are visitation memoranda used to record observations made of an employee's on-the-job performance. Fifth are formal assessment instruments used to evaluate the employee's overall performance.

The documentation of an employee's behavior and performance can be used for several purposes. First, it provides a continuing record for an administrator to follow an employee's actions and performance and to identify strengths, weaknesses, and problem areas. Second, it enables the employee to understand what problems have been identified and what corrective steps are necessary. Third, if an employee's performance does not improve, it serves as specific evidence to support a recommendation for termination.

The documentation system described below assumes that a school district has an ongoing evaluation plan. The procedures are designed to keep the volume of documents to a minimum, yet meet the need for full and complete documentation. The system attempts to be sensitive to the time constraints placed on school administrators.[2]

Memoranda to the File

Whenever an administrator observes an incident or behavior that is not of a significantly serious nature to require an immediate conference with the employee, but that should be considered in the employee's evaluation or at a later conference, it is appropriate for the administrator to prepare a short file memorandum. These file memoranda should be used sparingly. If an incident or series of incidents is in any way serious, the specific incident memorandum should be used. The memoranda to the file can be in various forms, such as a notation on a calendar or in a notebook with separate pages designated for specific individuals. They should include the name of the employee, the name or initials of the administrator making the entry, the date of the occurrence, and the facts of the event observed. These file memoranda can be used for the following limited purposes:

1. Conference with the employee concerning the incident or incidents and the preparation of a confirming memorandum

2. Assessment of the employee's performance
3. Refreshing the memory of the administrator for testimony at any proceeding or hearing relative to the employee's performance if the memos have not been incorporated into summary memoranda or other evaluation documents

Copies of these file memoranda need not be given routinely to the employee unless the employee requests them. Of course, under the public records acts in many states, the employee has the right to see them. There is no reason to keep these file memoranda secret from the employees. In fact, most administrators find it gives credibility to the system if employees are made aware of these memoranda and are encouraged to review any file memoranda made concerning their performance. Actually, the best practice is to incorporate the contents of these file memoranda into a summary memorandum or evaluation, which is given to the teacher at or following a conference. If a summary memorandum includes the information contained in file memoranda, the file memoranda should never have to be used again.

Even though it may not be the intention of the administrator to use these documents as evidence in future actions involving the employee, the memoranda should be written with the knowledge that copies may actually be introduced as evidence or a copy may be made available to the employee under the state's public records act. For example, if file memoranda are being used to refresh an administrator's memory at a hearing, in most states the attorney for the employee is entitled to see copies of the documents. Therefore, care should be taken not to write or record anything in a manner that could cause future embarrassment. A good practice is to record facts rather than make judgments or jump to conclusions. A file memorandum kept in a notebook might look something like this:

Sample Memorandum to the File

Teacher: Willie Makit
School: Theodore Inskeep Technical School
Grade: 8th
Subjects: Health & Sex Education, American History

9/20/81 — Did not sign in upon arriving at school. Arrived at 8:10 — 20 minutes late. (P.P.)

9/26/81 — In hallway near cafeteria at lunchtime. Did not challenge student who was in hall without permit. (P.P.)

10/2/81 — Talking with Bettie Wont in his classroom 45 minutes after school out with door closed. (P.P.)

10/3/81 — Talking with Bettie Wont in classroom 30 minutes after school out. No other students around and door open. (P.P.)

10/9/81 — Arrived 10 minutes late to school. Did not sign in until being reminded to do so by secretary Ida Spy. (P.P.)

10/10/81 — Failed to turn in weekly lesson plans by 4 p.m. (P.P.)

10/17/81 — Failed to turn in weekly lesson plans by 4 p.m. (P.P.)

10/21/81 — Arrived 20 minutes late to school. (P.P.)

10/27/81 — Did not sign in upon arrival. Secretary Ida Spy said arrived about 5 minutes late. (P.P.)

11/1/81 — Failed to turn in weekly lesson plans by 4 p.m. (P.P.)

Specific Incident Memoranda

If the administrator observes an incident involving an employee, or has a complaint from a third party, a specific incident memorandum may be appropriate. This memorandum should be sent *only* after the administrator holds a conference with the employee at which the incident is discussed and the facts and all viewpoints are considered. The memorandum should summarize the third party's complaint, the administrator's observation(s) of action by the employee, the employee's response, the administrator's determination, and any directives and/or reprimand to the employee. If the incident is so serious that termination is to be recommended immediately, the memorandum should so state. To avoid talking with an employee about an incident, in the hope that it will go away, is self-defeating and naive. Thirty minutes spent when the incident occurs may lead to corrective action by the employee and could help to avoid a two-day hearing or a week-long trial at some later date.

Also, the failure to confront problems, infractions, and deficiencies at the time they occur can greatly weaken a later action recommending termination. For example, suppose several incidents occur in the fall of a school year but are not mentioned to the employee by the administrator. An attempt to use those incidents as evidence for a termination recommendation in the spring of that school year may prove to be unsuccessful. The employee can claim unfair treatment because the reason(s) for termination were never disclosed during the school year. This makes the administrator appear to be acting in an arbitrary or devious manner and could call into question the grounds used to justify termination.

It is a good practice to have the employee acknowledge receipt of the specific incident memorandum by signing the copy. If the employee does not agree with the facts stated in the memorandum or the action taken, the employee should be given the opportunity to respond in writing either on the memorandum itself or through the submission of a separate document. This can be accomplished by inviting the employee to prepare a written statement within a specified time concerning any differences of fact or opinion expressed by the administrator in the memorandum. For example, the final paragraph of a memorandum might conclude, "If you disagree with the facts or conclusions stated in this memorandum, please advise me in writing no later than (date) so we can meet and work out any differences." By so doing, any disagreement can be noted, and the differences can be resolved promptly. In serious situations where the employee has proven to be recalcitrant or is of questionable integrity, one might consider a final sentence such as "If you do not respond, I can only assume you agree with the facts as stated in this memorandum." A statement of this nature should be used sparingly because it tends to polarize the positions of the administrator and the employee, thus making future communications more difficult.

If the specific incident concerning the employee comes from a third party such as a parent or student, care must be taken to examine fully the facts and determine whether the third party's information is correct. It is improper and legally disastrous to base a decision to terminate on information from a third party when the truthfulness of the allegation has not been established.

Upon the receipt of a third-party complaint, the administrator should make an investigation and conduct whatever informal hearings are necessary to determine whether the complaint is true. The preferred practice to follow when one receives a complaint from a third party is to get the complaint in writing. The third party should be advised at this point that if adverse action is taken against the employee based on this incident, the third party must be available to testify before the board, an arbitrator, or a court. If the third party will not agree to appear as a witness, other independent evidence must be available to establish the relevant facts at a hearing; otherwise, action adverse to the employee should not be undertaken.

The next step is to get the employee's side of the story. If there is a discrepancy in the third party's story and the employee's story, the administrator should interview any witnesses and attempt to determine what occurred. It may be necessary to have the employee confront the complainant in an informal conference to determine what actually occurred. Although the results of a polygraph test cannot be used in a termination proceeding in most states, in really serious situations an employee might be allowed voluntarily to take a polygraph test to aid in establishing innocence. When the reasons are very compelling, consideration can be given to requiring the employee to give a sworn statement or to submit to a polygraph examination as a condition of continued employment. This process should be used sparingly and only with the advice of legal counsel and board policy.

In many cases it will simply not be possible for the administrator to have agreement concerning what happened, so the administrator has to act as a judge and determine whose story to believe. If agreement is eventually reached or if the administrator has enough information to make factual determinations, a specific incident memorandum can be prepared. Such a memorandum should explain the findings made by the administrator and the reasons for those findings. Specific directives or suggestions to the employee might also be included in the memorandum if appropriate.

It is important to establish on the face of the specific incident memorandum that the employee received a copy of the document. In employee termination hearings, a dispute will often arise over whether the employee ever received a copy of some document. It is essential, therefore, to have the employee sign the memorandum acknowledging its receipt. If an employee refuses to sign, the administrator should have an adult witness present who will sign the document verifying that the employee was given a copy of the memorandum but refused to sign it acknowledging its receipt. It should be made clear to the employee, either on the face of the document or orally, that his or her signature, verifying that a copy of the memorandum has been received, does not constitute agreement with its contents. As noted previously, the employee should be given the opportunity to respond in writing to the memorandum.

Giving the employee an opportunity to disagree with the contents of the memorandum by responding in writing puts the employee on notice of the facts and findings stated in the memorandum. If no disagreement is noted in writing by the employee, a presumption is created that the contents of the memorandum accurately reflect the facts. A judge examining this situation will normally take the view that a reasonable person who received such a memorandum and who disagreed with the facts would have prepared a written response to the items with which there was disagreement. If the employee does not respond within the time stated in the memorandum, it becomes difficult to argue at a termination hearing that the employee now disagrees with the content of the memorandum or disagreed when the memorandum was written. A specific incident memorandum might be written as follows:

Sample Specific Incident Memorandum

To: Willie Makit

From: Paul Principal

Date: October 23, 1981

Re: Allegation of misconduct made by Mrs. Harvey Wont,
Mother of Bettie Wont, Student

You will recall that Mrs. Wont called me on October 20, 1981, to complain that you had molested her daughter, Bettie, while you were visiting their home one afternoon after school. No one else was at their home besides you and Bettie. Specifically, Mrs. Wont alleged that Bettie stated that you embraced her and then began fondling her private parts while suggesting that the two of you become "better acquainted" upstairs.

I called you in on October 21, 1981, to discuss the matter with you. You told me that you had not molested Bettie in any way and had made no suggestions to her concerning getting "better acquainted." You told me that you had taken Bettie to her home that afternoon, but only because Bettie requested that you do so. You also told me that the reason for taking Bettie home was because she was very upset about not making the cheerleading squad and seemed to want to talk to someone. I asked you about the times I had seen you in your classroom with Bettie after the other students had been dismissed. You responded that you had, in fact, on several occasions counseled her about various matters and that she had come to regard you as a friend and con-fidant. In regard to the specific alleged incident, you stated that you and Bettie had been talking and that you were ready to leave, when she came over and embraced you. She then told you she loved you and wanted you to stay with her. You said you told her that you could not do so and left.

On October 22, 1981, I had a conference with Mrs. Wont, you, and Bettie. After a long discussion and after careful questioning, Bettie admitted that you had, in fact, not molested her or made suggestions to her. She said she was angry at you for not staying with her, so she told her mother those things. Mrs. Wont apologized for the incident, as did Bettie.

Based on this investigation. I have determined that you did not in any way molest Bettie Wont. However, I do find that your conduct in this matter is not totally in keeping with proper pro-fessional standards. You are surely aware that girls of Bettie's age are very impressionable. You should be very careful in your relations with female students not to encourage any infatuations they may hold. Furthermore, unless absolutely essential, you should avoid driving a female student home without someone else being present. More importantly, to avoid situations like this from arising, you should not visit a female student in her home when her parents are not there. I will expect you to abide by these directives. I am also transferring Bettie from your Health and Sex Education Class into Felix Feelgood's class.

Because of this incident, I think both of you will be more comfortable with this move.

If you disagree with the facts, conclusions, or directives contained in this memorandum, please advise me in writing no later than _____, so we can meet and work out any differences.

/s/ _____
Paul Principal

I have received a copy of this memorandum.

/s/_____   _____(Date)_____

Visitation Memoranda

It is a common practice to summarize a visit to a teacher's classroom with a visitation memorandum. The content of such a memorandum should be reviewed with the teacher, and the teacher should be given a copy. Suggestions for improvement should be made in a conference and noted in the memorandum. A visitation memorandum may be used in the eventuality of a termination hearing, but the results of a visitation are normally compiled in a summary memorandum or an assessment document.

Summary Memoranda

Summary memoranda are ideal ways to record the results of conferences covering several incidents, a series of classroom visitations, or overall employee performance. Through such memoranda, the matters referred to in the file memoranda (which may not have previously been given to the employee) can be incorporated; matters not reflected in other memoranda can be put in writing; directives can be given; understanding of standards can be established; and evidence that a conference was held and the subjects discussed can be established. A copy of each summary memorandum should be given to the employee, and the employee should acknowledge receipt. As with the specific incident memorandum, the employee should be given an opportunity to put in writing any differences in the facts and conclusions stated in the memorandum. If an employee disagrees and files a response, a subsequent conference should be held with a follow-up memorandum to try to resolve any differences that may exist. The same comments applicable to the specific incident memoranda are also applicable to summary memoranda, with the major difference being that summary memoranda are designed to cover general conferences with the employee on several matters rather than only on a specific incident. A summary memorandum with specific directives might be written as follows:

Sample Summary Memorandum with Specific Directives

To: Willie Makit

From: Paul Principal

Date: May 5, 1983

Re: Conference of May 1, 1983

Over the past two years you and I have discussed your performance as a teacher at Theodore Inskeep Technical School. We have had numerous conferences to discuss specific incidents that have arisen as well as our scheduled assessment conferences. As we neared the end of this school year it became apparent to me that you were continuing to experience difficulties in complying with directives and in meeting the school district's standards in certain instructional and noninstructional areas. With this in mind, we had a conference in my office on May 1, 1983, to discuss your performance. At that conference we discussed the following areas, and I gave you specific directives for improvement.

1.   Preparation and submission of lesson plans. Since your arrival two years ago, you have experienced difficulty in submitting lesson plans in a timely fashion. You have acknowledged this on prior occasions such as in our conferences of November 5, 1981; March 16, 1982; and September 30, 1982. In this conference you again acknowledged this was a problem, but you stated that your night classes at graduate school kept you from consistently completing the lesson plans on time. You stated that you felt this was a legitimate excuse. I explained to you that, while taking further coursework was a good thing, its demands do not excuse failure to meet the requirements of your job. I advised you that I must have the clearly written and completed lesson plans in my box by 4:00 p.m. every Friday.

2.   Teacher-student relations. This is another area of continuing difficulty. We discussed your initial failure to challenge a student for a hall pass on November 5, 1981; your failure to discipline students for setting fire to a trash can in your room on January 15, 1982; and your disruptive classes, which caused Mr. Teacher and Ms. Teacher to complain on numerous occasions in the spring of 1982. We discussed these incidents in detail at your evaluation conference on March 10, 1982. You have acknowledged that these incidents occurred and have promised

to make corrections, but you continue not to ask students in the hall for passes (January 6 and 25, 1982; and April 1, 16, and 25, 1983), and your classes have continued to be distractive to other teachers and students. As we discussed, these types of incidents and your failure to deal with them cannot continue. You must make the necessary corrections immediately.

3. Classroom work and the issuance of grades. As we discussed, this is the most serious problem you have as a teacher. At the end of four nine-week grading periods you were from one to two days late in getting your grades into my office (October 15, 1981; April 1, 1982; October 17, 1982; and March 30, 1983). After each of these incidents I had a conference with you, and, once again, you blamed your night classes for the delay. I once again explained that that reason was not sufficient. After the last of these conferences, April 2, 1983, you acknowledged that you had no daily or test grades for Health Education Period 1 and only two grades for Health Education Period 3. As has been explained at the first faculty meeting of each year and as contained on page 6 of the Faculty Handbook, you must have at least six daily grades and two test grades for each nine-week reporting period. I specifically directed you to comply with these requirements.

Mr. Makit, the situation is serious. As I told you, I recommended your employment for the 1983-84 school year only because of your assurances that you will correct these deficiencies and follow these directives and school board policy. You have been given a growth plan in connection with your assessment, and numerous aids have been made available to you. As you and I discussed, I want this to work out so you become a successful teacher and that you continue to teach here. However, if you fail to follow any of the directives we discussed at our conference and which I have outlined in this memorandum, I will have no choice but to recommend that your employment with the district be terminated immediately.

If you have any questions concerning these directives or if you disagree with the facts or conclusions stated in this memorandum, please advise me in writing no later than _____ so we can meet and work out any differences.

/s/ _____

Paul Principal

I have received a copy of this memorandum.

/s/ _____   _____ (Date)

The Assessment or Evaluation Document

The assessment or evaluation document should be completed as prescribed by the policies and procedures of the school district. A summary narrative or memorandum ideally should supplement each negative assessment noted in the document. This can be done on the assessment document or on an attachment. If the assessment is such that the employee might be terminated if no improvement is shown, the employee should be advised that failure to improve could result in a recommendation for termination. The failure to warn of possible termination can result in claims by the employee that he or she would have improved if advised of the seriousness of the situation. Furthermore, it is wise to include instructions or specific directions for improvement. Such a practice not only is helpful to the employee, but, if the administrator's actions are later questioned, it also strengthens the argument that the employee has been treated fairly. Through the use of such evaluation documents, the employee will be put on notice that he or she has deficiencies which could result in a recommendation to terminate should those deficiencies not be remedied according to the instructions given for improvement.

In order to avoid difficulties with ratings on the evaluation, an employee should not be rated too highly when initially employed or assigned to a school. Rather, a straightforward and truthful evaluation should be made. It is much easier to raise evaluations in subsequent years than it is to lower high ones. Furthermore, a fair system of evaluation requires the setting of standards and expectations at the beginning of the school year, with the administrator following through with the implementation of those standards through the evaluation process.

Documentation in General

In preparing any memorandum, report the facts and avoid conclusionary statements not supported by the facts. For example, in a classroom visitation memorandum, reporting that a teacher's classroom was "disorderly," without any further explanation, is not very helpful. Rather, a principal should note such specifics as seeing three children talking during class recitation and one child playing in the back of the room. The principal should note that these acts were unnoticed by the teacher or were not corrected by the teacher. Furthermore, inflammatory words should not be used. For example, rather than characterize an action as "insubordination," the action should be factually described, and should be referred to as failure to comply with official directives and/or school board policy.

It is the specificity of the memorandum and not the quantity of words or the number of pages that counts. Directives in a memorandum should be clear, to the point, and not couched in jargon. For example, when directing a sometimes tardy employee to arrive at school on time, state: "You are required to be at school by (time) and you will be expected to have signed in by that time," rather than, "You are required to be at school on time." Instead of stating, "Your lesson plans are due once a week," one might say, "Your lesson plans are due in my box by 4:00 p.m. on each Friday, and I expect you to have them there beginning this Friday." When written in a constructive atmosphere, precise directives like these tend to clear the air and avoid real or imagined confusion about what is expected.

The specific incident memorandum, the summary memorandum, the visitation memorandum, and the assessment document should be written in the first person and personalized as much as possible. The use of "we" or "they" should be avoided unless two or more persons are involved in the supervisory roles and then the others should be identified by name. The key to the success of a documentation system is to provide an opportunity for the administrator and the employee to sit down and mutually work out the problem and determine the future actions of the employee.

Care should be taken to treat all employees alike, especially when dealing with absences and tardiness. It is destructive and embarrassing to have a teacher's attorney present a school's sign-in sheet at a hearing and show that other teachers have been tardy or absent more often than the teacher who is being proposed for termination for excessive tardiness or absences.

Another thought to keep in mind is that one should never write a memorandum to an employee when one is angry. It is much better to reflect for a day or so or to call in a third party to review a memorandum prior to sending it in circumstances where the administrator is angry or personally involved. By doing so, the administrator can avoid statements that might later be regretted, especially when the tone of the memorandum is being scrutinized by a judge or jury. In order to be effective, however, any memorandum must be prepared and sent to the employee soon after the incident and the subsequent conference occurs. Under no circumstances should a memorandum be prepared after the decision to terminate has been made and then backdated to reflect the incident on which the proposed termination will be based.

As in all employee matters, the evaluator should be careful to ensure that the employee feels he or she has been fairly treated. One should remember that if the employee's performance does not improve and a recommendation for termination is made, the fairness of the process will be judged by the members of the board and, possibly, by a state commissioner of education, an arbitrator, a judge, or a jury. In evaluating whether an employee has been treated fairly, one should attempt to view it from the perspective of a reasonable person who, after receiving all the facts, determines whether the process was fair. Another helpful standard for judging fairness is for the administrator to treat the employee as the administrator would like to be treated in the same circumstances.

Normally, the only documents that would be used as evidence at a termination hearing are summary memoranda and the evaluation or assessment instruments. Occasionally, specific incident and visitation memoranda might be used; however, it is a better practice to incorporate these types of memoranda and include them in a subsequent summary memorandum or evaluation instrument. If the employee has not received a copy of a file memorandum, it should not be used as evidence at a hearing. But it can be used to refresh the administrator's memory while testifying about the specific facts of an event. Again, if summary memoranda properly reflect the incidents recorded in the file memoranda, the file memoranda should never have to be referred to at a hearing.

Factors to Consider in Termination Proceedings

If an employee's performance does not improve to an acceptable level or if the employee does not comply with administrative directives and board policies, the administrator will have to determine whether to recommend termination. Before a final recommendation is made to the board, the employee's immediate supervisor and the next-level administrator should hold a conference with the employee. The employee should be confronted with the inadequacies or problems that have been identified and be given an opportunity to respond. This is a hedge against misunderstanding the basic reasons for the proposed termination, and it provides an opportunity to consider any additional facts or viewpoints an employee may wish to present. With this final effort to examine the situation more closely, there could be a reconsideration as to whether termination is the proper alternative. For example, if there is a personality conflict between the administrator and the employee, rather than a professional performance problem, a transfer to another school or department might be appropriate.

If it is determined after the conference with the employee that there is not sufficient evidence to support a termination, or the administrator's supervisor feels the employee can improve and become successful, a recap and summary memorandum of the conference can be prepared setting out specific standards and directives for the employee and also stating specific policies that, if violated, could result in a recommendation for immediate termination in the future.

If, after hearing the employee's side of the story, the administration decides to go forward with the recommendation for termination, the employee should be advised of this decision and offered an opportunity to resign. If there are other consequences of resignation such as the forfeiture of future employment opportunities, this should be made clear. To help avoid "constructive discharge" (i.e., forced resignation) claims, the employee, if choosing not to resign, should be advised of the right to a hearing before the board (if applicable under the contract or board policies). A resignation must be voluntary, and it is for this reason that it is advisable to have the administrator's immediate supervisor present at the meeting so any discussions concerning resignation can be witnessed. Providing the employee with an opportunity to resign gives the employee a professionally acceptable avenue of escape prior to the recommendation for termination.

If, after the conference with the employee, the administrator and supervisor determine that a termination recommendation should be made, it should be prepared for review by the school attorney. When the recommendation is made, the administration should submit to the school attorney a letter to be sent to the employee setting out the proposed termination. Also at this time, again for approval by the school attorney, the administration should prepare a statement of reasons supporting the proposed termination and a list of witnesses, together with their testimony, which will be presented if the employee requests a hearing before the board. The documents that support the reasons for the proposed termination should also be submitted at this time. The preparation of these letters and the gathering together of the documents prior to presenting the proposed termination to the board will aid the administrator in evaluating all facts and in determining whether a termination recommendation really should be made. The procedures also help ensure that the administrator remains in control of the employment situation and gives the administrator confidence in carrying out unpleasant but necessary personnel procedures.

Conclusion

Like all personnel procedures, the documentation system described here is not fail-safe. Since it must be implemented by humans, it is subject to error. However, this system does provide an opportunity for an administrator to communicate effectively with employees about their performance, it is hoped to improve it, but if necessary to provide the proper documentation for termination. In working with this system, the school board members, the state commissioner of education, arbitrators, judges, or jurors will evaluate the termination recommendation on the basis of fairness and reasonableness. To ensure an effective documentation system, administrators should keep in mind the following action steps:

1. Develop and adopt an educationally justifiable evaluation system and implement it.

2. Provide inservice for all administrative personnel in supervisory positions on the evaluation policies and the documentation system described in this chapter.

3. Apply the school's evaluation policy and documentation system in a way that preserves the personal dignity of employees and treats them like the supervisory administrator would expect to be treated in similar circumstances.

Footnotes

1. For a sample case illustrating the importance of documentation, *see* Childers v. Independent School Dist. No. 1, 645 P.2d 992 (Okla. 1982).
2. The system recommended in this chapter is only one possibility. For other possible documentation systems, *see* Ronald Ruud and Joseph Woodford, *Supervisor's Guide to Documentation and File Building for Employee Discipline* (Crestline, Calif.: Advisory Publishing, 1982); Chester Nolte, *How to Survive as a Principal* (Chicago: Pluribus Press, 1983), chap. 7; and William C. Carey, *Documenting Teacher Dismissal: A Guide for the Site Administrator* (Salem, Ore.: Options Press, 1981).

7
State Regulation of Educator Evaluation

Laura Means Pope

Evaluation as a form of accountability is an important element in the employment relationship between school boards and professional staff. Many legal issues are involved in the evaluation procedure. During the 1970s statutes on public sector management accountability were added to more than half of the state education codes. This chapter will examine the legal issues involved in state evaluation statutes as interpreted by the judiciary.

The questions below provide the basis for the discussion that follows.

1. What are evaluation statutes? How do they relate to tenure laws, administrative regulations, board policy, and collective bargaining agreements?

2. What is statutory due process, and what are the consequences of failing to provide it?

3. What standards of judicial review apply? What degree of compliance is required? And what remedies do courts employ?

4. Who determines the evaluation criteria? Who should do the evaluating, for what purpose, and how often? And what evaluative instruments or processes are used?

5. When is professional performance or behavior considered remediable? When is a remediation period required? And what length of period is reasonable?

Laura Means Pope is an assistant professor in the Graduate School of Education, University of California, Los Angeles. The author acknowledges the assistance of William De La Torre and Magan Van Alstine in the preparation of this chapter.

6. What pattern and content of evaluations are necessary to substantiate dismissal decisions?

The chapter concludes with recommendations for the administration of evaluations in order to improve teaching and supervision and, if necessary, to substantiate demotion or dismissal decisions.

Evaluation Statutes

Education is a state function authorized by the constitutions in all 50 states. Generally, state constitutions require state legislatures to establish a system of education. In some instances the constitution itself establishes part of that system. For example, in California the office of the superintendent of public instruction is established by the constitution.[1] Except in Hawaii, which is a single school district, all states provide a system of local school districts governed by locally elected or appointed boards of education, sometimes called school committees.

State statutes generally stipulate that certificated personnel have a right to employment after a probationary period, and they specify the reasons for demoting or dismissing persons with continuing contracts and the procedures that must be followed prior to making such decisions.[2] The purpose of such so-called tenure laws is "to assure teachers of experience and ability a continuous service and rehiring based upon merit rather than upon reasons that are political, partisan or capricious."[3]

During the 1970s management concepts stressing evaluation and accountability exerted increasing influence on education legislation. About half the states enacted evaluation statutes to "improve the quality of instructional, administrative, and supervisory services in the public schools,"[4] and to ensure uniformity of evaluation, at least within school districts.[5] This was a time when the deepening economic recession resulted in budget cuts, and declining enrollments led to teacher layoffs. By the mid-1970s and early 1980s, cases involving tenure and evaluation statutes and policies had burgeoned.

State statutes governing evaluation of educators vary widely in terms of form, content, length, and specificity. For example, the Iowa statute, in two sentences, requires boards of education to "establish evaluation criteria and implement evaluation procedures" and to "negotiate in good faith with respect to those procedures."[6] In contrast, the Kansas statute included everything from the legislative purpose to a penalty section.[7] Generally, the legislature requires local school boards to establish the evaluation criteria,[8] but some specify what is to be assessed. Alaska lists "teaching or administrative skills . . . interpersonal relationships with students, parents, peers and supervisors, as well as those additional factors which the school board considers relevant."[9] California includes "the progress of students toward the established standards" and "maintenance of a suitable learning environment."[10]

Frequently, statutes require boards to consult with professional personnel in developing criteria.[11] Sometimes the task of developing criteria is assigned to professionals. Louisiana law requires the state superintendent of education to produce a comprehensive plan for an education accountability program including goals, procedures, and evaluation instruments.[12] Washington also assigns the duty to the state superintendent of schools but provides for legislative review of the initially set minimum criteria.[13]

Statutes regulating evaluation may be an integral part of the tenure laws,[14] or they may be created by separate acts and coded near tenure laws.[15] In some states evaluation is part of the statutory duties of superintendents or principals.[16] State board of education administrative regulations on evaluation may be as binding on local boards as statutes are.[17] Typically, the statutes or regulations specify the minimum frequency of evaluation. Under some statutes or regulations probationary teachers must be evaluated more often than tenured personnel;[18] but in others, such a status distinction is forbidden.[19] Many evaluation statutes apply to all certificated personnel, except in some instances the superintendent,[20] and a number expressly protect employee privacy.[21]

Tenure and Evaluation: An Administrator's Dilemma

Many evaluation statutes were enacted as a result of public pressure to legislate better education; but inevitably, all evaluation statutes and regulations become, in operation, integral to the fair dismissal or tenure laws. Taken together, tenure and evaluation statutes create an administrative dilemma. On the one hand, conscientious administrators who want to help employees improve must demonstrate faith in their ability to do so and must emphasize the positive aspects of their performance as well as identify their weaknesses. On the other hand, to improve the school system may require decisions adverse to the employee; and the administrator must document weaknesses and give express notice that, unless corrected, they may lead to nonrenewal, demotion, or dismissal. This is the administrator's dilemma: to do justice to both the person and the system in the interest of public education.

The Iowa Supreme Court addressed this dilemma recently when it affirmed a trial court's ruling that the evidence presented substantiated a school board's decision to terminate its contract with a tenured elementary principal with 14 years of service. The court's ruling on the case is interesting:

> Probably no inflexible "just cause" definition we could devise would be adequate to measure the myriad of situations which may surface in future

litigation. It is sufficient here to hold that in the context of teacher fault a "just cause" is one which directly or indirectly significantly and adversely affects what must be the ultimate goal of every school system: high quality education for the district's students. It relates to job performance including leadership and role model effectiveness. It must include the concept that a school district is not married to mediocrity but may dismiss personnel who are neither performing high quality work nor improving in performance. On the other hand, "just cause" cannot include reasons which are arbitrary, unfair, or generated out of some petty vendetta.[22]

Restrictions on the Power of School Boards

As prelude to discussing the significance of evaluation in the whole employment process, some consideration of school boards' power to make employment decisions is necessary. Today, boards may employ their relatives, loyal constituents, or lovers to teach, but only if they hold state certification. Boards may choose not to renew a teacher's contract without explanation, but only in the probationary years of service. Boards may fire educators during the term of their contracts, but only for a few very good reasons. Boards may transfer educators without their consent, but not if they agreed otherwise at the bargaining table. School boards have considerable power in employment decisions; but constitutions, statutes, state agency regulations, and negotiated contracts have been used to tame the exercise of that power. All these restraints are products of the belief that something simply is not fair.

School officials often feel hampered by the myriad laws and due process requirements. Superintendents and principals say, "I'm responsible for this operation, but I don't have the authority to do anything about it!" Fairness is at the heart of the matter, but people disagree about what is fair. Yet, if school officials approach all the rules and regulations as simply a consensus on what is deemed "fair," they can develop an approach to administration that is equitable to all and will be so recognized by individuals and institutions alike.

Our society tends to resolve disagreements about what is fair by first determining how the decision should be made and by whom, a resolution known in the law as due process. The U.S. Constitution enshrines this concept in the 14th Amendment: "No State shall . . . deprive any person of life, liberty, or property, without due process of law."[23]

These proscriptions have significant implications for administrators making employment decisions. Chapters 3 and 4 explore both substantive and procedural due process flowing from the U.S. Constitution. Since state constitutions generally contain the same or similar language as the 14th Amendment, this chapter discusses statutory due process, which is broadly defined here to include the procedural rights and correlative duties prescribed by statute and administrative policy or regulation promulgated pursuant to statute.

Before a school board can make any employment decision adverse to the interests of an educator, it must follow the statutory procedures and state administrative regulations. To do otherwise risks reversal of the decision by an administrative agency and/or court.[24] Hundreds of suits challenging public school employment decisions form the case law interpreting statutory due process. School board members, superintendents, and taxpayer groups increasingly bemoan the high cost of such disputes. In three recent fiscal years the California Office of Administrative Hearings charged school districts $582,000 for 91 dismissal hearings in which school boards won 50 of the cases.[25]

In addition to statutory due process or public law restraints on school board discretion, collective bargaining agreements have the force of public law but are binding only to the parties involved. Some agreements prescribe particular procedures concerning evaluation or criteria for reduction-in-force decisions. A school board may not relinquish its duty to make employment decisions,[26] but neither can it act in ways contrary to a negotiated contract.[27] Both state agencies and courts can reinstate, at least temporarily, a dismissed teacher, even if nontenured, but the complainant must show that "the violation substantially and directly impaired his or her ability to improve himself or herself and attain continuing contract status."[28]

The Court's Role in Employment Decisions

At this point, a brief description of how courts view their role in public employment disputes may help the reader understand the outcomes.

Scope of Judicial Review. Courts uniformly reiterate that in the review of the administrative acts of a board of education they will not substitute their judgment for that of the board. One appellant argued before a federal district court that the board had denied him equal protection of the law when its policies and practices allowed teachers with less satisfactory evaluations than his to be appointed as permanent teachers. The court rejected the claim and declared: "The Board could properly refuse to renew plaintiff's contract without regard to the performance evaluation."[29] It further expressed its belief "that federal courts should not sit as 'super-Tenure Review Committees' when a plaintiff employs the 'I'm just as good as you are' argument."[30] The plaintiff lost because school administrators and the board had followed prescribed procedures and the board by law had the authority not to renew the contract, regardless of merit.

Had the school authorities failed to evaluate the plaintiff pursuant to the evaluation statute, quite another balance would be struck, even without tenure involved. An appellate court in a California case, while eschewing interference with the merits of a nonrenewal decision, nonetheless held the board strictly accountable for compliance with the evaluation statute. Failure to meet announced notification deadlines and to provide the teacher with written evaluations prompted the court to grant review of the board's decision as the only means to enforce evaluation statutes in the absence of a statutory right to arbitration or judicial review of a nonrenewal decision.[31]

The West Virginia Supreme Court is typical in its strict construction of both tenure statutes and evaluation regulations in favor of employees. A state board of education policy requires "open and honest evaluation of [every employee's] performance on a regular basis."[32] In an appeal of a board's refusal to renew an elementary teacher's contract and to grant her a continuing contract of employment, the supreme court reinstated the teacher.[33] Both the state superintendent of schools and circuit court had affirmed the board's decision, but the supreme court viewing the events as a whole found that despite regular evaluation, the principal had failed to give the plaintiff evaluations that were "open and honest" enough to apprise her of how she was performing as a teacher. The court ruled that every decision involving competency under the statutes governing employment of teachers must be based on evaluations conducted pursuant to the state board of education policy and that both statute and policy would be strictly construed in favor of the employee. The evaluations met the form required but lacked the substance guaranteed.

If school authorities have followed the statutes and the employee knows about his deficiencies and has had opportunity and help to improve, the court will not substitute its judgment for the board's. One tenured teacher was dismissed for insubordination because, after 16 sessions on daily lesson plans with the principal, he refused to attend additional sessions. He lost his appeal of the dismissal for insubordination.[34] The Arizona appellate court rejected the charge that a scheme of harassment was set up to force him out of the system. Even though the teacher's charge had some substance, the court found that the daily meetings with the principal were a reasonable means of supervision, that holding them during preparation time created no unusual burden, and that the principal had noted improvement during those sessions.

Standards of Compliance. The courts nearly always require strict compliance with statutes governing dismissal of employees. Substantial compliance, on the other hand, has sufficed in at least one jurisdiction, the District of Columbia school system, which is governed by a code enacted by Congress. At the time of the events in question, the code prohibited discharge of any school employee "except upon written recommendation of the superintendent of schools."[35] Based on several communications from the administrator of the district where the appellant worked, the superintendent of schools instructed the director of personnel to dismiss a community aide because of poor performance. The letter of dismissal notified the employee of the reason for the action and his right to a hearing. It also served as the superintendent's recommendation to the board, but was not actually signed by the superintendent. In a reversal of the superior court, the appellate court found no dereliction in duty nor improper delegation of power, because the superintendent had actually made the decision.[36] Compliance with the substance, if not the form, of the code sufficed.

Another federal court accepted substantial compliance as meeting the evaluation statute but required strict compliance with the tenure law. In that case a tenured teacher, dismissed as incompetent, appealed the board's decision and charged lack of due process and racial discrimination. Pursuant to Louisiana law, the board had adopted an evaluation policy providing that if "at any time during the evaluation process the teacher is charged with incompetence or willful neglect of duty, the evaluation procedure as implemented under [the evaluation statute] is superseded by the tenure statute."[37] The court found that the school authorities had substantially complied with the board's policy on evaluation and strictly complied with the tenure law, once the superintendent decided to recommend dismissal for incompetency and willful neglect of duty. The record showed multiple observations, post-observation consultations, specific recommendations for improvement, and warnings about unacceptable performance over a period of nearly two years. The only lack of compliance with board policy was the principal's failure to assist the teacher in establishing her personal goals for 1979-80. In this case both the board and the court viewed the evaluation and dismissal processes as distinctly separate and as calling for a different level of compliance in providing statutory due process. Even so, the substantial evidence that justified dismissal consisted primarily of the record of observations made pursuant to the evaluation statute. The evidence of fair treatment seems to be the key to understanding this case rather than the standard of compliance.

As the foregoing cases illustrate, the right to judicial review, the kind of review, and the standards of review and compliance depend on particular state statutes and case law.

The Significance of Criteria. Evaluation statutes frequently require professional educators to establish the criteria for evaluation or require boards of education to consult with professional staff before establishing them. Legislators, teacher unions, state boards of education, local school boards, superintendents and other administrators, and teaching staff have all contributed to the criteria currently in use. These criteria are crucial in determining the contours and quality of the educational enterprise. If used repeatedly, they serve as a powerful influence in the school system and in the lives of the professionals who strive to match performance to the criteria. They also temper the subjectivity of professional evaluation and ferret out unacceptable bias.

The absence of appropriate criteria on which to base evaluations can undermine the rationale used for employment decisions. For example, a trial court, in a recent suit challenging promotion policies as racially discriminatory in a district undergoing court-ordered desegregation, observed: "[T]he Board has not adopted any such non-racial objective criteria and, until this is done, the Court will never be in a position to adequately consider the propriety of any principal selection made by the Board."[38] The federal appellate court agreed that it was impossible for the defendant board to justify its selections for principal because it had no criteria on which to make its evaluations and decisions. The only objective evidence on record showed the black complainant to be "clearly superior" to the white principals selected for the positions he had sought. The court ordered the board to instate the complainant as a principal and to grant back pay based on the differential between his salary as a teacher and the salary he would have received as a principal.[39]

Compare the results of the above case with another board's decision to terminate the contract of a temporary teacher on the basis of unsatisfactory performance ratings. She successfully challenged the board's first attempt to dismiss her because of its faulty hearing procedure; there was no transcript of the proceeding, and the district presented no evidence. Almost two years later, the board followed mandated hearing procedures and again terminated her contract. This time the decision withstood legal attack, primarily because the main testimony supporting dismissal was based on proper evaluations. Both the superintendent and principal rated her performance a number of times and conferred with her in an effort to improve her performance. At the hearing, several teachers testified on her behalf, but the court held their testimony to be of less weight because they had not made actual classroom observations and "none had a certified qualification to evaluate another teacher."[40] The court upheld the board's action based on the supervisory ratings and on the fact that the plaintiff offered no evidence that the ratings or discharge resulted from "fraud, arbitrariness, or were contrary to law."[41]

Evaluator Qualifications. Judicial emphasis on the qualifications of the evaluator raises an interesting issue. Everybody feels qualified to make judgments about the schools. Whether professionals or the public represented by the board should make decisions concerning employment is a matter of long-standing tension. Statutes and case law embody the compromises. The school board makes the final decision on hiring, firing, assignment, and promotion, but under many laws only on recommendation of the superintendent.[42]

With respect to evaluations, state law may specify that evaluation of teachers is a duty of particular administrators or may simply declare that teachers are to be evaluated. In the latter case, state courts interpret the vague language to mean evaluation by persons trained and qualified to do so. The West Virginia state policy illustrates the point. The West Virginia Supreme Court has repeatedly ruled that if a board fails to follow the evaluation procedures in the state policy, it cannot discharge, demote, or transfer an employee for reasons having to do with prior misconduct or incompetency.[43] A trial court recently interpreted the proscription to mean that only the board could do the evaluating. The supreme court's reversal emphasized that school board members are generally not qualified to supervise the professional work of educators and that the law "clearly contemplates that professionally trained teachers, principals, and superintendents shall have exclusive control of these matters."[44]

Public Pressure in the Process. Political pressure frequently surfaces in dismissal decisions. Board members cannot ignore voters who urge firing someone, and this form of pressure permeates some cases. A classic one is the case of a wrestling coach whose team had a losing season. Soon after the booster club met with the principal, he confided in the coach that it looked as if either the coach, the superintendent, or the principal would have to go. Predictably, it was the teacher-coach who had to fight all the way to the state supreme court to keep his job. The court noted: "There was evidence, too, that [the coach] was simply the latest target of an overzealous booster club."[45]

Another case involved a tenured teacher who urged her fast-track students toward ever greater achievement. Some parents complained about the pace and her methods. All of her evaluations rated her performance "satisfactory," the highest possible rating. Without prior notice or a hearing the board terminated her contract when she refused to sign an individual plan for improvement. The agreement provided that any breach would result in immediate termination of her contract by the superintendent. A federal district court found that at the time she was advised that she could have an impartial hearing, the board had already made its decision, so such a hearing was impossible. The court ruled there was a violation of constitutional due process as well as of the substance of the tenure law. It ordered the board to reinstate the teacher and enjoined it from taking any action of any nature against the teacher based on an anything that led to her removal in the first place.[46]

In another case a tenured teacher, on the basis of two parental complaints, was evaluated by her assistant principal; and the assistant superintendent, who made three classroom observations, gave her notice of eight areas of deficiency and subsequently observed her classroom twice. The board gave her notice of its resolution to terminate her contract, granted a public hearing, and fired her. In the court's view, 17 years of teaching in that district went down the drain in eight weeks. The Minnesota Supreme Court dissected the charges in light of the evidence and ordered the board to reinstate the teacher because of the lack of reasonable time to improve.[47]

One suit specifically raised the issue of what weight can be given to public complaints supported by teachers versus evaluation by a county superintendent. The West Virginia Supreme Court ruled in favor of a principal whose competency was challenged by two citizens. The charge was supported by several teachers. The county superintendent testified on behalf of the principal; but the board, after the hearing, voted to terminate his contract. The state superintendent ordered reinstatement, but the circuit court affirmed the board's action. In its analysis of the evidence, the supreme court emphasized the right to professional evaluation by supervisors. The county superintendent's evaluation outweighed the citizen's complaints. The court also held that under the accountability sections of the state constitution, citizen complaints could result in the dismissal of public employees based on a competent evaluation. The court concluded that "a county board of education may receive complaints against any school employee from citizens and that the board should act upon these complaints, order an evaluation, and discharge an employee if an improvement period proves to be in vain."[48] The process sounds reasonable; nonetheless, unless administrators can withstand political heat in making professional judgments about subordinates' performance, expensive judicial review will be the last resort.

Evaluator Performance. The professional evaluator who is derelict in duty, spiteful, or simply inept risks exposure in a judicial review. Such was the fate of one apparently threatened superintendent who wanted to rid the district of a new, but well-experienced, principal. The superintendent's chatty, ungrammatical, somewhat peevish letter of evaluation asking for resignation upon threat of recommending dismissal is reproduced in its entirety, misspellings and all, in an appellate court decision. However, more important to the outcome of this case was the board's failure to adopt a written policy establishing evaluative criteria for principals. The court noted:

> In the absence of established evaluative criteria, the principal serves at the whim and pleasure of the superintendent. The principal has no guidelines against which to measure his or her performance and may thereby be deprived of a legitimate opportunity for improvement. Without knowledge of the criteria to be employed in a discharge or nonrenewal hearing, the principal is further handicapped in his or her ability to dispute the propriety of the termination decision. This was not the intent of the legislature. Futhermore, established evaluative criteria and prior evaluations are important for purposes of judicial review.[49]

The court ordered reinstatement of the principal. The record is silent on the superintendent's fate.

Administration of Evaluations. How often should supervisors evaluate subordinates? Statutes may set the minimum frequency,[50] board policy may demand greater diligence,[51] and good administrative practice may require even greater effort. One court observed that the state policy required evaluations to be "regular" and reasoned that "to be effective, [evaluations] must be more frequent than annual."[52] Recent case law suggests that effective administrators identify deficiencies through regular evaluations, conduct numerous observations and consultations during a suitable remediation period, and further evaluate the employee at the end of the period to determine whether other action is appropriate.

From a due process perspective, the regularity of evaluations must at least meet statutory or policy standards. The quality and frequency of observations during a remediation period are evidence of good faith administration of evaluation laws. If contract termination is deemed necessary, the board should rely solely on post-remediation period evaluations to support a finding that cause for dismissal or demotion exists.[53]

Remediability. Fairness to both students and educators raises the issue of whether an employee's personal behavior or professional performance, when determined to be unacceptable, is remediable. If not, the board can take immediate action, subject to procedural requirements. If the behavior or performance is remediable, the board must give the employee reasonable time to correct the deficiency and the administration must offer help in the improvement process. What is reasonable will vary, depending on the total circumstances of each case.

Judging behavior to be irremediable risks judicial disagreement. Citing numerous cases, an Illinois appellate court explored several definitions. The court explained that "[w]hether causes for dismissal are remediable is a question of fact and its initial determination lies within the discretion of the board."[54] It continued: "A cause is irremediable when irreparable damage has already been done and cannot be remedied. . . . Causes, remediable when considered alone, will be deemed irremediable where combined with other remediable causes if continued over a long period of time during which the teacher refuses or fails to remedy them."[55] In this case involving a physical education teacher, the court considered the pattern of evaluations, the teacher's attitude, and the long period between the last evaluation in October and the filing of charges in May, and ruled for the teacher with this rationale:

> We believe that the causes charged against plaintiff were remediable in nature because the Board failed to establish either that the plaintiff's causes severely damaged the students, faculty or school or persisted for a suffi-

cient time period so that they could not have been corrected if a warning had been given.[56]

In another Illinois case a board dismissed a black teacher with 25 years of service who failed to improve her classroom organization, teaching techniques, and student discipline within 64 school days after notice of deficiency. Despite multiple observations and suggestions by specialists and supervisors, her attempts to change were ineffective. The court concluded that the teacher's

> [D]eficiencies were fundamental and of long standing, having to do with her own mental discipline and her lack of grasp of her subjects. . . . Moreover, her defensive attitude — founded on her belief that some of the criticism against her was racially motivated — created an atmosphere which definitely worked against remediation since she was thereby led to assign the criticism to outside influences she could not control.[57]

The attitude of the employee toward the supervisor's criticisms and suggestions for remediation are an important factor in judges' opinions about the remediability of deficiencies.[58]

Another school board, prodded by complaints from parents, discharged without warning an elementary teacher with nearly 20 years of experience. The board's decision was based on the teacher's alleged cruelty to students and unlawful corporal punishment, which the board concluded was irremediable. The teacher had used physical force in directing children to their seats or directing them in the hall. The board relied on the precedent of four corporal punishment cases in which irremediable behavior justified peremptory discharge. The court disagreed and ordered reinstatement of the teacher. The court distinguished this teacher's acts from those in the four cases cited by the board in which the charges were, respectively, striking students on the face and head, using a cattle prod to shock students, paddling a student twice in 20 minutes, and striking students with five pieces of balsa wood taped to a curtain rod. The court held that the board failed to "demonstrate the damage to the students, faculty or school was so severe that it could not have been corrected."[59]

Considered as a whole, the cases cited so far suggest that to be fair the length of time a board must give an employee to correct deficiencies varies with the remediability of the behavior, the attitude of the teacher, the damage to students and the school system, the clarity and specificity of charges, timely notice, and what reasonably can be expected of an employee. The attitude and helpfulness of the administration and board also weigh in the determination. The courts may count the number of school days given to the employee for correcting the deficiency, but what happens before, during, and after that period seems to determine whether the time allotted is deemed fair.

Methods of Evaluation. One aspect of evaluation not challenged in these cases is the instrument used. Some states (e.g., West Virginia, Pennsylvania, and Louisiana) require use of particular rating instruments developed at the state level. Other states require local boards to develop an evaluation program. Generally, the professional staff develops the evaluation instrument. Regardless of the instrument used, the courts comment approvingly when supervisory observations are documented by written anecdotal comments and buttressed by additional observations by other competent evaluators.

Judges look at the record as a whole. They look at the pattern of evaluation to determine whether the ratings and conferences warn employees of unacceptable performance and explain what is unacceptable. They take a very dim view of surprises. This is illustrated by the court's reaction to the dismissal of a teacher charged with lack of student control and objectionable body odor. The principal's early evaluations were complimentary but recommended clamping down on talkative students. No criticisms appeared in the second and third evaluations. All these observations occurred in the fall of 1976. In January 1977 the principal compiled a "Teacher Appraisal Instrument" and rated the teacher "plus" on 36 of 37 items. The one minus concerned body odor. Six more observations between October 1977 and February 1978 all praised the teacher. In April 1978 the school board entered a tenure contract with the teacher for 1978-79. A November 1978 rating was all complimentary. The December rating suggested that students sharpen their pencils before class. On 31 January 1979 the principal asked for the teacher's resignation. Predictably, the court reversed the board's termination of the teacher's contract.[60]

In summary, good administration requires establishment of criteria, attentive implementation of evaluation procedures, documentation of observations, and candid communication with employees. Consider the case of a teacher with two good annual evaluations and one critical one, which led to nonrenewal of her contract. Asked why his early evaluations were not critical, the principal testified:

> Well, the first year most beginning teachers have difficulties of some sort or another. They like to be popular and that gets them into trouble real fast and also Mrs. Wilt was pregnant the first year which I think contributed to part of her problem and trying to be a halfway decent, humane person, I did not want to wipe her out totally the first year or second year.[61]

The court's response is a message for all evaluators:

> For an evaluation to properly inform the school employee about his or her job performance, it must be as accurate and truthful as the evaluator can make it. Otherwise a teacher or school employee will not know how his

or her job performance is actually viewed by the administrator and also will not know how he or she can improve.

We find this statement by Greenfield to be disturbing because it indicates that the evaluations of the appellant for the first two years may not have been done openly and honestly, as required by [regulation]. These evaluations and observations are very subjective in nature because the areas intended to be measured cannot be objectively quantified. If these evaluations and observations were simply paperwork cranked out to feed the hungry bureaucrat, then we would not have spent so much time discussing them in this opinion. However, as evidenced by the facts of this case, a person's very livelihood can depend on where the evaluator places his checkmark on the form.

We would hope that in future cases, administrators, supervisors and principals will fully realize the importance of observations and evaluations and understand the significance of [the regulation] in this regard.[62]

Recommendations

The message of the evaluation statutes and case law is simple: Within the framework of the law, set standards, develop a regular process, and be fair. Practicing the last principle is hard because we all look at a decision from different perspectives. Being fundamentally fair, however, can take much of the sting out of adverse, but sometimes necessary, decisions.

More specifically, the lessons of the case law reviewed in this chapter can be condensed into the following guidelines:

1. Establish specific written criteria for the selection and evaluation of certificated personnel.
2. Use trained supervisory personnel to conduct evaluations.
3. Evaluate all certificated personnel regularly. To be effective, "regular" must be more often than annual.
4. If a particular instrument is prescribed by law, regulation, or policy, be careful that making the requisite judgments is not perfunctory. Supplement the instrument with anecdotal information.
5. Discuss openly and candidly with the person being evaluated all aspects of the evaluation and make specific recommendations for improvement as needed.
6. If the deficiencies in the educator's performance are so serious that failure to change could lead to demotion, nonrenewal of contract, or dismissal, give the person a written explanation to that effect, counsel him or her, and set a reasonable timetable for future observations and a reasonable deadline for correcting the deficiency. What is reasonable varies with the danger to students and staff, how long the behavior has been tolerated, how difficult change will be, and the employee's attitude.

7. Rely primarily on evaluations made after the period of remediation to determine whether demotion, reassignment, nonrenewal of contract, or dismissal is appropriate.
8. Listen to complaints from parents, but rely on the opinions of qualified evaluators if there is disagreement.
9. Observe all the relevant procedural and substantive requirements set forth in statutes, regulations, board policies, and collective bargaining agreements when making an employment decision that is adverse to the employee.
10. Move with deliberate speed and without surprises to balance consideration for the employee, the welfare of the students, and the progress of the educational system.

Footnotes

1. Cal. Const. art. 9 § 2. The constitution establishes the system.
2. Arval Morris, *The Constitution and American Education* (2nd ed.) (Racine, Wisc.: West Publishing Co., 1980), p. 620.
3. Board of Educ. of School Dist. No. 131 v. Illinois State Bd. of Educ., 403 N.E.2d 277, 279 (Ill. 1980).
4. Fla. Stat. Ann. § 231.29 (West 1982). For a list and discussion of such state statutes, *see* Joseph Beckham, *Legal Aspects of Teacher Evaluation* (Topeka, Kans.: National Organization on Legal Problems of Education, 1981), apps. B, C.
5. Cal. Educ. Code § 44660 (West 1978).
6. Iowa Code Ann. § 279.14 (West Supp. 1982).
7. Kan. Stat. Ann. §§ 72-9001 — 9006 (1976). The 1982 amendment, *inter alia*, repealed the legislative intent section, *id.*, §§ 72-9002 — 9006 (1982).
8. *See, e.g.*, Ariz. Rev. Stat. Ann. § 15-537(B) (West 1982); Cal. Educ. Code § 44660 (West 1978); Okla. Stat. Ann. tit. 70, § 6-102.1 (West 1982).
9. Alaska Admin. Code tit. 4, § 19.020 (1975).
10. Cal. Educ. Code § 44662 (West 1978).
11. *See, e.g.*, Cal. Educ. Code § 44661 (West 1978) (advice of district's certificated personnel); Fla. Stat. Ann. § 231.29 (West Supp. 1983) (Florida Council on Educational Management); Nev. Rev. Stat. § 391.3125 (1979) (elected representatives of teacher personnel).
12. La. Rev. Stat. Ann. § 391.3 (West 1982).
13. Wash. Rev. Code Ann. § 28A.67.065 (West 1982).
14. *See, e.g.*, Conn. Gen. Stat. § 10-151b (West Supp. 1983).
15. *See, e.g.*, Okla. Stat. Ann. tit. 70, 6-102.2 (West 1982).
16. *See, e.g.*, W. Va. Ann. Code § 18A-2-9 (Supp. 1983).
17. *See, e.g.*, Trimboli v. Board of Educ. of Wayne Cty., 280 S.E.2d 686 (W. Va. 1981). The board failed to follow the administrative regulations of the state board of education so the state supreme court ordered reinstatement of a transferred employee.
18. *See, e.g.*, Ariz. Rev. Stat. Ann § 15-537(D) (West 1982); Kan. Stat. Ann. § 72-9003(d) (1982).

19. *See, e.g.*, 4 Alaska Admin. Code § 19.030 (1975).

20. *See, e.g.*, Conn. Gen. Stat. § 10-151b(a) (West Supp. 1983).

21. *See, e.g.*, 4 Alaska Admin. Code § 19.040 (1975): "Unless mutually agreed otherwise by both the person evaluated and the school board (or its designee), no portion of an evaluation may be made public, except as evidence in a proceeding relative to an evaluated person's certification or employment, or as otherwise allowed or required by a court of law."

22. Briggs v. Board of Dir. of Hinton Commun. School Dist., 282 N.W.2d 740, 743 (Iowa 1979).

23. U.S. Const. amend. XIV, § 1.

24. *See, e.g.*, Wilt v. Flanigan, 294 S.E.2d 189 (W.Va. 1982) (no "open and honest" evaluation as required by administrative regulation); Cantrell v. Vickers, 495 F. Supp. 195 (N.D. Miss. 1980) (hearing not "impartial" because board decision previously made); Orth v. Phoenix High School System No. 210, 613 P.2d 311 (Ariz. App. 1980) (written "reminder" not sufficient preliminary notice of inadequacy).

25. *Cal-Tax Research Bulletin* (November 1981): 3, 4.

26. *See, e.g.*, Wesclin Educ. Ass'n v. Board of Educ., 331 N.E.2d 335 (Ill. App. 1975).

27. *See, e.g.*, Fries v. Wessington School Dist. No. 2-4, 307 N.W.2d 875 (S.D. 1981).

28. *Id.* at 879.

29. Derrickson v. Board of Educ. of the City of St. Louis, 537 F. Supp. 338, 342-43 (E.D. Mo. 1982).

30. *Id.* at 343.

31. *See, e.g.*, Anderson v. San Mateo Commun. College Dist., 151 Cal. Rptr. 111 (Cal. App. 1978).

32. W. Va. Board of Educ. Policy No. 5300(6)(a).

33. Wilt v. Flanigan, 294 S.E.2d 189 (W. Va. 1982).

34. Siglin v. Kayenta Unified School Dist., 655 P.2d 353 (Ariz. App. 1982).

35. D.C. Code § 31-102 (1973), repealed 25 D.C. Reg. 6055 (1978).

36. District of Columbia v. White, 435 A.2d 1055 (D.C. 1981).

37. Jones v. Jefferson Parish School Bd., 533 F. Supp. 816 (E.D. La. 1982).

38. Lee v. Conecuh Cty. Bd. of Educ., 634 F.2d 959, 963 (5th Cir. 1981).

39. *Id.* at 964.

40. Kudasik v. Board of Dir., Port Allegheny School Dist., 455 A.2d 261, 263 (Pa. Commw. 1983).

41. *Id.* at 264.

42. *See, e.g.*, Fla. Stat. Ann. tit. 15, § 231.36(3)(a)3 (West Supp. 1983); Mass. Ann. Laws ch. 71, § 42 (Michie/Law. Coop. 1978); N.Y. Educ. art. 61 § 3012 (Consol. 1979).

43. Trimboli v. Board of Educ. of Cty. of Wayne, 254 S.E.2d 561 (W. Va. 1979).

44. Trimboli v. Board of Educ. of Wayne Cty., 280 S.E.2d 686, 688 (W.Va. 1981), quoting Rogers v. Board of Educ., 25 S.E.2d 537, 542 (W. Va. 1943).

45. Munger v. Jesup Commun. School Dist., 325 N.W.2d 377, 380 (Iowa 1982).

46. Cantrell v. Vickers, 495 F. Supp. 195 (N.D. Miss. 1980).

47. Ganyo v. Independent School Dist. No. 832, 311 N.W.2d 497 (Minn. 1981).

48. Mason City Bd. of Educ., 274 S.E.2d 435, 439 (W.Va. 1981.)

49. Hyde v. Wellpinit School Dist. No. 49, 611 P.2d 1388, 1391 (Wash. App. 1980).

50. *See, e.g.*, Fla. Stat. Ann. § 231.29(a) (West 1982) (each employee at least once a year).

51. Childers v. Independent School Dist. No. 1 of Bryan Cty., 645 P.2d 992, 995 (Okla. 1982) (statute required evaluation of tenured personnel every three years; board policy required evaluation of all teachers twice a year).

52. Lipan v. Board of Educ., 295 S.E.2d 44, 45 (W.Va. 1982).

53. Board of Educ. of School Dist. No. 131 v. Illinois State Bd. of Educ., 403 N.E.2d 277, 281 (Ill. 1980).

54. Morris v. Board of Educ. of the City of Chicago, 421 N.E.2d 387, 392 (Ill. App. 1981).

55. *Id.*

56. *Id.* at 393.

57. Community Unit School Dist. No. 60 v. Maclin, 435 N.E.2d 845, 851 (Ill. App. 1982).

58. *See* discussions of the evidence in Munger v. Jesup Commun. School Dist., 325 N.W.2d 377 (Iowa 1982); Siglin v. Kayenta Unified School Dist., 655 P.2d 353 (Ariz. App. 1982); and Board of Dir. of the Sioux City Commun. School Dist. v. Mroz, 295 N.W.2d 447, 449 (Iowa 1980).

59. Board of Educ. of School Dist. No. 131 v. Illinois State Bd. of Educ., 445 N.E.2d 832, 837 (Ill. App. 1983); *accord*, Williams v. Colorado Springs School Dist., 641 F.2d 835 (10th Cir. 1981).

60. Hollingsworth v. Board of Educ. of School Dist. of Alliance, 303 N.W.2d 506 (Neb. 1981).

61. Wilt v. Flanigan, 294 S.E.2d 189, 194 n.5 (W.Va. 1982).

62. *Id.*

63. *Id.*

8

Good Cause Basis for Dismissal of Education Employees

W. Lance Landauer, John H. Spangler,
and Benjamin F. Van Horn, Jr.

All states have some statutory provisions regarding teacher dismissals, but few cite exactly the same causes. The reasons specified for dismissal vary from the very specific to the very general, with a great deal of ambiguity and overlap among the causes. The most frequently cited causes for teacher dismissal are immorality, incompetence, and insubordination. The discussion in this chapter concerning these three causes encompasses the general judicial principles found in teacher dismissal cases.

Immorality

School boards in 38 states are statutorily authorized to dismiss a teacher on a direct charge of immorality and/or moral turpitude. No other single charge is as widespread in dismissal statutes. In the remaining 12 states statutory grounds of good or just cause, unfitness to teach, or unprofessional conduct may be used to dismiss a teacher for immoral conduct. While legislatures have chosen to cite immorality as a cause for dismissal, they have been reluctant to define the term or to discuss its ap-

---

W. Lance Landauer is the principal of New Oxford Junior High School in New Oxford, Pennsylvania.

John H. Spangler is an assistant principal at New Oxford Junior High School.

Benjamin F. Van Horn, Jr. is the superintendent of the Fannett-Metal School District in Willow Hill, Pennsylvania.

plication to specific conduct. Consequently, the definition of immorality and application to specific conduct have been left to the judicial system. As a 1952 Pennsylvania decision pointed out: "Exact definitions of such abstract terms [as immorality] are obviously quite impossible."[1] Because of the imprecise nature of the term, school boards, when contemplating dismissal of personnel on such charges, need to be aware of what the courts have said about conduct considered to be immoral.

A survey of relevant cases reveals that actions that form the basis for dismissals based on immorality generally fall into one or more of the following discrete categories of conduct:

1. Heterosexual misconduct with students
2. Heterosexual misconduct with nonstudents
3. Homosexuality
4. Nonsexual misconduct with students
5. Physical abuse of students
6. Classroom discussion or use of materials that are sexual in nature
7. Use of profanity
8. Misconduct involving drugs
9. Misconduct involving alcohol
10. Other criminal misconduct
11. Misappropriation of funds
12. Cheating
13. Lying

While the categories of conduct which the courts have construed as immoral cover a broad range of behavior, certain guidelines can be identified that the courts will generally apply to cases involving a dismissal for immorality.

Sexual Misconduct with Students. Sexual misconduct with students may not be engaged in by teachers, and such misconduct justifies removal of the teacher from the classroom. No other category of conduct used as a basis for immorality dismissals has generated such unanimous disapproval in court decisions as sexual misconduct by a teacher with students. A Washington court observed in 1973 that "[i]t is difficult to conceive of circumstances which would more clearly justify the action of the Board than the sexual misconduct of a teacher with a minor student in the district."[2] A 1982 decision in the same state held that sexual misconduct with students "is inherently harmful to the student-teacher relationship."[3]

The dismissal of a Colorado teacher was upheld where it was found that he engaged in mutual tickling of the genitals, sexually suggestive dialogue, and other sexually related horseplay with female students on a field trip. The court responded to the teacher's argument that the activities were good-natured and a positive influence by stating that "[i]t is difficult to conceive of a single positive aspect that such behavior might have in an educational context."[4]

A 62-year-old history teacher with 18 years of satisfactory service in the Texas schools was dismissed because of an improper sexual relationship with one of his students. Concerning his immediate removal from the classroom and his dismissal, the Fifth Circuit Court of Appeals said, "a male eighth-grade teacher charged with sexual misconduct with his teenage female students should not be in contact with them in the teaching process."[5]

The fact that a student's parents are aware of, or even encourage, the relationship between their child and a teacher may not be enough to mitigate a finding of immorality. A Washington junior high school counselor met a high school girl through social contacts with her parents. With the parents' approval the two began to date. The girl became pregnant and the school administration learned that the counselor was the father of the child. The teacher was questioned and admitted the truth of the allegations. Shortly thereafter the couple was married but the counselor was dismissed, nevertheless. The counselor appealed the dismissal but the court upheld the action of the school board, reasoning as follows:

> While the argument that "immorality" *per se* is not a ground for discharge without a showing of adverse effect upon "fitness to teach" or upon the school has merit, we decline to set such a requirement where the sexual misconduct complained of directly involved a teacher and a minor student. In our view, the School Board may properly conclude in such a situation that the conduct is inherently harmful to the teacher-student relationship, and thus to the school district."[6]

Sexual Misconduct with Nonstudents. Private, discreet sexual conduct is viewed in terms of its adverse effect on the school and on the teacher's ability to perform the teaching function. A divorced Nebraska teacher was dismissed because she had, at various times, allowed single men, single women, or couples to stay at her apartment overnight. In overturning the dismissal, a federal court ruled that for the board "to justify a dampening of the rights of assembly or association and privacy the state . . . must show that the termination . . . was caused by conduct which 'materially and substantially' interfered with the school's work."[7]

A South Dakota school board that sought to dismiss a teacher for cohabitation presented as evidence a petition condemning the teacher's action, as well as evidence of adverse student reaction and general controversy within the school and community because of the teacher's living arrangements. The court upheld the dismissal, ruling that "it would seem reasonable for the School Board to conclude that controversy between the plaintiff and the parents and the community members of this locale would make it difficult for the teacher to maintain the proper educational setting in her classroom."[8]

In 1969 the California Supreme Court ruled that a one-week, private homosexual relationship was not sufficient reason to revoke a teacher's certificate. The court reasoned that the definition of a term such as immorality or moral turpitude is so broad that the term must be related "to the issue of whether, on the job, the employee had disqualified himself."[9] The court provided a check list of factors that may be used in determining the adverse effect on a teacher's fitness:

> In determining whether the teacher's conduct thus indicated unfitness to teach the board may consider such matters as the likelihood that the conduct may have adversely affected students or fellow teachers, the degree of such adversity anticipated, the proximity or remoteness in time of the conduct, the type of teaching certificate held by the party involved, the extenuating or aggravating circumstances, if any, surrounding the conduct, the praiseworthiness or blameworthiness of the motives resulting in the conduct, the likelihood of the recurrence of the questioned conduct, and the extent to which disciplinary action may inflict an adverse or chilling impact upon the constitutional rights of the teacher involved or other teachers.[10]

A board's ability to prove an adverse effect on the teacher's ability to function, using the factors outlined by the court, is of extreme importance in dismissals focusing on private conduct. The courts have repeatedly stressed that even though a teacher occupies a special position and "as a consequence of that elevated status, a teacher's actions are subject to much greater scrutiny than that given to the activities of the average person,"[11] the basis for dismissal must rest on a teacher's ability to perform the teaching function. As one Ohio court stated: "The private conduct of a man, who is also a teacher, is a proper concern to those who employ him only to the extent that it mars him as a teacher, who is also a man."[12]

Teacher Profanity in the Classroom. Speech that is profane, sexual, or vulgar and cannot be shown to have a valid educational purpose is not constitutionally protected and may serve as a basis for dismissal. Generally, a teacher enjoys a measure of freedom in classroom instruction. However, when a teacher chooses to discuss topics of a sexual nature not related specifically to the course of study, the conduct may be questioned.[13] For example, when a Florida band teacher discussed virginity, premarital sex, and various sexual activities with his coed classes, the school board dismissed him and the court upheld the dismissal. In an opinion quite critical of a federal judicial trend toward permissiveness, the court stated that it was "still of the opinion that instructors in our schools should not be permitted to so risquely discuss sex problems in our teenage mixed classes."[14]

A Pennsylvania teacher's dismissal was upheld when it was proven that he called one of his students a slut and had implied to the class that the student was a prostitute. The court ruled that his language failed to foster and elevate the ideals and attitudes a teacher should develop in his students and that his conduct evidenced a moral failure in his own character.[15]

A California teacher who told his class that the school bell system "sounded like a worn-out phonograph in a whorehouse" and that the color of his classroom walls looked like someone had "peed on them and then smeared them with baby crap" was judged by the courts as being so vulgar that his fitness to teach was impaired.[16] The court ruled that the teacher's vulgarity had reached the point where the effect on his fitness and ability to teach was sufficient to warrant his dismissal. On the other hand, the courts have generally ruled that when a teacher's use of sexual references or profanity does not "transcend his legitimate professional purpose,"[17] the speech will be considered constitutionally protected and a dismissal based on this conduct will be overturned.

Privacy Rights as a Defense. The constitutional right to privacy cannot be claimed as a defense against dismissal if the conduct was of a public, bizarre, or flagrant nature. When the private conduct of a teacher becomes public knowlege or when the claim of privacy is applied to conduct that, in fact, is not private, the courts generally have held that the conduct is not protected from school board scrutiny by a right to privacy. For example, a Massachusetts teacher who took a mannequin to a spot on his front lawn under a street lamp and proceeded to undress it, caress it in a lewd fashion, and place it between his legs, claimed the board's dismissal violated his right to privacy. A federal court upheld the dismissal, ruling that "the right to privacy . . . may be surrendered by public display. The right to be left alone in the home extends only to the home and not to conduct displayed under the street lamp on the front lawn."[18]

An Oregon teacher claimed that his dismissal, which was based on publicized homosexual acts at an adult bookstore, violated his right to privacy. The court stressed that he "was not dismissed because of his sexual preference, but rather because of the manner and place in which he exercised that preference with the resultant notoriety surrounding his activities."[19]

A federal court in Illinois found unconvincing a teacher's argument that his right to privacy included publication in a swinger's magazine of a photograph showing him and a female companion nude from the waist up. The court ruled that the public nature of such a photograph made it constitutionally permissible for the board to inquire into the moral character of the teacher.[20]

A 1973 New York decision ruled that it was an error to assume that there is an absolute right to privacy. The court went on to provide instances where a teacher's right to privacy might be limited:

> In our view what otherwise might be considered private conduct beyond the licit concern of school officials ceases to be such in at least either of two circumstances — if the conduct directly affects the performance of the professional responsibility of the teacher, or if, without contribution on the part of school officials, the conduct has become the subject of such public notoriety as to significantly or reasonably impair the capability of the particular teacher to discharge the responsibilities of his position.[21]

While immorality is the most frequently cited legislative cause for dismissal, its application and definition have generally been left to the courts. A major consideration for the judiciary is proof of a nexus between conduct and fitness to teach. Where this nexus is demonstrated by the board, the dismissal action has a greater chance of being sustained in the courts even when constitutional challenges to the dismissal are claimed.

Incompetence

A review of appellate court decisions rendered over the past 30 years reveals that the courts have permitted school boards to use a broad interpretation of incompetence. The conditions or behaviors that have successfully been applied to incompetence fall into four general categories: inadequate teaching, poor discipline, physical or mental disability, and counterproductive personality traits.

Since the courts have permitted a broad interpretation of incompetence, the critical factor in a successful dismissal is the evidence produced to substantiate the charges. The following evidentiary guidelines should be applied when considering the dismissal of a tenured professional employee on the grounds of incompetence.

1. A comparative standard of performance is applied by school boards where incompetence is alleged.

A teacher must be measured against a standard used for other teachers in a similar position, not against some hypothetical standard of perfection. A Nebraska school board decided to dismiss a physical education teacher who received good ratings in all areas except discipline and organization. In ruling for the teacher's reinstatement the Nebraska Supreme Court provided the following rationale: Incompetence is not measured in a vacuum, against a standard of perfection; it must be measured against the performance of others in a similar position.

Although the teacher's conduct may have been minimal, it was not incompetent, and there was no evidence that the teacher's conduct was below the standard of performance required of others. Finally, there was no expert testimony providing sufficient evidence of incompetence.[22]

A similar rationale was applied in the reinstatement of a Tennessee kindergarten teacher. The newly assigned elementary principal, formerly an assistant junior high school principal, recommended that the teacher be dismissed due to her lack of classroom control. The principal had no prior exposure to kindergarten classrooms or training in this area. A state supervisor testified that, although more classroom structure was needed, the teacher was providing an adequate readiness program and was using acceptable teaching techniques. The Tennessee Supreme Court reinstated the teacher because of the lack of any persuasive testimony that the teacher's performance was ineffective or below the standards of efficiency maintained by other kindergarten teachers.[23]

2. There should be substantial evidence to justify incompetence.

To determine whether there is substantial evidence, the courts have often applied the "reasonable man" test. This test poses the question: Would a reasonable man have reached the same decision upon examination of the record as a whole?

The record as a whole, rather than any single incident, should be used to establish substantial evidence. A discharged elementary principal argued that the 67 instances cited by the school board as the basis for its dismissal decision were no more than petty daily errors. However, the record as a whole provided substantial evidence to support the school board's decision, and it was the Minnesota Supreme Court's opinion that the dozens of errors attributed to the principal indicated that his problems exceeded those of petty daily errors.[24]

Even testimony leading to inconsistent conclusions does not prevent a school board's dismissal decision from being supported if there is substantial evidence. An elementary principal was dismissed for deficiencies in teacher supervision, student discipline, decision making, and long-range planning. These problems were documented by two totally negative evaluations made by the superintendent. However, 34 teachers and many parents signed a letter of support, and a former superintendent wrote a letter attesting to the principal's leadership skills. Nevertheless, the Iowa Supreme Court found sufficient evidence on the record to support the findings of the school board.[25]

3. School boards and administrators should document a pattern of incompetent behavior. (See Chapter 6.)

Most successful dismissals for incompetence are based on a pattern of behavior rather than a single critical incident. An Illinois teacher was dismissed for deficiencies in planning, lesson presentation, and classroom discipline. The appellate court clarified that the momentary lapses in discipline or a single day's lesson gone awry is insufficient reason for a teacher's dismissal. However, if a pattern of unacceptable behavior is established, a dismissal will be upheld.[26]

A Washington teacher was dismissed for unacceptable disciplinary practices. On one occasion the teacher kicked the leg of a student's chair causing the student to fall backward and strike his head on a table. The teacher's past record revealed other instances of improper discipline, and he had been notified of the consequences for repeated violations of district regulations. In upholding the teacher's dismissal, the court of appeals stated "sufficient cause for discharge may be evaluated in light of the teacher's record as a whole, which may be said to demonstrate a continuing pattern of unacceptable teaching practices."[27]

4. School boards should ascertain whether the behavior in question is irremediable before terminating employment.

Under some state statutes, school boards must first decide if a charge is remediable or irremediable before making a dismissal decision. If a school board considers the charges remediable, then the teacher is entitled to a notice of the charges and a period of time to correct the unacceptable conduct. If the charges are considered irremediable, then dismissal proceedings can be initiated without the preliminary notice of charges and a remediation period. However, the determination of irremediability is subject to judicial review. Irremediable charges are those that could not have been corrected even if a warning had been issued or charges that have had a damaging effect on students, faculty, or school.[28]

The dismissal decision of a New Mexico school board was overturned because it failed to show that the teacher's behavior was not correctable. The teacher on several occasions had violated the district's disciplinary policy, for example, hitting one student with a drumstick and kicking another student. However, the administrators failed to follow the conference procedure required by state statutes. In reinstating the teacher the court of appeals stated, "Although the situation was serious, the question remains: was it correctable? There is neither evidence nor finding that it was not, and no evidence that any effort was made at any conference to correct the teacher's unsatisfactory work performance."[29]

An Illinois teacher was reinstated when the court disagreed with the school board's decision that the dismissal causes were irremediable. This physical education teacher had poor classroom discipline, presented disorganized lessons, and ridiculed awkward students. Since there was no evidence of irreparable damage to students, the court found the school board in error for not providing notice and an opportunity for remediation.[30]

5. *In jurisdictions that require an effort at remediation, school boards must be sure that a reasonable period for remediation has been provided.*

A teacher of mentally handicapped students was dismissed for lack of instructional planning, lack of positive learning activities, and lack of cooperation with colleagues. A period of 15 school days lapsed between the notice to remedy and the last formal evaluation. An Illinois appellate court did not consider this a reasonable period for assessing improvement and stated further that an evaluation should have been made at the end of an agreed upon remediation period.[31]

In another case a high school English teacher was given notice to remedy her classroom discipline, communication skills, and record-keeping. After a lapse of five school weeks she received a formal evaluation and was dismissed. Statements from students, teachers, and the principal indicated that she was making an effort to improve. The Minnesota Supreme Court found this remediation period unreasonable and reinstated the teacher.[32]

An Illinois elementary teacher was dismissed because of poor discipline and ineffective instruction. Over a remediation period of eight school weeks several administrators and supervisors observed the teacher and provided assistance. The teacher exhibited a defensive attitude toward suggestions for improvement and no progress was noticed in her performance. In this case the court found the remediation period reasonable and upheld her dismissal.[33]

6. *School boards should seek to establish that an employee's conduct had an adverse effect on the efficient operation of the school.*

Historically, the courts have studied the administrative record to determine if there were sufficient facts to support the alleged inadequacies of the teacher and limited their review to the teacher's condition or conduct. However, during the past decade the courts have frequently asked school boards to support their charges of incompetence by also showing an adverse effect on the students, the teaching process, and the school in general.

A kindergarten teacher was dismissed for reasons related to her teaching philosophy, classroom discipline, and uncompromising attitude. However, the teacher was able to show that the achievement level of her students was equal to that of their peers. The Michigan Court of Appeals overturned the dismissal and tenure revocation decision of the school board and the state tenure commission with the following reasoning:

> Because the essential function of a teacher is the imparting of knowledge and of learning ability, the focus of this evidence must be the effect of the questioned activity on the teacher's students. Secondarily, the tenure revocation proceeding must determine how the teacher's activity affects other teachers and the school staff.[34]

A mathematics teacher in Tennessee was dismissed for publicly expressing her hatred for blacks. She openly stated her feelings to the elementary school principal and his assistant, both of whom were black. As a result of her racial biases, she would often turn her head and look away when the principal attempted to speak to her. When assigned a black aide the teacher rejected her and failed to give her work to do. The court emphasized that the school board's interests in maintaining an efficient school system outweighed the teacher's First Amendment interest of free speech. The teacher's dismissal was upheld because her remarks and behavior had a detrimental effect on the school and community.[35]

The dismissal of a Minnesota teacher was overturned because an adverse effect on the students could not be established. This third-grade teacher was suspended immediately for allegedly holding pins under the outstretched arms of a student until he admitted to throwing a crayon. Several factors contributed to the teacher's reinstatement. First, the school board had not considered the remediability of the teacher's conduct. This teacher had taught for 23 years with an unblemished record, and there was no written discipline policy in the school district. Second, there was no evidence of actual physical or psychological harm. No children in the class, including the disciplined student, expressed a fear of returning to her class nor did they report the incident to their parents.[36]

The process of dismissing incompetent teachers is considerably more complicated than the application of a technical or legal definition. Nevertheless, school boards and administrators should not misinterpret the role of the judiciary as an obstacle to the dismissal process. The courts have been careful not to intrude upon the discretionary powers of school boards to determine a teacher's incompetence, and they have accepted a broad interpretation of this ground for dismissal. However, courts have required that a school board's findings be supported by substantial evidence and be in conformance with the employee's statutory and constitutional rights.

Insubordination

Insubordination is listed as a separate cause for the dismissal of teachers in the statutes of 21 states. Violation of school law and policy or good or just cause are often substituted for a charge of insubordination or in a dismissal action when insubordination is not specifically listed as a cause for teacher dismissal in a state's school laws. Violation of school law or policy is listed as a separate cause for dismissal in 17 states. Good or just cause is specified in 28 states. Insubordination does not necessarily have to be cited as a part of state statute in order for courts to uphold a dismissal action for insubordination.

Regardless of statutory provisions, insubordination is a judicially acceptable cause for the dismissal of a teacher in all states. The U.S. Supreme Court affirmed the action of the Pennsylvania Supreme Court regarding the dismissal of a teacher who refused to answer his superintendent's questions regarding his loyalty. The Pennsylvania court supported the dismissal on the basis of incompetency. It reasoned that the teacher's lack of frankness and candor and insubordination made him incompetent. The U.S. Supreme Court indicated that "the Pennsylvania statute, unlike those of many other States, contains no catch-all phrase, such as conduct unbecoming a teacher, to cover disqualifying conduct not included within the more specific provisions. Consequently, the Pennsylvania courts have given incompetency a broad interpretation."[37] Judicially defined insubordination can be classified as follows: absence from duty, refusal to follow established procedures for classroom or nonclassroom activities, improper use of corporal punishment, improper grooming, refusal to sign loyalty oaths and to participate in loyalty-related activities, improper union activity, and criticism of authority.

Persistence of the Violation. Generally, school boards are required to demonstrate the presence of a persistent willful violation of a reasonable rule or order emanating from a proper authority in order to receive judicial affirmation for the dismissal of a tenured teacher. The Wyoming Supreme Court affirmed the dismissal for insubordination of a teacher who refused to accept a teaching assignment made by the principal. An industrial arts teacher was directed to teach a first-period welding class in one school and to teach the remainder of his schedule in another school located in the same district. Transportation was provided by the district and the teacher was certified to teach welding. The teacher was informed by the principal of his probable schedule several weeks prior to the start of school with the final schedule being confirmed at the beginning of the school term. The teacher reported to the first-period class as directed for the first four days of school. Thereafter, he repeatedly refused to report to class claiming that he was not properly prepared to teach welding, that materials were inadequate, and that he was not directed by the board or superintendent to teach welding. The court ruled the action to be insubordination by applying the following rationale:

1. Persistence: The action of the teacher was persistent in that he verbally refused the assignment and, in fact, failed to report for class as directed.
2. Willful: There was no misunderstanding or negligence; the teacher intended not to obey a direction that he fully understood.
3. Reasonable rule or order: Other teachers traveled between buildings, the teacher was certified in the subject, transportation

164

was provided, and the time for travel was sufficient. There was nothing unreasonable about the direction.

4. Proper authority: The board and superintendent properly delegated the authority of class assignments to the principal.[38]

"Persistence" is often difficult to define. One view of persistence focuses on the intention of the teacher. For example, teachers may be dismissed for violation of rules regarding their attendance at school. The Maine Supreme Court affirmed the dismissal for insubordination of a teacher who absented herself from school despite the denial of her leave request. The teacher had made several requests and had announced her intention to disregard the board's denial of her leave request. She had no record of similar transgressions. The court reasoned that although there was no persistence of action, there was a persistence of intent. She intended to disobey and, despite opportunity to correct her action, she followed through with her insubordinate act.[39]

The Connecticut Supreme Court defined persistence differently. The court ordered the reinstatement of a teacher who had absented herself from duty despite the denial of her leave request. In this case the teacher twice requested leaves of absence, and on both occasions the requests were denied. The Connecticut court ruled that a persistence of action had to be demonstrated in order to sustain a dismissal for insubordination. Since the act appeared in isolation, it was reasoned not to be sufficient to demonstrate persistence.[40]

Willful Violation. Insubordinate acts must be willful in order to sustain dismissal actions. Unless a rule or directive prohibiting an action is clearly and properly communicated in an understandable form or is readily apparent in administrative-employee relationships, a dismissal action for insubordination is not possible. In general, if teachers are unaware of the presence of a rule or directive prohibiting certain kinds of behavior, courts will not judge them as being willfully insubordinate.

An Alabama appeals court upheld a school board's dismissal of a tenured guidance counselor for insubordination upon a review of evidence that established that the counselor refused to meet his assigned duty as a supervisor of children prior to the beginning of the school day. The supervision assignment was rotated among employees, but the counselor contended that counselors should be exempt from the duty. A formal reprimand was issued, which prompted the counselor to file a grievance. The grievance was sustained on procedural grounds, but the court, in considering the counselor's conduct, reached a decision that there was sufficient evidence of a willful refusal to obey a reasonable order to justify dismissal.[41]

Reasonable Orders from Acceptable Authorities. Statute law, regulation, policy, and practice often designate specific officials and administrative bodies to make rules governing certain kinds of actions. For an action to be considered as insubordinate, the rule governing the action must come from an acceptable authority. Further, rules and orders must be reasonable both in design and application. If a teacher is able to demonstrate that a rule or order was capricious, arbitrary, or violative of constitutional rights, then courts may reverse the school board's dismissal decision.[42]

Teachers can be compelled to follow reasonable directives in the operation of their classes. Rules or directives pertaining to corporal punishment and general classroom operation must be followed. In a corporal punishment case, the North Dakota Supreme Court ruled that written guidelines and administrative admonitions were sufficient to justify dismissal of a teacher who repeatedly used corporal punishment with his students. Written guidelines specified that corporal punishment is allowed only with the permission and under the supervision of the principal. On five occasions the teacher had slapped students' faces and pulled their hair despite being directed by the principal to discontinue such actions.[43]

When considering a dismissal action for insubordination a school district must be sure that it is based on a legitimate school concern. In order to limit a teacher's use of a specific teaching method or kind of material, a school district must demonstrate the likelihood of a substantial or material interference with the operation of the school before grounds for insubordination can be established. Factors related to such a concern would include the age of the students,[44] the relationship of course material or teaching method to the subject of study, the kinds of materials or methods available in the general school curriculum and library,[45] expert opinion about the material or method, and the degree of interference or disruption the material or method may engender relative to the orderly operation of the school.[46]

Substantial Evidence. School boards must demonstrate the existence of "substantial evidence" to support the dismissal of a teacher for insubordination. In demonstrating substantial evidence, courts apply the reasonable man test. If reasonable persons could agree that the evidence supported the charge of insubordination, the courts will accept the existence of substantial evidence to confirm charges of insubordination. Therefore, it is essential that dismissal for insubordination be based on verifiable fact and documentary evidence.[47]

Nonclassroom Directives. Teachers can be required to follow nonclassroom directives that can be shown to bear a rational relationship to the functions of the school. Violations of valid regulations governing medical and psychological examinations, residency requirements, and requirements to confer privately with administrators have all resulted in judicial affirmation of the dismissal of teachers. School boards are compelled to follow prescribed regulatory and statutory procedures affecting nonclassroom directives. For example, many states accept the right of a school board to enact regulations requiring teachers to reside in their district of employment. However, the New Hampshire Supreme Court declared an ordinance requiring district residency to be a violation of a teacher's fundamental constitutional rights.[49]

The Mississippi Supreme Court ruled that a teacher's refusal to sign an attachment to a regular employment contract was sufficient to demonstrate insubordination. The attachment contained a statement, approved by the school board, indicating that the teacher agreed to follow the provisions of a newly enacted board policy manual. The provisions were explained at a teachers' meeting and all teachers, except the plaintiff, signed the attachment. The superintendent asked her to sign the attachment on several occasions. She refused. He finally wrote to her instructing her to sign the attachment or he would recommend her dismissal for insubordination. She still refused, and she was dismissed. The court affirmed the dismissal, reasoning that the teacher's persistent insubordinate refusal to sign the contract attachment was sufficient to warrant dismissal. The court rejected the teacher's contention that the dismissal action was arbitrary, capricious, and an abuse of the school board's discretion.[49]

Uncooperative Behavior. Uncooperative behavior can serve as a cause for the dismissal of a teacher on grounds of insubordination. A charge of uncooperative behavior is usually characterized by a series of insubordinate acts, which may be combined with some other category of offense. The offenses may or may not be related to one another. Although a specific statutory cause for dismissal must be listed, a pattern of uncooperative behavior should be established. A single offense may not be sufficient to warrant dismissal action. A pattern of inappropriate actions on the part of a teacher carries more weight in judicial actions than single charges of uncooperative behavior.

A Massachusetts appellate court affirmed the dismissal of a teacher for incapacity, conduct unbecoming a teacher, and insubordination. The evidence presented showed that the teacher entered other teachers' classrooms on occasions, demanding materials and disrupting the normal operation of those classes; pushed a student in the presence of other students and confronted him with legal difficulties he was having outside of school; entered a classroom without the permission of the teacher and searched for teaching materials; and exhibited verbally abusive behavior toward the principal, a teacher aide, and the librarian. The court stated that the misdeeds taken in isolation were not very significant; however, when viewed in combination over a 12-month period, they were sufficient to warrant discharge. The court concluded that the teacher's inability to cooperate and get along with her colleagues as evidenced by the series of incidents was sufficient to warrant dismissal.[50]

Constitutional Protections. A teacher may not be dismissed for insubordination if the motivating reason for the dismissal was the exercise of behavior that is constitutionally protected. The teacher has the initial burden of proving that the challenged behavior was constitutionally protected. Once demonstrated, a school board must either demonstrate a compelling reason for the limitation of the protected behavior or demonstrate that, even in the absence of the protected behavior, other specified charges would have resulted in the teacher's dismissal.[51]

The United States Supreme Court has established a standard for a compelling reason to limit constitutionally protected behavior. A school board must demonstrate an actual disruption of the operation of the school to limit constitutionally protected behavior. Teachers may engage in unpopular constitutionally protected behavior without being dismissed from public employment.[52] If a teacher engages in constitutionally protected behavior that is part of the cause for his or her dismissal, the dismissal can still be affirmed if the school board is able to demonstrate, by the preponderance of evidence, that the teacher would have been dismissed even in the absence of the protected behavior.[53]

Insubordination is a frequently cited cause for the dismissal of teachers. Insubordinate behavior can lead to the dismissal of a teacher in all jurisdictions whether or not it is specifically listed in the statutes governing teacher dismissal. However, care must be taken to thoroughly document all charges. A documented series of inappropriate acts demonstrating a pattern of uncooperative behavior provides the strongest case for dismissal for insubordination. Further, all insubordination dismissal actions must provide evidence of a persistent, willful refusal to obey a reasonable rule or order emanating from a proper authority.

Footnotes

1. Albert Appeal, 92 A.2d 663, 664 (Pa. 1952).
2. Denton v. South Kitsap School Dist. No. 402, 516 P.2d 60, 65 (Wash. App. 1973).
3. Pryse v. Yakima School Dist. No. 7, 632 P.2d 60, 65 (Wash. App. 1982).
4. Weissman v. Board of Educ. of Jefferson Cty. School Dist. No. R-1, 547 P.2d 1267, 1274 (Colo. 1976).
5. Moore v. Knowles, 482 F.2d 1069, 1073 (5th Cir. 1973).
6. Denton v. South Kitsap School Dist. No. 402, 516 P.2d 1080, 1082 (Wash. App. 1973).
7. Fisher v. Snyder, 346 F. Supp. 396, 401 (D. Neb. 1973).
8. Sullivan v. Meade Cty. Indep. School Dist. No. 101, 387 F. Supp. 1237, 1247 (D. S.D. 1975).

9. Morrison v. State Bd. of Educ., 461 P.2d 375, 382 (Cal. 1969).

10. Id. at 386.

11. Chicago Bd. of Educ. v. Payne, 430 N.E.2d 310, 315 (Ill. App. 1982).

12. Jarvella v. Willoughby-Eastlake City School Dist. Bd. of Educ., 233 N.E.2d 143, 146 (Ohio C.P. 1967).

13. Penn-Delco School Dist. v. Urso, 382 A.2d 162, 167-68 (Pa. Commw. 1978).

14. Pyle v. Washington Cty. School Bd., 238 So. 2d 121, 123 (Fla. App. 1970).

15. Bovino v. Board of School Dir. of Indiana Area School Dist., 377 A.2d 1284, 1288 (Pa. Commw. 1977).

16. Palo Verde Unified School Dist. v. Hensey, 88 Cal. Rptr. 570, 572 (Cal. App. 1970).

17. Mailloux v. Kiley, 323 F. Supp. 1387, 1391 (D. Mass. 1971), aff'd, 448 F.2d 1242 (1st Cir. 1971).

18. Wishart v. McDonald, 500 F.2d 1110, 1113-14 (1st Cir. 1974).

19. Ross v. Springfield School Dist. No. 19, 641 P.2d 600, 608 (Ore. App. 1982).

20. Weissbaum v. Hannon, 439 F. Supp. 873, 879 (E.D. Ill. 1977).

21. Jerry v. Board of Educ., 324 N.E.2d 106, 111 (N.Y. 1974).

22. Sanders v. Board of Educ. of the South Sioux City Comm. School Dist. No. 11, 263 N.W.2d 461 (Neb. 1978).

23. Williams v. Pittard, 604 S.W.2d 845 (Tenn. 1980).

24. Lucan v. Board of Educ. and Indep. School Dist. No. 99, 277 S.W.2d 524 (Minn. 1979).

25. Briggs v. Board of Dir. of the Hinton Commun. School Dist., 282 N.W.2d 740, 743 (Iowa 1979).

26. Board of Educ. of Minooka Commun. Consol. School Dist. No. 201 v. In-geles, 403 N.E.2d 277 (Ill. App. 1980).

27. Sargent v. Selah School Dist. No. 119, 599 P.2d at 29 (Wash. App. 1979).

28. See, e.g., Gilliland v. Board of Educ. of Pleasant View Consol. School Dist. No. 622, 365 N.E.2d 322 (1977).

29. Morgan v. New Mexico State Bd. of Educ., 488 P.2d 1210, 1213 (N.M. App. 1971).

30. Morris v. Board of Educ. of the City of Chicago, 421 N.E.2d 387 (Ill. App. 1981).

31. Board of Educ. of School Dist. No. 131 v. Illinois State Bd. of Educ., 435 N.E.2d 845 (Ill. App. 1982).

32. Ganyo v. Independent School Dist. No. 832, 311 N.W.2d 497 (Minn. 1981).

33. Community Unit School Dist. No. 60 v. Maclin, 435 N.E.2d 845 (Ill. App. 1982).

34. Beebee v. Haslett Pub. Schools, 239 N.W.2d 724, 728 (Mich. App. 1976), rev'd on other grounds, 278 N.W.2d 36 (Mich. 1979).

35. Anderson v. Evans, 660 F.2d 153 (6th Cir. 1981).

36. Kroll v. Independent School Dist. No. 593, 304 N.W.2d 338 (Minn. 1981).

37. Beilan v. Board of Educ., School Dist. of Philadelphia, 357 U.S. 399, 406 (1958).

38. Board of Trustees of School Dist. No. 4 v. Colwell, 611 P.2d 427, 434 (Wyo. 1980).

39. Fernald v. City of Ellsworth School Comm., 342 A.2d 704 (Me. 1975).
40. Tucker v. Board of Educ. of the Town of Norfolk, 418 A.2d 933 (Conn. 1979).
41. Jones v. Alabama Tenure Comm., 408 So. 2d 145 (Ala. Civ. App. 1981).
42. Brown v. Portsmouth School Dist., 451 F.2d 1106 (1st Cir. 1971).
43. Lithun v. Grand Forks Pub. School Dist. No. 1, 307 N.W.2d 545 (N.D. 1981).
44. *See, e.g.*, Parducci v. Rutland, 316 F. Supp. 352 (N.D. Ala. 1970).
45. *See, e.g.*, Burns v. Rovaldi, 477 F. Supp. 270 (D. Conn. 1979).
46. *See, e.g.*, Nigosian v. Weiss, 343 F. Supp. 757 (S.D. Mich. 1971).
47. *See, e.g.*, Briggs v. Board of Dir. of the Hinton Commun. School Dist., 282 N.W.2d 740 (Iowa 1979).
48. Donnelly v. City of Manchester, 274 A.2d 789 (N.H. 1971).
49. Sims v. Board of Trustees, 414 So. 2d 431 (Miss. 1982).
50. Springgate v. School Comm. of Mattapoisett, 415 N.E.2d 888 (Mass. App. 1981).
51. *See* Chapter 3.
52. Tinker v. Des Moines Indep. Commun. School Dist., 393 U.S. 274 (1977).
53. Mount Healthy City School Dist. Bd. of Educ. v. Doyle, 429 U.S. 274 (1977).

9

The Law on Reduction In Force: An Overview and Update

Perry A. Zirkel

A 1980 monograph provides a detailed analysis of legislation and litigation relating to reduction in force (RIF).[1] This chapter will provide an overview of the prior material covered in the monograph and a focus on cases decided since 1980.

A glance at the literature reveals that the widespread problem of and local response to RIF have remained matters of substantial concern.[2] The incidence of reported court cases further reflects the expanding interest in this area. A reading of these court decisions also reveals that state statutes continue to be the primary source of the law concerning RIF. Thus they are an appropriate starting point for this chapter. Other sources of law, such as constitutional protections and collective bargaining agreements, will be included in the summary of the relevant case law.

The primary focus of the chapter will be on the loss of positions by public school teachers for nonpersonal reasons (in contrast to such personal reasons as incompetency, immorality, or insubordination).[3] Related actions, such as the demotion of administrators based on budgetary cutbacks, will be included only as they relate to the primary focus.

Overview of RIF Statutes

Although seldom labeled expressly as "reduction-in-force" requirements, such provisions are often found in tenure laws or other

Perry A. Zirkel is University Professor of education and former dean at the School of Education, Lehigh University.

teacher employment statutes. The scope and specificity of these provisions vary considerably. A primary distinction exists between those statutes that permanently say "adiós" through terms like dismissal, nonrenewal, or termination, and those that, more hopefully, say "hasta la vista" through terms like suspension, layoff, leave, or furlough. Statutes in the dismissal-type category include those of Alabama, Colorado, Connecticut, Delaware, Kansas, Maine, Massachusetts, Nevada, and Virginia. Less numerous are statutes in the suspension-type category, such as those in Kentucky, Minnesota, Pennsylvania, and Rhode Island, which typically have provisions for recall or restoration.

Table 1 (pages 174-175) shows the variations in the RIF statutory pattern across the 50 states. For a more complete interpretation, readers are urged to examine the specific wording of their respective state statutes in consultation with an appropriate attorney.

A large majority of states (42) have some form of statutory RIF provisions, and some of these statutory reasons for RIF overlap. The most common statutory reason for RIF is decline in enrollment (22). Other reasons are fiscal or budgetary constraints (7); reorganization or consolidation of school districts (10); change in the number of teaching positions (8); curtailment or alteration of program or services (6); discretion of the school board (9); and the catchall category of "good or just" cause (16).

The order of release is statutorily specified in 18 states. Six states specify that nontenured employees must be released before their tenured colleagues within their area(s) of qualification. Ten states have statutes that require that RIF be accomplished within the same area(s) of qualification in inverse order of seniority. No state statutorily specifies merit as the sole, overriding criterion for determining who will be released; therefore, most statutes leave the matter of merit up to local policy or bargained agreement and to the common law of the courts. The six states in the "other" column have legislated special provisions for order of release. For example, California's statute formerly called for a lottery method in situations where two persons had the same seniority, but this method was replaced recently with an amendment that stipulates the determination be based on "the needs of the district and students." Rhode Island's statute provides a limited exception to seniority for teachers needed in technical subjects. Florida's statute lists several merit-type criteria such as efficiency and capacity to meet the educational needs of the community as among the criteria to be used, but otherwise leaves the order of release to local school board discretion. Louisiana's statute specifically states that seniority is not relevant. Oregon's legislation does not specify an order for release but has a seniority-plus-merit formula for the transfer of employees in RIF situations. Missouri provides for merit as the criterion for retention among tenured teachers.

Sixteen of the "hasta la vista" statutes establish the order for recalling suspended teachers, should vacancies arise for which they are qualified. Eight states have mandated that suspended teachers be given first consideration for subsequent vacancies in their area(s) of qualification. However, 11 states are more strict, specifying inverse seniority as the determining factor for recall to such vacancies. Michigan and Minnesota provide that suspended teachers be reinstated for the first vacancy for which they are qualified. Missouri accords tenured teachers who were laid off priority for recall over nontenured teachers.

These various legislative patterns take on specific meaning in terms of what they do and do not state when subject to litigation. Below are summarized court decisions, with an emphasis on cases decided since 1980, in the areas of reasons for RIF, order of release, and order of recall, plus one other major area — due process procedures. Within each of these four areas, other nonstatutory contexts, such as relevant constitutional provisions and local collective bargaining agreements, will also be discussed.

Statutory Reasons for RIF

Enrollment Decline. In a Pennsylvania case that tested that state's requirement of a "substantial enrollment decline" as a reason for RIF, an intermediate appellate court ruled that a five-year reduction in school district population from 3,443 to 3,064 (10%) was sufficient to meet the statutory standard.[4] Although not cited by this court, previously recorded decisions on this issue provided a range of enrollment declines, which the facts of this case fit.[5] Thus the judicial deference typical to this area was consistent, although not extended, with this decision.

California's RIF statute is complex. A decline in average daily attendance is one of two permissible reasons under the statute. The second — reduction or discontinuance of particular kinds of services — is discussed in a subsequent section.[6] Previous cases have held that positively assured attrition must be considered when calculating the number of certified employees who can be laid off due to a decline in average daily attendance.[7] In a recent California case the intermediate appellate court held that certified employees laid off because of the second statutory reason does not affect the number of such employees who can be laid off based on the attendance-decline reason.[8]

Fiscal or Budgetary Basis. Although there have not been any new decisions in this area, two relatively recent cases decided prior to 1980 illustrate two important lessons. In a Pennsylvania case, the intermediate appellate court reversed the trial court decision that had sustained the

Table 1. OVERVIEW OF STATE STATUTORY PROVISIONS FOR RIF

	Proper Reasons							Order of Release			Order of Restoration		
	Enrollment	Fiscal	Reorganization	Elim. of Position	Curric. Change	Board Discretion	Other	Nontenured First	Inverse Seniority	Other	Preference List	Inverse Seniority	Other
Alabama	X					X							
Alaska	X												
Arizona		X										X	
Arkansas	X						X					X	
California				X	X		X	X	X				
Colorado				X			X	X		X			
Connecticut							X						
Delaware	X		X										
Florida	X				X	X	X			X			
Georgia	X				X								
Hawaii						X	X	X			X	X	
Idaho						X		X			X		
Illinois						X							
Indiana													
Iowa							X						
Kansas													
Kentucky			X			X			X			X	
Louisiana				X						X			
Maine													
Maryland	X						X						
Massachusetts							X						X
Michigan	X		X*				X						X
Minnesota	X	X		X					X		X	X*	

174

State													
Mississippi													X
Missouri	X	X	X		X		X		X		X	X	
Montana													
Nebraska	X		X	X			X						
Nevada	X	X	X	X			X		X			X	
New Hampshire													
New Jersey	X	X	X	X			X		X		X	X	X
New York	X X	X X	X X	X X			X X		X†		X X	X X	X
North Carolina	X	X	X			X	X				X	X	
North Dakota	X		X		X			X		X			
Ohio	X	X	X				X				X	X	X
Oklahoma													X
Oregon	X	X	X	X X		X X	X X	X	X	X		X X	
Pennsylvania	X						X		X	X			
Rhode Island	X												
South Carolina													
South Dakota													
Tennessee	X			X	X		X		X		X		
Texas	X	X	X			X							
Utah	X	X	X										
Vermont													
Virginia							X						
Washington							X						
West Virginia	X		X	X		X			X†		X	X	
Wisconsin	X X											X X†	
Wyoming							X						
District of Columbia	(X)		(X)			(X)	(X)	(X)	(X)				
TOTALS	22	7	10	8	6	9	16	6	10	6	8	11	3

*Only in non-first-class city districts

†Only in Milwaukee

suspension of a business education teacher based on the school board's purported managerial right to release employees for reasons of economy. Pointing out that the governing statute specified three reasons for RIF, which do not include fiscal grounds, the court reinstated the teacher with back pay, commenting:

> We can fully appreciate the unwillingness of the hearing court to reach a result in this case where a teacher whose . . . services are no longer needed, and who will have no scholars to teach must be paid his salary indefinitely. However, according to the decided cases, the legislature has so commanded.[9]

The judgment was affirmed by an equally divided Pennsylvania Supreme Court.[10] The lesson from this case is that if the state statute expressly enumerates proper reasons, they should be strictly followed.

Where fiscal grounds are specified in the statute and followed, the question becomes a matter of proof, i.e., whether the actual circumstances meet the statutory standard for fiscal justification. For example, Missouri statutes specify "insufficient funds" as a reason for RIF. In interpreting this language, a Missouri appellate court held that a local board had satisfied this standard when it placed 10 nontenured teachers on leave because of an "erosion of expected sources of revenue."[11] Thus, as in the college and university sector where RIF is commonly termed "fiscal exigency," courts tend to give local authorities the benefit of the doubt.[12]

Reorganization or Consolidation of School Districts. When a new district is created by the consolidation of former school districts, the question arises as to whether tenured teachers carry their permanent status into the new district. Even where statutes attempt to provide the answer, courts have split in interpreting cases where ambiguity exists. For example, the New Mexico Supreme Court interpreted an earlier version of its present statute in such a way that the consolidated district was considered a continuation of the constituent districts, thus requiring the preservation of tenure rights.[13] In contrast, the Maine Supreme Court held that where a new regional school district was created by special legislation rather than the general laws of the state, teachers in the constituent area schools had no tenure rights with respect to the new school district.[14]

Where reorganization rather than consolidation is the reason for RIF, teachers may seek refuge in a strict interpretation of the statute. Such an approach was successful in a recent case, where an equally divided Pennsylvania Supreme Court upheld the reinstatement of two full-time and two part-time teachers suspended in a discretionary district reorganization. The reorganization was found not to qualify as a curricular alteration or required reorganization as specified in Pennsylvania's statute.[15]

Reduction in the Number of Teaching Positions. Elimination of position as a rationale for RIF inevitably leaves ambiguity in statutes that specify it as a basis. Inasmuch as elimination of a position could result from a variety of reasons, the scope of board discretion becomes the critical question. For example, in a recent case in Maine a local school board voted to limit its budget for the academic year to a two-mill increase, which resulted in the elimination of two teaching positions. In rejecting the suit of a tenured teacher whose position had been eliminated, the state's highest court ruled that:

> In reserving to the school board the right to terminate a contract when changes in local conditions warrant the elimination of the teaching position for which the contract was made, [Maine's statute] imposes on the board only an implied duty to exercise that reserved power in good faith for the best interests of education in the district.[16]

The Connecticut Supreme Court similarly sustained a local board's discretion in demoting a reading supervisor and refusing to hear her arguments as to the educational value of her position.[17] The result in other jurisdictions may differ from this posture, depending on such factors as the specific legislative language and history and the particular factual circumstances.

Other cases based on the elimination of position often involve administrators and specialists who allege that their positions have been merely disguised rather than dissolved. Although results again vary across statutory jurisdictions, in general, courts tend to accept the board's purported abolition of a position where the duties were largely redistributed to existing personnel; but they have looked with disfavor when the duties are allocated in the form of one or more functionally equivalent new administrative positions.[18] Similarly, courts have tended to look with disfavor on the elimination of teachers' positions when new teachers are hired for suspiciously similar positions.[19]

Curricular Changes. California continues to take the lead in this specific area of litigation. Its statute provides as reason for RIF the "reduction or discontinuance of particular kinds of services." In one recent case a California appeals court refused to interpret this phrase as permitting a school district to terminate a group of school nurses by transferring some of their particular services (e.g., health instruction) to other employees.[20] The court indicated that RIF could be justified by a difference in the method of providing such services or in the services themselves, but that merely a change in the persons providing these services was not sufficient to constitute such a difference. In a more recent case the appellate court did interpret the provision more broadly, allowing for its applicability to a curricular offering that could not be eliminated but could be reduced to a minimum level according to state requirements.[21]

Pennsylvania is another of the relatively few states providing a curriculum curtailment reason for RIF. In a long-litigated case two teachers filed a grievance challenging their suspension under a collective bargaining agreement that incorporated the RIF legislation. The school district contended that the matter was not arbitrable, but the Pennsylvania Supreme Court ultimately ordered the district to submit the issue to arbitration.[22] After the arbitrator upheld the suspension, the local teachers association challenged his decision because the suspensions were not prompted by a substantial decrease in enrollment. The state's intermediate appellate court upheld the arbitrator, based on his finding that the suspensions were in conformity with the specific requirements of the curriculum curtailment provision of the RIF statute.[23]

Other Good or Just Cause. Although board discretion as a reason for RIF has not been reported in recent court decisions, the other catchall provision in many state statutes, "other good or just cause," has been the basis for continuing litigation. Courts have tended to interpret such umbrella phrases broadly. For example, the Massachusetts Court of Appeals held that a school committee possessed the power under the statute's "good cause" provision to abolish a physical education teacher's position on fiscal grounds.[24] Similarly, Iowa's courts have interpeted the statutory term "just cause" to encompass not only personal faults as grounds for dismissal but also RIF reasons, such as budgetary needs.[25]

Nonstatutory Reasons for RIF

Collective Agreements. Local collective bargaining agreements sometimes specify reasons for RIF.[26] For example, a collective bargaining agreement for a school district in Michigan permitted a reduction in staff in the event of a reduction in financial resources. However, according to the state intermediate court of appeals, the phrase "reduction in financial resources" in this context did not apply to a reduction in the projected surplus of the district but rather applied when there was a shortfall in revenue.[27] In another case the collective agreement required the local board to negotiate procedures in the event of RIF, but it did not specify the justifying reasons. Looking to the statutory backdrop, the court concluded that RIF provisions in the contract referred to the decrease in teachers due to circumstances such as declining enrollments, not voluntary retirements or resignations. Inasmuch as the latter circumstances were at issue in this case, negotiations were not required.[28]

Bad Faith/Pretext. Whether the permissible bases of RIF stem from statutes, collective bargaining agreements, or other sources, courts have made clear that "we could not countenance a subterfuge by which an unscrupulous school board would use a fictitious necessity for discharging a teacher."[29] Proving pretext is not an easy matter. Courts tend not to probe aggressively for underlying impermissible motives if there seems to be sufficient evidence supporting the stated permissible reasons. For instance, in response to the plaintiff-teacher's claim that the real reason for his nonrenewal was the personal antagonism of the board members toward him rather than declining enrollment and diminishing funds, the Supreme Court of North Dakota stated:

> [Our precedent] requires only that the reasons for nonrenewal be sufficient to justify the contemplated action. That there may be other additional reasons for nonrenewal is immaterial.[30]

Similarly, an Iowa appellate court found preponderant evidence of justifiable reasons, reversing the trial court's finding of subterfuge.[31] Further, a federal district judge overturned a jury verdict in favor of a kindergarten teacher who claimed that she would not have been released except for the fact that she had filed a grievance against the superintendent. In strong language, the judge accused the jury of "twisted logic" and the plaintiff of "point[ing] to a phantom constitutional 'pea' under a hastily shifted shell," and concluded: "Perversions of the Constitution, like violations of the Constitution, should not be tolerated."[32] However, when faced with an RIF case (called "excessing" in New York City) involving a school district business administrator, who was also in the middle of protracted proceedings to terminate him for alleged incompetency and improper conduct, New York's intermediate appellate court found that there was no showing of a budgetary need for eliminating his position and that the proceeding against him instead stemmed from a personal dispute with the superintendent. Thus the court awarded him back pay and reinstatement and reminded the school authorities that "[e]xcessing may not be used as a device to resolve disciplinary problems."[33]

Some other courts have also found RIF to be a pretext for a violation of constitutional rights, statutory protections, or collective bargaining rights. Thus a federal appeals court upheld the reinstatement of a teacher found to be released in retaliation for her exercise of First Amendment rights.[34] A Michigan state appellate court upheld the reinstatement of a teacher found to be released based on his leadership of the local bargaining unit.[35] Statutory rights also extend to federal antidiscrimination legislation, as exemplified by recent decisions finding the Title VII claims of reassigned female plaintiffs sufficient to at least go to the jury.[36]

Order of Release

Once a bona fide reason for RIF is established, the next decision is the proper order of RIF. As stated earlier, some statutes clearly provide the order of RIF in terms of tenure, seniority, or other criteria. For example, 10 states by statute give teachers "bumping" rights over their less senior colleagues within the same area of qualification. The interpretation of these criteria has caused a spate of litigation.

Tenure Status. In cases involving the order of RIF between tenured and nontenured teachers where the statute is silent or ambiguous, the overwhelming majority of courts have accorded tenured teachers a priority.[37] However, the Maine Supreme Court recently ruled that the state statute, which is silent on this matter, does not implicitly require that probationary teachers be terminated before tenured teachers.[38]

Where local districts attempt to fill the statutory void by board policy or collective agreements, exceptions to the overall trend favoring tenured teachers must be clearly specified and applied. For example, a school board in South Dakota established a policy giving priority to continuing contract teachers over those not on continuing contract, with an exception for staff members needed to maintain an existing program. When a teacher with 11 years of service was released and a teacher not on continuing contract was assigned to part of the math program that the released teacher had instructed, the state supreme court held that the school board failed to support the exception with sufficient evidence.[39]

Inverse Seniority.[40] Where statutes are ambiguous on the order of RIF, courts have tended to favor a seniority standard within or across the tenured and nontenured categories.[41] Unlike the trend favoring tenured over nontenured teachers, courts have not markedly moved to read inverse seniority into statutes that are silent on the matter.[42] Further, courts have refused to carry over the seniority standard of RIF statutes to cases of demotion and transfer.[43]

A California appellate court departed from a strict seniority standard in its interpretation of a statutory provision that prohibits termination of senior employees "while any probationary employee, or any employee with less seniority, is retained to render a *service which said permanent employee is certificated and competent to render* [emphasis added]." The court construed this statutory language to authorize not only the bumping of junior employees by senior employees possessing the same skills, but also the retention of junior employees and administrators if they possessed a "special credential or needed skill."[44] In other cases administrators were similarly protected from the application of the seniority standard in California's complex RIF statute, based on a confidential relationship or special credential.[45] However, a California court recently rejected a local board's extension of "skipping rights" to junior teachers who were competent in Spanish but were not employed in a bilingual program, reasoning that such language needs applied to the statute's tie-breaking standard rather than to its "certificated and competent" language.[46]

Other Criteria. In 1979 Pennsylvania amended its statute to eliminate the merit portion of a seniority-plus-merit formula that had been used as the basis for determining the order of teacher layoffs. Under the old formula, seniority was quantitatively combined with merit when there was a substantial difference in teacher efficiency ratings, but seniority was used alone when there was no substantial difference in ratings. A case that after several years recently reached the Pennsylvania Supreme Court illustrates some of the difficulties of applying the old statutory standard. In this case the court held that two teachers were improperly released, because an eight-point difference in unweighted efficiency ratings was not found to be a substantial basis for suspending one of the plaintiff-teachers and because the efficiency rating for the other plaintiff-teacher was neither supported by anecdotal records nor based directly on classroom observations.[47] Further, a lower appeals court in Pennsylvania interpreted the old statutory provision as authorizing the use of seniority as the sole criterion where there was no substantial difference between prior performance evaluations and none was completed for the current year.[48]

As stated earlier, some state statutes still retain at least a limited role for merit. Oregon's statute requires the board, prior to RIF, to "make every effort" to transfer teachers, based on merit and seniority, to other positions for which they qualify. Under this statute, the state's intermediate appellate court held that the board failed to meet its burden when it "retained a teacher with factual but not legal qualifications while dismissing a permanent teacher with legal qualifications."[49] The plaintiff-teacher had certification in industrial arts but his experience in this area was limited to teaching woodworking and drafting courses, which were experiencing declining enrollments. The retained teacher, who had less seniority than the plaintiff, had college training and teaching experience in mechanical industrial arts courses, which were fully enrolled, but he had certification only in social studies. Thus seniority prevailed where merit was perhaps factual, but not legal.

In an Iowa case both merit and seniority were used in an RIF provision in a collective bargaining agreement. Under this provision the least qualified teacher was to be released first, but in the event of relatively equal qualifications, the teacher with least seniority in the affected area was to be released. The appellate court upheld the board's discretion in defining qualifications objectively by according points to years of experience and training, thus allowing seniority a partial role in the merit step, as well as the exclusive role in the second step, of the contractual sequence.[50]

Some authorities advocate that in the absence of statutory or contractual limitations, the school board should adopt an RIF policy that utilizes other factors than strict seniority to determine who will be released.[51] Illustrative of such an approach is a school board in Nebraska that adopted a list of several criteria in priority order for determining

RIF. The board's list included contribution to the district's extracurricular program and accorded it a higher priority than seniority. The state supreme court upheld the board's discretion to use contribution to the activity program as an RIF criterion in the absence of statutory or contractual restrictions.[52]

Scope of Bumping. Determining who will be released depends on not only the criteria for retention but also the scope of their application. Bumping rights are typically limited to the area(s) in which the affected teacher is qualified. In addition to legal qualification, another issue is whether and to what extent boards have a duty to realign their staff to effectuate bumping rights. A final issue is the relationship of RIF requirements to affirmative action mandates.

Courts have varied considerably in the interpretation they have accorded to the term "qualified" as it relates to RIF. They are generally agreed that certification is necessary, but some courts have not regarded it as sufficient. Thus, as the aforementioned Oregon case illustrates, factual and legal qualifications are not necessarily synonymous.[53]

Some courts have taken a restrictive view of legal qualification, limiting it solely to certification. For example, the Iowa Supreme Court interpreted the phrase "skill, ability, competence and qualifications" in a collective bargaining agreement RIF clause as distinguishing "qualifications" from the preceding terms, "skill, ability, competence," and thus limiting it to state certification. Inasmuch as the two released teachers in this case were certified to teach junior high as well as elementary school, the board was held to violate the collective bargaining contract by comparing them only to teachers in grades K-6 rather than those in K-8.[54] Similarly, the Minnesota Supreme Court interpreted "other positions . . . for which [the teacher] is qualified" in the RIF statute as intending bumping cross-departmentally where said teacher has more than one license, thus equating qualification with certification.[55]

The scope of the qualified comparison group becomes more complex with the introduction of the concept of "tenure area" in New York's seniority-based RIF statute. Some courts have used distinctions such as vertical (special) versus horizontal (academic) tenure areas to restrict the scope of bumping,[56] whereas other courts have been more expansive in interpreting New York's complex statutory scheme.[57]

In other contexts, some courts have gone beyond certification areas to require a higher standard for legal qualification. In a Pennsylvania case the intermediate appellate court upheld the additional consideration of maintaining a balance between male and female physical education teachers.[58] Similarly, courts in Illinois and Iowa have upheld the consideration of academic training as an element of legal qualification based on state education department regulations and collective bargaining agreement language, respectively.[59]

A related issue impinging on the scope of bumping rights is whether and to what extent a school board has a duty to realign staff to retain teachers on the basis of seniority as required by statute or bargaining agreement. Pennsylvania is a leading jurisdiction for development of this issue, starting with a 1956 decision by the state supreme court wherein this duty was established,[60] and extending through a recent amendment to the RIF statute, which requires the school district to "realign its professional staff so as to insure that more senior employees are provided with the opportunity to fill positions for which they are certified and which are being filled by less senior employees."[61] Intervening lower court decisions have generally interpreted the supreme court's *Welsko* decision restrictively. For example, in upholding the board's rejection of various realignment plans submitted by senior teachers who were slated for RIF, the intermediate appellate court stated: "*Welsko* does not require the board to realign teachers where such realignment is impractical, and we may not substitute our judgment for that of the School Board in this respect."[62] In another case the court allowed considerations of factual qualifications to determine whether realignment was practical. The court upheld the board's rejection of the two plans proferred by the plaintiff based on the fact that under both of them the plaintiff would be bumping another teacher into a position for which the other teacher was certified but had little or no recent experience.[63] In a case decided after the enactment of the aforementioned amendment, the court rejected an unrestricted reading of the new statutory provision, incorporating instead the limitations of the preceding case law. Thus emphasizing the impracticality of realignment across multiple certifications, the court concluded that "its effect on the educational process within the school district must be considered."[64]

Oregon's statute explicitly places a similar duty on boards facing RIF, stating that "[s]chool districts shall make every effort to transfer teachers of courses scheduled for discontinuance to other positions for which they are qualified."[65] An Oregon appeals court interpreted this statute as requiring only a reasonable effort, not extending to creating a vacancy by reshuffling, which the teacher could only fill after upgrading his qualifications, and also not extending to transferring him to a classified position that did not require teaching.[66]

Courts in Illinois have also faced the realignment issue, but without the benefit of statutory language explicitly establishing such a duty. In the absence of such language, the intermediate courts have found a limited realignment duty applicable to boards in RIF situations. In two recent cases Illinois appellate courts rejected realignment to preserve the positions of tenured plaintiffs where they were not strictly qualified under Illinois certification regulations for the reassignments that they proposed.[67] In a third case another judicial district of the same appellate level found failure to carry out realignment to be "palpably arbitrary and capricious" since "[t]he simple transposition of one class in English for one class in journalism [for which there was no special certification] would have had the effect of enabling each of the then existing faculty members to maintain a full class load without the necessity of dismissing [any of them]."[68]

Courts in other jurisdictions have varied in their resolution of this issue; although in the absence of applicable statutory or local contract language, they have not read in a substantial realignment duty. In a South Dakota case the state's highest court interpreted the school district's RIF policy to require reassignment of one course to effectuate the bumping rights of a tenured teacher.[69] Conversely, an Iowa appellate court rejected the plaintiff's proposed shifting of two other teachers to vacancies caused by resignations, finding the RIF clause in the collective bargaining agreement did not place "an affirmative duty on the Board to perform a wholesale arrangement of teaching assignments every time a vacancy occurs."[70]

A third possible limit on the effectuation of traditional RIF criteria, such as seniority and tenure status, is the principle of affirmative action in employing minority teachers.[71] Under a last-hired-first-fired RIF procedure, minority teachers would often be affected disproportionately due to earlier discriminatory barriers to their securing positions. There has been limited litigation, all of recent vintage, to reach an accommodation between these principles.

The leading cases have arisen within the context of court-ordered desegregation plans that incorporate percentage goals for the employment of minority educators. In a series of decisions by a federal district court in Michigan, the subordination of statutory and contractual seniority standards to a court-ordered, constitutionally mandated desegregation remedy was made clear.[72] The court based its reasoning on the educational interests of the students, concluding that the priority on attaining and retaining a goal of 20% of black teachers (where the student body was 28.5% black but the layoff had reduced the proportion of black teachers to 8.9%) in the Kalamazoo school district (where only 2% of the staff was black when the 1973 desegregation remedy was mandated) was needed to "provide the students with role models . . . [and] to prove to its Black students that Blacks are not always the ones who will bear the brunt of layoffs during times of financial hardship."[73] This role-model rationale was maintained through two successive rounds of layoffs in 1980-81 and 1981-82, and through the intervening grievances by the teacher association and individual nonminority teachers. However, in 1983 the Sixth Circuit Court of Appeals vacated and remanded the district court's decision in the *Kalamazoo* case. The appeals court ruled that a racial remedy may override seniority and tenure rights only where it is necessary, not merely reasonable.[74]

The rationale and result of the lower court's *Kalamazoo* decision were followed in an intervening opinion by the First Circuit Court of Appeals, affirming an order by District Judge Arthur Garrity, Jr. The opinion was that when RIF became necessary in the Boston schools, the school committee was required to maintain the current percentage of black teachers and administrators, many of whom had been hired in response to an affirmative action decree entered in the Boston school desegregation case.[75] The Boston Teachers Union, with the support of the American Federation of Teachers, asked the U.S. Supreme Court to review the First Circuit Court's decision, but in an October 1982 decision the Court declined to do so.[76] In a less publicized reverse discrimination case, a federal district court in New York similarly cited the *Kalamazoo* case and upheld the subordination of contractual and statutory dictates to those of a court-ordered desegregation remedy that mandated the hiring, recall, and promotion of underrepresented black teachers and administrators.[77] In light of the reversal of the Sixth Circuit Court's decision and the absence of a Supreme Court decision, this area of the law is in a state of flux.

A variation of competing interests in RIF actions occurs when the collective bargaining agreement incorporates an affirmative action layoff plan.[78] In such a case a federal district court in Michigan dismissed the constitutional and statutory claims of nonminority teachers, ruling that a prior judicial finding of race discrimination is not a prerequisite where there is substantial and chronic underrepresentation of minority teachers.[79]

It is less clear what the resolution of the competing interests would be in the absence of a court-ordered or contractual affirmative action provision.[80] In Cambridge, Mass., the school district adopted an affirmative action policy as part of a voluntary desegregation plan. However, the collective bargaining agreement called for seniority-based RIF. When the conflict between the policy and the contract arose in the form of a suit, the parties negotiated an out-of-court settlement whereby the affirmative action goals and procedures were supported.[81]

Guidance about these competing interests, particularly in the circumstances of a conflict between court-ordered affirmative action and statutorily established seniority systems, was expected from the Supreme Court as a result of its decision to hear the case of *Boston Firefighters Union v. Boston NAACP*,[82] in which the lower courts prohibited the police and fire departments from reducing the percentage of blacks and Hispanics below the level obtaining at the commencement of RIF despite a seniority-based state civil service statute; but the Court subsequently found the case to be moot.

Procedural Due Process

In addition to the questions of "why" and "who" in RIF policies, there is the issue of "how." Most states statutorily provide some form of procedural due process for educational personnel who are to be dismissed, namely, proper notice and the right to a hearing. These provisions typically are found in tenure statutes or administrative procedure acts rather than in statutory RIF policies. Thus the issues involved are whether the statutory due process provisions are applicable to RIF and, if not, whether the due process clause of the Constitution provides protection in such circumstances.

As discussed in chapter 4, the Supreme Court has established a two-part test relative to constitutional protections: 1) whether constitutional due process applies depends on whether the plaintiff shows either an objective "property" right in continued employment or a sufficient "liberty" interest in terms of his or her reputation, and 2) how much such process is due depends in part on the nature of the individual's interest at stake. Generally, the tenure and administrative procedure acts as well as the constitutional due process clause are not interpreted expansively in favor of RIF plaintiffs because 1) RIF statutes assume discontinuity rather than continuity in employment; 2) RIF is considered to be impersonal, that is, primarily attributable to the school district's condition rather than the merits of the individual teacher; and 3) under some statutes RIF implicates a lesser individual interest, i.e., suspension rather than dismissal. The bulk of the case law in this area is covered elsewhere;[83] only the issues raised in recent cases are summarized below.

Two recent decisions serve as examples of the threshold statutory and constitutional issues. In a Massachusetts case the state supreme court read the RIF legislation as an exception to the procedural requirements of the tenure statute. Thus the plaintiff, a tenured physical education teacher, was held to be entitled neither to the procedural guarantees of the tenure act nor — absent a statutory or contractual right to expect continued employment — to those of the U.S. Constitution.[84] In an Ohio case the federal district court dismissed the constitutional claims of two high school principals who had been demoted due to declining enrollments, finding that the RIF statute negated any property right to continued employment.[85] The court relied on an earlier decision by the Ohio Supreme Court, which held that the due process procedures of the tenure act were not applicable to suspensions under the RIF statutes and that the suspension procedure did not deprive the suspended teacher of a protected property interest.[86] Other recent decisions tend to deal with issues of notice or hearing requirements.

Notice. Lack of statutory compliance was alleged in two recent cases concerning proper notice. In a Michigan case the court of appeals held that the state's fair dismissal act, which requires that a nontenured teacher receive notice of unsatisfactory service at least 60 days prior to nonrenewal, does not apply to the nonrenewal of a nontenured teacher based solely on economic grounds.[87] Even where statutory nonrenewal procedures are applicable, notice requirements in some cases may not be strictly enforced in favor of suspended teachers. For example, in an Arkansas case, where the board of education accidentally sent a reappointment letter to a guidance counselor on the RIF list because of a computer programming error, the Eighth Circuit Court of Appeals upheld the district court's finding of "substantial compliance" with the statutory requirement of written notice within 10 days of the close of the school term. The court found such compliance because of two meetings and a letter within the required time period in which administrative personnel explained the mix-up and offered the guidance counselor a teaching position.[88] Because the counselor declined the teaching contract and signed and returned the counseling contract before the end of the school term, the plaintiff was left without any position as a result of the court's decision.

Hearing. The legitimacy of postsuspension hearings and mass hearings under Pennsylvania statute was recently tested at the intermediate appellate court level. In the postsuspension hearing case, the court found that both the tenured and nontenured employees had an enforceable expectation of continued employment, i.e., a property right under state law, entitling them to due process protection. Turning to the question of what process is due, the court analyzed the respective interests, alluded to the nonstigmatizing effect of impersonal reasons, and ruled as follows: "On balance, we conclude that a postsuspension hearing comports with due process by providing a reasonable accommodation of the competing interests."[89] In the other case the court upheld the legality of a mass hearing for 242 tenured employees demoted because of Philadelphia's budget crisis and refused to interpret the demotion statute strictly since the board provided the teachers with the opportunity for an individual postsuspension hearing.[90]

Another Pennsylvania case held that the exclusion of certain expert testimony at a suspended teacher's hearing constituted harmless error since it was merely cumulative to other testimony concerning whether budget cuts could be accomplished in a different way.[91] Other state courts have upheld RIF hearings against challenges to school boards' impartiality.[92] A California court similarly sustained the hearing procedures of a local school board with regard to challenges based on statutory requirements for an open meeting and for reading the transcript and seemed to look to substantial, rather than technical, compliance by the board.[93]

A statement of specific reasons is a related due process safeguard required in some circumstances. Although courts have generally found a requirement to state and support the reasons for undertaking RIF,[94] they have not tended to infer a requirement that boards articulate the reasons for selecting one teacher over another in implementing RIF. For example, the North Dakota Supreme Court refused to interpret that state's statutory requirement that school boards give "maximum consideration to basic fairness and decency" as requiring them to state the reasons for selecting one teacher over another in responding to financial difficulty.[95] Faced with a more explicit statutory scheme, California's intermediate appellate court held that a failure to give a written statement concerning the order of termination did not expand the legal rights and interests of suspended employees.[96]

In one of the few recently reported decisions that produced at least a partial victory on due process grounds for an RIF plaintiff, the Minnesota Supreme Court interpreted the statutory requirement for specific findings of fact and supporting evidence of reasons for RIF to preclude the board from introducing at a belated hearing evidence that occurred after the statutory deadline.[97]

Recall Rights

Due to ample coverage elsewhere,[98] only a sampling of recent cases relating to the recall of teachers subject to RIF will be treated in this section. Litigation in this area generally stems from suspension-type, rather than dismissal-type, RIF statutes. As summarized in Table 1, some statutes specify a preference or priority status for suspended teachers. A larger number specify that recall follows inverse order of seniority among qualified teachers when a vacancy arises. Interpretation of such statutory provisions accounts for the bulk of litigation concerning recall rights. Two recent decisions by the Minnesota Supreme Court are illustrative. In one case a suspended teacher argued that the requirement in the RIF statute for cities of the first class (e.g., Minneapolis) that teachers subject to RIF be given "first consideration" for vacant positions for which they are qualified should be interpreted as requiring recall in inverse seniority order. The teacher pointed out that the standard for layoffs in the same statute was inverse seniority and so was the standard for recall in the statute for cities not of first-class size. The Minnesota Supreme Court disagreed, accepting instead the school district's interpretation that "the statute requires it simply to evaluate a more senior teacher before considering other applicants but that the district retains discretion, when filling a special position, to reject a more senior teacher in favor of one who has the special qualifications required for that position."[99] In the other Minnesota case, the court held that a full-time teacher who had been suspended and then accepted a part-time position in the district remains on statutory recall status to the extent of the remainder of the full-time position.[100] Here, the teacher had accepted a three-fifths position in one of his areas of certification, physical education. Under Minnesota's statute for cities not of first-class size, the state supreme court held, upon rehearing, that he was entitled to reinstatement to a two-fifths opening in a girls' physical education position over a less experienced teacher, who was female and new to the district. As a comparison to analogous release rights cases reveals,[101] recall rights decisions are roughly but not exactly parallel.

Conclusions

With appropriate cautions for jurisdictional variations, certain generalizations seem to emerge concerning legal aspects of RIF:

1. RIF is primarily a matter of state statutes, thus the specific legislative provision should not be neglected in ascertaining legal developments nationally.

2. Statutory RIF reasons vary within a predictable pattern, ranging from enrollment decline to a catchall "good cause" category.

3. Where an RIF reason is statutorily specified, it should be strictly followed and factually supported.

4. Courts tend to defer to the evidence and decisions of local school boards unless the plaintiff-teacher can show the proferred reason to be a subterfuge for an impermissible basis (e.g., race discrimination or union activity).

5. A minority of statutes specify criteria with respect to the order for RIF. Where such criteria are specified, seniority and tenure status predominate; merit is given a relatively limited role.

6. Where statutes are silent or ambiguous about the order of release, courts tend liberally to read in an inverse seniority standard, to be more restrictive about inferring a tenure priority, and to allow but not generally require other criteria, such as merit.

7. Bumping rights provided by these criteria are limited by the court-construed contours of legal qualification, realignment duty, and affirmative action. Legal qualification generally is interpreted to mean certification; realignment duty is typically limited; and affirmative action tends to take priority over traditional RIF criteria.

8. Courts have tended not to interpret statutory and constitutional procedural due process protections expansively in relation to RIF plaintiffs.

9. Recall rights are legislated and litigated less than release rights, with roughly although not exactly parallel results.

Footnotes

1. P. Zirkel and C. Bargerstock, *The Law on Reduction-in-Force*, (Arlington, Va.: Educational Research Service, 1980). For a less statutory approach and one that formulates a sample local policy, *see* R. Phay, *Reduction in Force: Legal Issues and Recommended Policy* (Topeka, Kans.: National Organization on Legal Problems of Education, 1980).

2. *See, e.g.,* "Record Number of Teachers Face Layoffs," *Instructor* 92 (Sept. 1982):8. For a more conservative report, *see* Toch, "Survey Finds as Few as 6,500 Teacher Layoffs," *Education Week*, 8 September 1982, p. 1. *See also,* Johnson, "Seniority and Schools," *Phi Delta Kappan* (December 1982): 259-64; Toch, "Virginia District's Lay-Off Policy Gives Discretion to Principals," *Education Week*, 28 April 1982, p. 6.

3. E.g., Illinois RIF legislation refers to "honorable dismissal."

4. Andresky v. West Allegheny School Dist., 437 A.2d 1075 (Pa. Commw. 1981).

5. *See e.g.*, Phillippi v. School Dist., 367 A.2d 1133 (Pa. Commw. 1977) (district had a 27% decline over six years); Smith v. Board of School Dir., 328 A.2d 883 (Pa. Commw. 1974) (district had a 15.7% decline over 10 years).

6. *See* notes 20-21 accompanying text.

7. *See, e.g.,* Lewin v. Board of Trustees, 133 Cal. Rptr. 385 (Cal. App. 1976).

8. Brough v. Governing Bd., 173 Cal. Rptr. 729 (Cal. App. 1981).

9. Theros v. Warwick Bd. of School Dir., 401 A.2d 575, 577 (Pa. Commw. 1979); *cf.* Providence Teachers Union v. Donilon, 492 F. Supp. 709 (D.R.I. 1980). The *Donilon* court ordered a more specific statement of reason and, upon request, a hearing where the board suspended teachers for "program reorganization" under the Rhode Island statute, which specifies only declining enrollments as a reason.

10. Warwick Bd. of School Dir. v. Theros, 430 A.2d 208 (Pa. 1981); *see also* Eastern York School Dist. v. Long, 430 A.2d 267 (Pa. 1981) (equally divided state supreme court upheld reinstatement of teacher where reported reason of curriculum curtailment was not sufficient ground); Cumberland-Perry Area Vocational-Technical School Joint Operating Comm. v. Brinser, 430 A.2d 276 (Pa. 1981) (equally divided state supreme court upheld reinstatement of teacher suspended for solely economic reasons).

11. Frimel v. Humphrey, 555 S.W.2d 350, 352 (Mo. App. 1977).

12. *See. e.g.*, VanGieson and Zirkel, "The Law and Fiscal Exigency," *Journal of Teacher Education* 32 (1981):39-40. The term used generically in Great Britain is "redundancy."

13. Hensley v. State Bd. of Educ., 376 P.2d 968 (N.M. 1962); *see also* Nyre v. Joint School Dist., 45 N.W.2d 614 (Wis. 1951); *cf.* Acinapuro v. Board of Coop. Educ. Serv., 455 N.Y.S.2d 275 (Sup. Ct. App. Div. 1982). In this decision a special takeover statute was interpreted broadly to preserve tenure rights.

14. Beckett v. Roderick, 251 A.2d 427 (Me. 1969); *cf.* In re Closing of Jamesburg High School, 415 A.2d 896 (N.J. 1980). The court ruled that

where a school is closed for not meeting state standards and pupils are sent to other districts, tenured teachers have no carryover rights absent agreement by the receiving school districts.

15. Lake Lehman School Dist. v. Cigarski, 430 A.2d 274 (Pa. 1981).
16. Paradis v. School Administrative Dist. No. 33, 446 A.2d 46 (Me. 1982).
17. Yaffe v. Board of Educ., 380 A.2d 1 (Conn. Super. 1977).
18. *Compare, e.g.,* Ryan v. Ambach, 419 N.Y.S.2d 214 (Sup. Ct. App. Div. 1979) (upheld absorption of assistant principal's duties by existing personnel), *with* Board of Educ. v. Niagara Wheatfield Teachers Ass'n, 388 N.Y.S.2d 459 (Sup. Ct. App. Div. 1976) (rejected abolition of a nurse's position where no economy was achieved through the hiring of several health aides).
19. *See, e.g.,* Moser v. Board of Educ., 283 N.W.2d 391 (Neb. 1979).
20. Santa Clara Fed'n of Teachers, Local 2393 v. Governing Bd., 172 Cal. Rptr. 312 (Cal. App. 1981).
21. California Teachers Ass'n v. Board of Trustees, 182 Cal. Rptr. 754 (Cal. App. 1982); *see also* Palos Verdes Faculty Ass'n v. Governing Bd., 179 Cal. Rptr. 572 (Cal. App. 1982).
22. Rylke v. Portage Area School Dist., 375 A.2d 692 (Pa. 1977).
23. In re Portage Area Educ. Ass'n, 432 A.2d 1170 (Pa. Commw. 1981); *see also* Cedonic v. Northern Area Special Purpose Schools, 426 A.2d 186 (Pa. Commw. 1981).
24. School Comm. of Foxborough v. Koski, 391 N.E.2d 708 (Mass. App. 1979); *cf.* NEA Valley-Center v. Unified School Dist., 644 P.2d 381 (Kan. 1982); Sells v. Unified School Dist. No. 429, 644 P.2d 379 (Kan. 1982) (reorganization of special education services was good cause for nonrenewal).
25. Briggs v. Board of Dir., 282 N.W.2d 740 (Iowa 1979); Von Krog v. Board of Educ., 298 N.W.2d 339 (Iowa App. 1980).
26. The negotiability of RIF varies from state to state. *See, e.g.,* Zirkel, note 1, at 42; Pisapia, "What's Negotiable in Public Education?" *Gov't Union Rep.* 3 (1982):99. For recent cases, *see, e.g.,* Boston Teachers Union v. School Comm., 434 N.E.2d 1258 (Mass. 1982) (job security clause held enforceable for no more than one fiscal year); Board of Educ. v. Cam/Voc Teachers Ass'n, 443 A.2d 756 (N.J. App. 1982) (negotiability of impact of RIF to be decided by PERC).
27. Port Huron Area School Dist. v. Port Huron Educ. Ass'n, 327 N.W.2d 413 (Mich. App. 1982).
28. Stow Teachers Ass'n v. Stow Bd. of Educ., No. 9985 (Ohio App. June 17, 1981).
29. Hagarty v. Dysart-Geneseo Commun. School Dist., 282 N.W.2d 92, 98 (Iowa 1979).
30. Reed v. Edgeley Pub. School Dist., 313 N.W.2d 775, 779 (N.D. 1981). For related reasoning by the Supreme Court, *see* the discussion of the *Mt. Healthy-Givhan* line of cases in Chapter 3.
31. Von Krog v. Board of Educ., 298 N.W.2d 339, 342 (Iowa App. 1980).
32. Renfroe v. Kirkpatrick, 549 F. Supp. 1368, 1371 n.5 & 1373 (N.D. Ala. 1982).

33. Green v. Board of Educ., 433 N.Y.S.2d 434, 436 (Sup. Ct. App. Div. 1980); *see also* Currier v. Tompkins-Seneca-Tioga Bd. of Coop. Educ. Serv., 438 N.Y.S.2d 605 (Sup. Ct. App. Div. 1981); Genco v. Bristol Borough School Dist., 423 A.2d 36 (Pa. Commw. 1980); *cf.* Perlin v. Board of Educ., 407 N.E.2d 792 (Ill. App. 1980) (board's good faith as an issue subject to trial).

34. Zoll v. Eastern Allamakee Commun. School Dist., 588 F.2d 248 (8th Cir. 1978); *see also* Knapp v. Whitaker, No. 81-1185 (C.D. Ill. 1983), *cited in Nolpe Notes* 18 (April 1983):6.

35. Freiburg v. Board of Educ., 283 N.W.2d 775 (Mich. App. 1979).

36. *See, e.g.*, Padway v. Palches, 665 F.2d 915 (9th Cir. 1982); Rodriguez v. Board of Educ., 620 F.2d 362 (2d Cir. 1980). *But see* Gillespie v. Board of Educ., 528 F. Supp. 433 (E.D. Ark. 1981) (rejected sex discrimination pretext claim), *aff'd on other grounds*, 692 F.2d 529 (8th Cir. 1982).

37. *See, e.g.*, Witt v. School Dist. No. 70, 273 N.W.2d 391 (Neb. 1979); Fedele v. Board of Educ., 394 A.2d 737 (Conn. C.P. 1977); Coats v. Unified School Dist. No. 353, 662 P.2d 1279 (Kan. 1983).

38. Paradis v. School Administrative Dist. No. 33, 446 A.2d 46 (Me. 1982).

39. Schnabel v. Alcester School Dist., 295 N.W.2d 340 (S.D. 1980).

40. Litigation about the calculation of seniority is not covered in this chapter due to space limitations. *See, e.g.*, Andresky v. West Allegheny School Dist., 437 A.2d 1075, 1079 (Pa. Commw. 1981); Berland v. Special School Dist. No. 1, 314 N.W.2d 808, 814 (Minn. 1982).

41. *See, e.g.*, Lezette v. Board of Educ., 319 N.E.2d 189 (N.Y. 1974); State ex rel. Ging v. Board of Educ., 7 N.W.2d 7 (Minn. 1942); *cf.* Dinerstein v. Board of Educ., 408 N.E.2d 670 (N.Y. 1980) (upheld seniority right across areas of certification).

42. *See, e.g.*, Hill v. Dayton School Dist. No. 2, 532 P.2d 1154 (Wash. 1975); *cf.* Fercho v. Montpelier Pub. School Dist., 312 N.W.2d 337 (N.D. 1981) (upheld suspension of teacher who had nine years of tenure where there was no factual allegation of violation of contractual seniority standard).

43. *See, e.g.*, Bohmann v. Board of Educ., 443 N.E.2d 176 (Ohio 1983) (transfer or reassignment); Green v. Jenkintown School Dist., 441 A.2d 816 (Pa. Commw. 1982) (promotion).

44. Moreland Teachers Ass'n v. Kurze, 167 Cal. Rptr. 343, 347 (Cal. App. 1980).

45. Palos Verdes Faculty Ass'n v. Governing Bd., 179 Cal. Rptr. 572, 575 (Cal. App. 1982) ("often intimate and confidential relationship"); Santa Clara Fed'n of Teachers v. Governing Bd., 172 Cal. Rptr. 312, 317 (Cal. App. 1981) ("special credential or needed skill").

46. Alexander v. Delano Joint Union High School Dist., 188 Cal. Rptr. 705 (Cal. App. 1983). For a description of California's tie-breaking standard, *see* Overview of RIF Statutes section in this chapter.

47. Carmody v. Board of Dir., 453 A.2d 965 (Pa. 1982); *cf* Sto-Rox School Dist. v. Horgan, 449 A.2d 776 (Pa. Commw. 1982) (substantial difference test applicable only to unweighted ratings).

48. Fatscher v. Board of School Dir., 417 A.2d 287 (Pa. Commw. 1980).

49. Cooper v. Fair Dismissal Appeals Bd., 570 P.2d 1005, 1008 (Ore. App. 1977).

50. Von Krog v. Board of Educ., 298 N.W.2d 339, 343 (Iowa App. 1980).

51. *See, e.g.,* Phay, note 1, at 17.

52. Dykeman v. Board of Educ., 316 N.W.2d 69 (Neb. 1982).

53. *See* note 49 and accompanying text.

54. Ar-We-Va Commun. School Dist. v. Long, 292 N.W.2d 402, 403 (Iowa 1980); *cf.* Coats v. Unified School Dist. No. 353, 662 P.2d 1279 (Kan. 1983). The *Coats* court required, based on the board's past practice, comparison across K-12 rather than merely 9-12).

55. Berland v. Special School Dist. No. 1, 314 N.W.2d 809, 812-13 (Minn. 1982).

56. *See, e.g.*, Kelley v. Ambach, 442 N.Y.S.2d 616 (Sup. Ct. App. Div. 1981); Cole v. Board of Educ. 457 N.Y.S.2d 547 (Sup. Ct. App. Div. 1982); Rohin v. Board of Educ., 443 N.Y.S.2d 192 (Sup. Ct. 1981).

57. *See, e.g.*, Dinerstein v. Board of Educ., 408 N.E.2d 670 (N.Y. 1980); Oltsik v. Board of Educ., 450 N.Y.S.2d 518 (Sup. Ct. App. Div. 1982).

58. Fatscher v. Board of School Dir., 417 A.2d 287 (Pa. Commw. 1980).

59. *See, e.g.*, Newman v. Board of Educ., 424 N.E.2d 1331 (Ill. App. 1981); Von Krog v. Board of Educ., 298 N.W.2d 339 (Iowa App. 1980).

60. Welsko v. Foster Twp. School Dist., 119 A.2d 43 (Pa. 1956).

61. 24 P.S. § 11-1125.1(c). It is not settled whether this provision applies to promotions as well as suspensions. *Compare* Shestak v. General Braddock Area School Dist., 437 A.2d 1059 (Pa. Commw. 1981) *with* Green v. Jenkintown School Dist., 441 A.2d 816 (Pa. Commw. 1981).

62. Andresky v. West Allegheny School Dist., 437 A.2d 1075, 1078 (Pa. Commw. 1981); *see also* Sto-Rox School Dist. v. Horgan, 449 A.2d 796, 802 (Pa. Commw. 1982).

63. Proch v. New Castle Area School Dist., 430 A.2d 1034 (Pa. Commw. 1981).

64. Godfrey v. Penns Valley Area School Dist., 449 A.2d 765, 769 (Pa. Commw. 1982).

65. ORS 432.865 (1)(j). In such circumstances, as mentioned in the Overview of RIF Statutes section, this statute requires the determination to be based on merit and seniority. *See* note 49 and accompanying text.

66. Shandy v. Portland School Dist. No. 1, 634 P.2d 1377 (Ore. App. 1981).

67. Higgins v. Board of Educ., 428 N.E.2d 1126 (Ill. App. 1981); Herbach v. Board of Educ., 419 N.E.2d 456 (Ill. App. 1981). For references to Illinois' training-based regulations, *see* note 59 and accompanying text.

68. Peters v. Board of Educ., 435 N.E.2d 814, 817 (Ill. App. 1982).

69. Schnabel v. Alcester School Dist., 295 N.W.2d 340 (S.D. 1980).

70. Von Krog v. Board of Educ., 298 N.W.2d 339, 343 (Iowa App. 1980); *cf.* Fercho v. Montpelier Pub. School Dist. No. 14, 312 N.W.2d 337 (N.D. 1981) (realignment prior to notice is sound management but not a legal requirement).

71. This section focuses on reverse discrimination cases. For direct discrimination decisions, *see* note 36 and accompanying text. There is also a line of

cases starting with *Singleton* v. *Jackson Municipal Separate School District,* 419 F.2d 1121 (5th Cir. 1970), *cert. denied,* 396 U.S. 1032 (1970), requiring the use of nonracial objective criteria for conducting RIF in districts undergoing court-ordered desegregation. Such cases are covered in Chapter 2.

72. Oliver v. Kalamazoo Bd. of Educ., 498 F. Supp. 732 (W.D. Mich. 1980); 510 F. Supp. 1104 (W.D. Mich. 1981); 526 F. Supp. 131 (W.D. Mich. 1981).

73. 498 F. Supp. at 755.

74. 706 F.2d at 763.

75. Morgan v. O'Bryant, 671 F.2d 23 (1st Cir. 1982), *cert. denied,* 103 S.Ct. 62 (1982); *see also* separate affirmance in this case, 687 F.2d 510 (1st Cir. 1982).

76. *But see* note 81 and accompanying text.

77. Arthur v. Nyquist, 520 F. Supp. 961 (W.D.N.Y. 1981).

78. *Cf.* M. Ware, "Reduction in Force: The Legal Aspects," in *School Law in Changing Times,* ed. M. McGhehey (Topeka, Kans.: National Organization on Legal Problems of Education, 1982), pp. 132-141. This discusses a proposal by the director of NEA's Teacher Rights Programs for a partial exception provision requiring that proportional employment of an underrepresented group be, as nearly as possible, no less at any level after a layoff than what it was before the layoff.

79. Wygant v. Jackson Bd. of Educ., 546 F. Supp. 1195 (E.D. Mich. 1982).

80. Minnesota provides some direction by statute, permitting seniority to give way where it places the district in violation of its affirmative action program. MINN. STAT. ANN. 125.12(6b)(c)(1974).

81. *See* "Settlement Reached in Teacher Layoff and Minority Hiring Case," *Center for Law and Education Newsnotes* (August-September 1982):7.

82. 103 S.Ct. 293 (1982). The NEA filed a brief in support of the affirmative action plan in these circumstances. *See Education Week,* 9 February 1983, p. 7.

83. *See, e.g.,* Zirkel, note 1, at 33-39; Phay, note 1, at 33-42.

84. Milne v. School Comm., 410 N.E.2d 1216 (Mass. 1980); *see also* Boston Teachers Union v. School Comm., 434 N.E.2d 1258 (Mass. 1982). *But cf.* Ward v. Viborg, 319 N.W.2d 502 (S.D. 1982), which held that the due process procedures of the tenure statute are applicable where board policy incorporates them by reference.

85. Lacy v. Dayton Bd. of Educ., 550 F. Supp. 835 (S.D. Ohio 1982).

86. Dorian v. Euclid Bd. of Educ., 404 N.E.2d 155 (Ohio 1980).

87. Dailey v. Board of Educ., 327 N.W.2d 431 (Mich. App. 1983).

88. Gillespie v. Board of Educ., 692 F.2d 529, 531 (8th Cir. 1982); *cf.* Williams v. Seattle School Dist. No. 1, 643 P.2d 426, 432 (Wash. 1982). The *Williams* court stated: "We follow a functional analysis of the adequacy of notice."

89. Andresky v. West Allegheny School Dist., 437 A.2d 1075, 1078 (Pa. Commw. 1981); *see also* Sto-Rox School Dist. v. Horgan, 449 A.2d 796, 799 (Pa. Commw. 1982).

90. School Dist. of Philadelphia v. Twer, 447 A.2d 222 (Pa. Commw. 1982).

91. Chester Upland School Dist. v. Brown, 447 A.2d 1068 (Pa. Commw. 1982). Like the decision in note 90, this case arose under Pennsylvania's demotion, not RIF, legislation.

92. Reed v. Edgeley Pub. School Dist. No. 3, 313 N.W.2d 775 (N.D. 1981); Fercho v. Montpelier Pub. School Dist. No. 14, 312 N.W.2d 337 (N.D. 1981); Von Krog v. Board of Educ., 298 N.W.2d 339 (Iowa App. 1980); Nagy v. Belle Vernon Area School Dist., 412 A.2d 172 (Pa. Commw. 1980).

93. Santa Clara Fed'n of Teachers v. Governing Bd., 172 Cal. Rptr. 312, 319 (Cal. App. 1981).

94. *See e.g.*, Providence Teachers Ass'n v. Donilon, 492 F. Supp. 709 (D.R.I. 1980), in which the court ordered more specific reasons for RIF and, on request, a hearing where the board used "program reorganization" for a reason under Rhode Island statute, which only lists declining enrollment as a reason for RIF; Freeman v. School Bd., 382 So. 2d 140 (Fla. Dist. Ct. App. 1980), in which the court ordered a hearing if plaintiff can show that the reason was pretextual.

95. Reed v. Edgeley Pub. School Dist. No. 3, 313 N.W.2d 775 (N.D. 1981).

96. Palos Verdes Faculty Ass'n v. Governing Bd., 179 Cal. Rptr. 572 (Cal. App. 1982).

97. Herfindahl v. Independent School Dist. No. 126, 325 N.W.2d 36 (Minn. 1982).

98. *See* Beckham, "Reduction-in-Force: A Legal Update," in *School Law Update 1982*, ed. T. Jones and D. Semler (Topeka, Kans.: National Organization on Legal Problems of Education, 1983).

99. Berland v. Special School Dist. No. 1, 314 N.W.2d 809, 816 (Minn. 1982).

100. Walter v. Independent School Dist. No. 457, 323 N.W.2d 37 (Minn. 1982).

101. *See* note 58 and accompanying text.

Glossary

agency shop: an arrangement whereby employees must become union members or pay a service fee to the union as a condition of continued employment. (An agency shop is as restrictive as a union shop or closed shop.)

arbitrability: refers to whether a particular grievance is substantively and procedurally eligible under a collective bargaining agreement to be heard and decided by an arbitrator.

bumping rights: power given by contract or statute to have priority for a position over other employees in the same area of qualification when there is a reduction in force.

cert. denied: discretionary denial by the Supreme Court to review a case when the losing party petitions for appeal by a writ of "certiorari."

cf.: footnote signal to indicate that a cited court decision offers related, not direct, support for the statement(s) in the text.

continuing contract: a contract that is automatically renewed, thus having the effect of tenure.

de facto: literally, "in fact," i.e., actually occurring although not officially sanctioned.

de jure: literally, "by law," i.e., occurring as a result of official government action.

de novo: hearing or trying a matter anew, as if it had not been heard or tried previously.

dictum: statement in a judge's written opinion that goes beyond the holding, or principle, of the case and thus has no binding effect on subsequent cases.

due process: short for "due process of law" in the 14th (and 5th) Amendment, which has been interpreted to mean private procedural and substantive rights protected from governmental interference.

equal protection:	short for "equal protection of the laws" in the 14th Amendment, protecting the individual from invidious discrimination by the government.
equitable relief:	a special remedy, such as an injunction, ordered by a court when ordinary, legal remedies, such as money damages, are inadequate.
infra:	literally, "below," i.e., signifying a cross-reference to a subsequent part of the document or chapter.
injunction:	a court order, based on equitable considerations, requiring the defendant to do or, more typically, to refrain from doing a specified act.
invidious:	illegal, typically used in relation to discrimination that is not permitted by law.
irrebuttable presumption:	a conclusive presumption that requires a finding of the proved fact, and thus is not subject to being rebutted, once the underlying evidence is presented.
liquidated damages:	the sum that the party to a contract agrees to pay if he breaches his obligations under the contract, the sum being an estimate of the probable damages that will ensue.
moot:	referring to a case that presents no actual controversy, typically where the issues have ceased to exist.
plaintiff:	the complaining party, i.e., the person(s) bringing the suit at the trial level (against the defendant).
post facto:	after the fact.
post hoc:	literally, "after this," i.e., afterward.
prima facie:	literally, "on its face," i.e., evidence that establishes a sufficient case for the suing party such that the burden shifts to the

defending party to produce rebuttal evidence.

RIF:

abbreviation for "reduction in force," a term for temporary or permanent loss of position(s) due to the condition of the employing school district rather than to the actions of the employee educator.

supra:

literally, "above," signifying cross-reference to an earlier part of the document or chapter.

suspect:

a classification, such as race, that merits strict scrutiny by the court and thus requires compelling justification by the defendant governmental agency.

Index